Dynamics
of Dependence:
U.S.-Israeli Relations

Studies in International Politics

Leonard Davis Institute for International Relations,
The Hebrew University, Jerusalem

Dynamics of Dependence:
U.S.-Israeli Relations
edited by Gabriel Sheffer

Despite Israel's enormous dependence on the United States, relatively little has been written by Israeli scholars about relations between the two countries. In this book of original essays, contributors discuss the social, ideological, and political groups in the United States that support or oppose Israel, examine how they influence policy decisions, and review U.S. public opinion toward Israel. In addition, the politics of supplying arms and economic aid to Israel are analyzed in historical perspective. Finally, the contributors explore the range of U.S. interests in the dispute over the West Bank.

Gabriel Sheffer is editor of *The Jerusalem Journal of International Relations* and associate director of the Leonard Davis Institute for International Relations.

STUDIES IN INTERNATIONAL POLITICS
LEONARD DAVIS INSTITUTE FOR INTERNATIONAL RELATIONS
THE HEBREW UNIVERSITY, JERUSALEM

Dynamics of Dependence: U.S.-Israeli Relations

edited by Gabriel Sheffer

Westview Press • Boulder and London

Studies in International Politics, Leonard Davis Institute for International Relations, The Hebrew University, Jerusalem

This Westview softcover edition is printed on acid-free paper and bound in softcovers that carry the highest rating of the National Association of State Textbook Administrators, in consultation with the Association of American Publishers and the Book Manufacturers' Institute.

Copyright © 1987 by Westview Press, Inc.

Published in 1987 in the United States of America by Westview Press, Inc.; Frederick A. Praeger, Publisher; 5500 Central Avenue, Boulder, Colorado 80301

Library of Congress Cataloging-in-Publication Data
Dynamics of Dependence.
    (Studies in international politics / Leonard Davis
Institute)
    Includes index.
    1. United States—Foreign relations—Israel.
2. Israel—Foreign relations—United States. I. Sheffer,
Gabriel. II. Series: Studies in international politics
E183.8.I75U24 1986   327.7305694   86-9123
ISBN 0-8133-7215-1

Composition for this book was created by conversion of the editor's word-processor disks. This book was produced without formal editing by the publisher.

Printed and bound in the United States of America

The paper used in this publication meets the requirements of the American National Standard for Permanence of Paper for Printed Library Materials Z39.48-1984.

6   5   4   3   2   1

Contents

List of Tables and Figures ix

INTRODUCTION: SHARED VALUES AS THE BASIS
FOR THE U.S.-ISRAELI "SPECIAL RELATIONSHIP,"
Gabriel Sheffer 1

1   ISRAEL'S IMAGE,
    Gabriel Sheffer and Menachem Hofnung 7

2   TRENDS IN AMERICAN ATTITUDES
    TOWARD ISRAEL,
    Eytan Gilboa 37

3   ISRAELI MILITARY PROCUREMENT
    FROM THE UNITED STATES,
    Mordechai Gazit 83

4   U.S. AID TO ISRAEL:
    PROBLEMS AND PERSPECTIVES,
    Leopold Yehuda Laufer 125

5   U.S. AID TO THE WEST BANK AND GAZA:
    POLICY DILEMMAS,
    Leopold Yehuda Laufer 165

About the Contributors 201
Index 203

Tables and Figures

Tables

1.1 Pro-Israeli groups and factors 32
1.2 Ambivalent groups and factors 33
1.3 Anti-Israeli groups and factors 33

2.1 Sympathy with Jews or Arabs, 1947–1949, 1964 40
2.2 Jewish immigration to Palestine, 1945 42
2.3 Blame for the Arab-Israeli Conflict, 1953–1957 44
2.4 Favorability rating toward Israel, 1956 46
2.5 Sympathies toward Israel and the Arabs, 1967–1977 48
2.6 Sympathies toward Israel and the
    Arab nations, 1978–1982 56
2.7 Peace intentions, 1977–1979 58
2.8 Sadat and Begin: Handling of
    peace negotiations, 1977–1978 59
2.9 Israeli favorability rating, 1976–1981 60
2.10 Sympathies toward Israel and the
    Arab nations, 1982–1984 66
2.11 Beirut massacre 68
2.12 Attitudes toward the war in Lebanon,
    June–September 1982 70
2.13 Opinions on Israeli uses of force 72
2.14 U.S. support to Israel or the Arabs? 1977–1982 74

4.1 U.S. assistance to Israel, 1950–1983 126
4.2 Forecast of Israel's foreign debt service, 1978–1983 159

5.1 U.S. government assistance to the West Bank and Gaza 170
5.2 Food relief programs, fiscal year 1983 171

ix

5.3 AID funded programs of U.S.
     private voluntary organizations 180

Figures

4.1 U.S. assistance to Israel, 1949–1983...................... 128
4.2 U.S. assistance to Israel, 1949–1970...................... 132
4.3 U.S. assistance to Israel, 1971–1983...................... 135

INTRODUCTION

Shared Values as the Basis for the U.S.-Israeli "Special Relationship"

GABRIEL SHEFFER

Despite the tremendous and constant growth of Israeli dependence on the United States, Israeli scholars and writers have contributed surprisingly little to the expanding literature on U.S.-Israeli relations, and even less to the literature on dependence. This volume, which includes studies resulting from research conducted at the Leonard Davis Institute for International Relations of the Hebrew University, adds Israeli scholars' views on some of the complex issues arising out of Israeli dependence on the United States. These contributions are meant both to complement the knowledge of the specific Israeli case and add to the understanding of the dependence phenomenon in general.

Even a cursory review of the theoretical and empirical literature on modern dependence shows that, in comparison to other cases of patron-client relationship in the Western block, U.S.-Israeli relations have indeed assumed unique features and special dimensions. Israel is a very small state located in a remote region far from American borders; it is involved in a continuing conflict with many of its regional neighbors, some of which (Egypt, Jordan and, of course, Saudi Arabia) have recently become close American allies; it is culturally quite different from the United States; and finally, despite its paramount reliance on American goodwill, it uses defiance as a major weapon and tactic in an attempt to influence its patron's policies. Nevertheless, the general trend in the development of U.S.-Israeli relations is that of growing intimacy that is evident in a number of spheres. While certain episodes (e.g., the 1975 Ford-Kissinger

1

"reassessment"; the 1981 Israeli bombing of the Iraqi nuclear reactor; the latter stages of the 1982–1983 war in Lebanon, especially during the occupation of Beirut; and most recently the 1985 Pollard espionage scandal) have led to a temporary deterioration in these cordial relations, the overall subsequent adverse effects of all these incidents have been negligible. Moreover, despite intermittent predictions by Israeli, American, and European observers that U.S.-Israeli relations would not develop beyond certain previously given levels (such predictions stemming at times from wishful thinking on the part of critics of various Israeli government policies) it seems that, at least in the short run, virtually nothing can frustrate the continuing intimacy between the two countries.

The prima facie conclusion that Israel is indeed regarded as a special U.S. ally, or client, is borne out by various indicators. Israel receives a large chunk of the total U.S. foreign and military aid package, as well as enjoying a great deal of U.S. attention. Despite the recent setback caused by the Pollard affair, it has established and maintained close cooperation with the United States in the sphere of strategic and military intelligence. Since the late 1960s Israel has been able to buy or acquire almost any form of U.S. military or military-related equipment. Through means of the recently established free trade zone, Israel can more easily promote its commercial and trade interests in the United States. And finally, occasional acts of defiance notwithstanding, Israel appears to enjoy almost endless political patience on the part of its patron, relying on the United States to ward off diplomatic attacks in the UN and in other international forums often antagonistic to it.

A special interpretation is needed to explain this incomparably special position, since most conventional interpretations are at best only partially applicable. Such interpretations tend to focus either on common national or strategic interests between patron and client, or else argue the existence of an "economic investment trap" that ties the patron to its client. In this case, however, none of these interpretations seem sufficient.

The argument that U.S.-Israeli relations are deduced from mutual national interests, for example, suffers from both theoretical and empirical weaknesses. From the theoretical and methodological viewpoints this argument is simply too vague and ambiguous, the ambiguity deriving from the difficulties inherent in defining the national interests of a huge nation. From a practical point of view it is also difficult to accept the national interest interpretation, since both Israel and the United States are highly pluralistic in their social, ideological, and political makeup. It is almost impossible to point to consensus on any aspect of these relations, except perhaps for the very general feeling in Israel that continued close ties with the United States are in fact desirable. Otherwise, there are deep divisions both in Israel and in the United States, in government circles and among the public at large, concerning almost every aspect of U.S.-Israeli relations. There is no consensus, for example, concerning the exact level of military or economic aid to be given to Israel, or about political or diplomatic commitments from either side. Perhaps most important and pertinent, there is also no consensus about the manner in which close U.S.-Israeli connections serve immediate American interests—or more accurately, to what extent this intimacy may in fact clash with other perceived U.S. interests. Certain segments in the United States, for example, do not welcome the U.S. involvement in rescuing Soviet Jews, arguing that the United States should pursue its own interests before those of a foreign state. Similarly, a growing number of critics question what they view as unequivocal U.S. commitments to Israel, especially when the latter acts in defiance of U.S. wishes.

The more specific argument concerning Israel's strategic importance to the United States also fails to fully explain the intensity of the friendship between the two states that has developed during the last two decades. Certain Israeli governments and political parties (generally those defined as more right-wing and aggressively nationalistic) have tried at times to invoke the impression that Israel renders strategic services to the United States that are more important than the benefits it receives in return. One major proponent of this approach, former Defense Minister Ariel Sharon, maintains, for instance, that Israel serves to block Soviet advances in the region, along with explicitly and implicitly supporting and protecting the pro-Western regimes in the region. Such a proposition, however, is debated by Israeli and American analysts and politicians— which seems to indicate that "soft" rather than "hard" strategic factors might be the basis for the continuing affinity between the two countries. Moreover, from a purely strategic viewpoint, Israel's capability to assist the United States seems limited to certain parts of the Middle East, the best indication of this being its non-existent or marginal role in the Iran-Iraqi war, in the continuing Egyptian-Sudanese controversy, and in various attempts to check Lybian adventures abroad. The Soviet Union also does not seem particularly perturbed by Israeli actions or statements as it pursues its own interests in the Middle East and the region's peripheries.

Finally, the "economic investment trap" explanation is insufficient in accounting for the longevity of U.S.-Israeli relations. An "investment trap" refers to a situation in which a superpower (or any other patron) maintains a certain commitment to a troubled client not because of the latter's current strategic attraction or other major contributions to the well-being of the former, but rather in an effort to protect earlier political and economic investments, to save face, or to maintain a certain level of prestige. Such was the case, for example, during the latter stages of U.S. involvement in Vietnam, when the United States acted in an effort both to maintain its prestige and, to a certain extent, protect its previous economic and military investments. But this model is hardly applicable as a complete explanation of U.S.-Israeli relations. While it might explain certain aspects of the complex relations between the two states—and probably the rationale of a few American politicians and bureaucrats— it certainly does not account for the fact that the vast majority in Congress consistently votes to either maintain or increase the level of U.S. support for, and aid to, Israel.

If none of the interpretations described above is adequate, what can, in fact, account for the enduring intimacy of U.S.-Israeli relations? The answer may lie in the shared values of the two countries—that is, various soft and intangible factors that serve to influence the U.S. administration in favor of Israel (for example, attitudes towards democracy, respect for pluralism, urge for political stability, etc.). This is not to say that cost benefit calculations concerning strategy, trade, commerce, Jewish voters, or cooperation in intelligence or scientific exchanges do not count. Indeed they do count—but among the variety of contributing elements, the non-quantifiable soft factors count more.

The article by Gabriel Sheffer and Menachem Hofnung that appears in this volume defines and categorizes some of the salient clusters and factors exerting great influence on the U.S. administration. Some of these factors work in favor of Israeli interests, some against it and some can turn either way. The most outstanding pro-Israeli groups are, of course, the American Jewish community—whose attachment to Israel can be explained only on the basis of the assumptions of the "shared values" interpretation—certain fundamentalist Protestant groups, philo- Semitic groups and other social and political segments supporting Israel for liberal or humanitarian reasons. In comparison to these quite wide circles, the groups who wholeheartedly support Israel for strategic or commercial reasons are relatively small. Similarly, there are only a few groups that can be characterized as clearly anti-Israeli; Sheffer and Hofnung suggest that the majority of organized political and social groups showing interest in Israel should in fact be classified as "ambivalent" groups that can swing either way. The authors feel that although no major changes or deterioration in support will take place in the near future, there are factors contributing to very gradual erosion of the close U.S.-Israeli relations.

A slightly different view concerning the stability of U.S.-Israeli relations is suggested by Eytan Gilboa in his study of U.S. attitudes towards Israel as revealed in public opinion polls. Gilboa also deals with "soft" factors that fit the "shared values" model. Based on his research, Gilboa concludes that the American public has continuously supported Israel over the Arab states, by wide margins, even during events such as the war in Lebanon. This is not to say that U.S. support is either total or blind; during the peace-making process with Egypt, and on various occasions when Israel has used force against its adversaries in the Middle East— particularly when these are moderate Middle Eastern states—there has been a drop in U.S. support. Moreover, as in other areas of foreign policy, the American public tends to follow the views expressed by the White House and the American mass media. On the whole, however, the degree of U.S. support as revealed in public opinion polls is impressive. In analyzing his data, Gilboa concludes that the existence of common values is the single most important basis for the intimacy in U.S.-Israeli relations. Gilboa's prediction, based on his analysis of the past, is that there will be no deterioration in U.S.-Israeli relations.

The two other contributors to this volume, Mordechai Gazit and Leopold Yehuda Laufer, have dealt with what may be termed the "harder" factors influencing U.S.-Israeli relations. Gazit discusses what he terms the most sensitive issue in these relations, namely arms sales, delineating four stages in the development of the arms sales pattern. According to Gazit, the sum total of U.S. military aid to Israel amounts to approximately $20 billion. However, this impressive scope of military assistance does not ensure the stability of future arms sales. As Gazit demonstrates, intangible factors have influenced each administration's military aid policy, and the possibility always remains of either fluctuations in aid or temporary sanctions against Israel, should the administration feel that such action is warranted.

In his first paper, Laufer examines U.S. economic aid to Israel. In view of Israel's tremendous dependence on the United States, he finds, both patron and client have few options regarding either the continuation or diminution of intimacy and support. According to Laufer, the U.S. administration has opted for the status quo in its policy towards Israel, preferring to continue with given levels of economic support rather than risk clashing with Congress, public opinion, or the Jewish lobby. The use of economic aid as a lever to exact certain Israeli behavior is only partially effective; in Laufer's view, only a radical change in Israeli policies concerning the West Bank or the Palestinians could cause a major shift in U.S. policy vis-à-vis its small ally. Once again, it is the "shared values" model that seems to best explain the rationale behind U.S. economic aid to Israel.

In his second paper, Laufer discusses a neglected subject—namely, U.S. aid to the West Bank and Gaza—focusing on the complexities of the Israeli government's position and the implications concerning the general fabric of U.S.-Israeli relations. More specifically, Laufer has found

that a majority of U.S. funding in the West Bank and Gaza is earmarked
for a special program designed to maintain and strengthen direct links
between the United States and the Palestinians. Understandably, this
program has created unrest among Israeli policymakers.

In terms of the future of U.S.-Israeli relations, the paramount question
is how long the trend of growing intimacy between patron and client
can be expected to continue. From the analysis offered in this volume,
it emerges that fluctuations in the warmth of these relations are in fact
possible, especially if Israel chooses to pursue policies that clash with
established U.S. interests or frustrate U.S. intentions. From the Israeli
point of view, there are both advantages and disadvantages in the fact
that ideological and emotional factors form the underpinnings of U.S.-
Israeli intimacy. The major advantage is that, since Israeli commitments
to its patron are relatively undefined, its freedom of action is wide and
well ensured. On the other hand, intangible factors not only make it
difficult to accurately gauge the future levels of U.S. support, but leave
open the possibility that a sharp shift may occur at any time. Gilboa's
analysis shows, for example, that U.S. public support for Israel fell
during and after crises arising out of Israeli actions undertaken in 1973,
1975, and 1983 (and, one can add, in 1985).

Generally speaking, Israeli leaders have been able to count on U.S.
support even during periods of Israeli defiance. But given the fact that
U.S.-Israeli relations are based on the ambiguous reality of shared values,
U.S. support for Israel could be drastically reduced if and when Israel
opts to contradict or continuously frustrate highly cherished American
values. A radical change in Israeli policy vis-à-vis the West Bank (e.g.,
moving to annex it), or continued resistance to the resumption of the
peace process with the joint participation of Jordanians and Palestinians,
could lead to such a shift. With this in mind, Israeli leaders may be
well advised to consider their actions in light of the whole web of U.S.-
Israeli relations in order to guard against the possibility of a wide-scale
deterioration of U.S. support.

ONE

Israel's Image

GABRIEL SHEFFER
MENACHEM HOFNUNG

Introduction

Purpose and Terminology

In the course of the past four decades, complex and multifaceted relations have existed between the United States and Israel. Until now, however, there have been large gaps in the research pertaining to these relations. Most studies have focused on political and diplomatic issues from a historical point of view, ignoring, in the main, the question of how various social groups have influenced U.S. policy towards Israel. This chapter is an attempt to fill in the gap through means of a detailed examination of the ways in which U.S. policy are affected by various groups and factors operating within the American political system.

The influence of the U.S. administration, bureaucracy, and Congress will not be dealt with at great length in this study. Rather, an attempt will be made to create as complete an inventory as possible of views and attitudes pertaining to Israel, whether these are held by specific groups or are rooted in U.S. culture and more general traditions. The importance of each of these views and its influence on U.S. policy will be evaluated. A number of new developments and shifts in attitudes towards Israel will also be analyzed; in this context, the question of whether Israel is in a position to manipulate various groups will be examined.

Specific views, attitudes, and perceptions are rarely the exclusive property of any one group. Nevertheless, it is possible to identify groups that are basically pro-Israel or anti-Israel. There are also groups whose perception of Israel is somewhat contradictory. At times these groups may regard Israel as a democracy and ally worthy of U.S. support and on other occasions as a balky, intransigent state in need of U.S. guidance and/or sanctions. As such, they will be termed "ambivalent" groups, since their actions may serve either to promote or thwart Israeli interests. Attitudes maintained by amorphous or marginal groups, along with those rooted more generally in U.S. culture and traditions, will be identified in this study as "perceptions" or "factors" influencing U.S. policy.

Whenever possible, groups will be analyzed in terms of their membership, structure, and basic attitudes. Within the three categories (pro-Israel, anti-Israel, and ambivalent groups and factors), what are perceived as the most influential groups and factors will be analyzed first, with the rest discussed in descending order of importance.

A number of specific terms will be used in the analysis that follows. The first is the "direction of influence" of various groups and factors; as indicated above, this refers to the basic orientation of a group or factor as pro-Israel, anti-Israel, or ambivalent. The "nature" of a given group's influence may be tangible or intangible—i.e., expressed in concrete ways as support or opposition to specific acts of the U.S. government, or more abstractly, in general support or opposition to Israel in public opinion polls and in trends in public attitudes towards Israel. The "time range" refers to the length of activity or existence of a group or factor. A "short-term" action of a group or a factor is one of two years or less. Groups and factors which are active in the short-term are generally connected with specific events in the Middle East; groups or factors which are active for longer periods are associated with relatively stable views, perceptions, and ideologies regarding relations between the United States and Israel.

Finally, it should be noted that there are three important assumptions underlying the analysis throughout. The first is that the United States will continue to maintain a strong involvement in the Middle East. The second is that despite a number of recent adverse developments, U.S.-Israeli relations will remain reasonably friendly. And third, that changes are in fact underway in various groups' attitudes towards Israel, and in the factors and perceptions affecting U.S. governmental policies.

Groups and Perceptions Influencing Pro-Israeli Policies

Pro-Israeli Groups

American Jewry. Understandably, the American Jewish community is the main ethnic-religious group displaying a continuous commitment to

Israel by means of its massive moral, economic, and political support. Many individual American Jews demonstrate great concern for Israel's political and economic well-being, as do most of the large American Jewish organizations. In the short range, this well-organized and well-defined group will undoubtedly continue to positively influence the nature of both formal and informal U.S.-Israeli relations, since it is hard to foresee a catastrophic development that would lead to a critical change in American Jewish commitment to Israel. In the long-term, however, a number of highly significant new processes occurring in the community could have adverse effects on its relations with Israel.

On the one hand, the traditional rivalry and lack of consensus that once characterized Zionist, anti-Zionist, and non-Zionist organizations has almost totally disappeared. Large American Jewish organizations display a unity and consistency in their support of Israel, and one may assume that this support will undergo no significant change in the foreseeable future. On the other hand, some of these large organizations (e.g., the UJA, Hadassah, and the Conference of the Presidents of the Major Jewish Organizations) are actually "umbrella" organizations consisting of a number of smaller bodies. The risk here lies in the fact that these smaller organizations have the capability of bolting their federation frameworks against a backdrop of communal friction and adopting new attitudes concerning the aid they extend to Israel. In fact, such a development has already occurred in the case of the American Jewish Joint Distribution Committee (JDC), whose relationship with Israel cooled during the 1970s as a result of its activities on behalf of the absorption of Soviet Jews into the American Jewish community. A second risk connected with umbrella organizations is that the rank and file may change their views while the organization leadership continues to pursue old policies. Such a situation would lead to a growing gap between the grass roots and the organization leadership, and subsequently to a gradual deterioration in these organizations' capacity for efficient political and economic action on behalf of Israel.

A number of social and cultural trends in the American Jewish community in recent years could also influence the behavior of major Jewish organizations in the long range. The first of these trends is assimilation, accompanied by intermarriages and the drifting away of "marginal Jews."[1] Growing assimilation has two interrelated effects on American Jewish organizations: the first, a general decline in membership and the second, a subsequent decrease in the organizations' ability to influence the U.S. government and/or extend substantive economic aid to Israel. Growing assimilation also requires a reallocation of the community's efforts and resources in an attempt to fortify its internal position and prevent further demographic losses. An additional, clearly negative, development is the hostility displayed by many American Jewish youths towards institutionalized and established Jewish activities. A new generation of leaders and activists has emerged that is alienated from the Jewish establishment. A portion of these new activists have opted for involvement in alternative political and social frameworks, most of which are democratic, voluntary, non-institutionalized, and non-establishment. Examples include Briera, the New Israel Fund, and support for the Israeli Peace Now movement. In the meantime, those who have remained active in communal organizations and functions have evinced changed attitudes leading to a diminished unity and a weakened capacity to mobilize for political action.

Other changes in the American Jewish community are related to the establishment of new communities that quite naturally devote their efforts and resources to developing and strengthening local institutions rather than focusing on Israeli-related affairs. There is also the need to strengthen existing aging communities. Finally, new ideological groups have emerged within the Jewish community that exhibit new attitudes towards various Israeli policies, especially with regard to the solution of the Arab-Israeli conflict. These groups have not accepted the major Jewish organizations' self-imposed restriction against public criticism of Israel but have taken Israel to task both for its attitudes towards the Palestinians and its settlement policies in the West Bank. Moreover, since the late 1970s, there has been growing support within the American Jewish community as a whole for recognition of the Palestinians' right for self-determination, a view obviously in opposition to traditional official Israeli government policies. This has led to mounting tension between the Israeli political leadership and some prominent leaders of the American Jewish community (Raab 1982–1983, 46–97).

The social, demographic, and ideological processes just described have weakened the traditional ties between the organized American Jewish community and the state of Israel. In the future, the relationship may well deteriorate further. American Jewry's nearly unchallenged support for Israel has been slowly but steadily eroding. A major factor behind this phenomenon is the increasing controversy concerning Israeli government policy. As noted, the major American Jewish organizations have generally refrained from public criticism of Israel. On a number of occasions, however, American Jewish leaders have voiced sharp criticisms of Israeli policies behind closed doors and in talks held with Israeli politicians and officials. Concealed at first, the dispute between leaders of the organized American Jewish community and Israeli leaders has slowly come out into the open; during the last years of the Likud government in Israel, dissent was voiced much more bluntly and openly (Sheffer 1983–1984, 30–37). Although the level of criticism has died down somewhat in the wake of the Cahan Commission's report on the Sabra and Shatila massacre and in view of the results of the 1984 elections in Israel, there is no reason to assume that this debate has abated altogether, since it focuses on a number of essential doctrinal aspects of the relations between Israel and American Jewry.

Differences of opinion among various segments of the American Jewish community and the lack of coherence in this community's political attitudes could clearly lead to negative long-term developments in the U.S. administration's attitude towards Israel, since internal disputes weaken the efficacy of Jewish organizations' influence on Congressmen, senior politicians, and bureaucrats. With this in mind, rigorous analysis and accurate definition of the problems interfering with intimate relations between Israel and American Jewry would seem to be necessary in order to enhance mutual understanding and agreement between the two sides. Israeli recognition of the Jewish community's emotional sensitivities and ideological tendencies is vital, as is the strengthening of ties between the Israeli and American Jewish elites.

Finally, it should be reemphasized that the Jewish community's commitment to Israel is not to be taken for granted. Rather, it is subject to severe fluctuations. Under the current conditions of tremendous Israeli economic, military, and political dependence on the United States, much depends on Israel's ability to maintain the present level of American Jewish commitment. Although other sources of support for Israel exist, these are not only of lesser importance but are subject to contradictory and adverse influences, and can be mobilized only with great efforts relative to the measures needed to rouse the sympathies of the American Jewish community.

Philo-Semites and World War II Veterans. Certain gentile groups in the United States whose members are chiefly in the older age brackets still feel and express sympathy for Israel as a Jewish state. The attitudes of these groups are connected to a number of factors, the most important of which is a feeling of guilt over the fate of the Jewish people in general, and their fate during World War II in particular. Philo-Semitic groups are generally most active during times of anti-Semitic or neo-Nazi outbursts or attacks on Jewish institutions, or in the wake of anti-Israeli resolutions of international organizations. A number of U.S. politicians have also articulated philo-Semitic feelings, notably the late Senator Henry Jackson and President Ronald Reagan. Senator Jackson's exposure to anti-Semitism was particularly direct and brutal—he was one of the first to enter the concentration camps upon their liberation—and this experience was one of the bases of his later unflinching support of Israel. President Reagan has also occasionally cited the Holocaust as one of the factors behind his sympathy for Israel; it would appear that guilt over this issue can at times be a positive influence on U.S. policy towards Israel.

Nonetheless, the Holocaust issue can cut both ways. Former Israeli prime minister Menachem Begin, for example, habitually brought up the topic of the Holocaust in his talks with both Jewish and gentile groups and leaders. The reactions were sometimes positive, but more often negative. There are two basic reasons for this ambiguity: first, that as time elapses, the memory of World War II and its horrors recedes; and second, that recurrent harping on the Holocaust can render it banal and even ludicrous.

It is undeniable, however, that guilt feelings, pro-Israeli tendencies and philo-Semitism are closely related. The question is how to transform these feelings into effective political influence. Most philo-Semitic groups are relatively amorphous and unorganized. There is one outstanding exception: World War II veterans, who have displayed ongoing and durable sympathy for Israel. It is only proper to note that Jewish veterans are among the most prominent and active members of this group, which has mobilized on numerous occasions in support of Israel (even to the extent of holding several conventions in Israel).

Other philo-Semitic groups, found mainly in the Bible Belt, are motivated in the main by their esteem for Jewish traditions, skills, and achievements. Philo-Semitism is thus essentially a cultural-ideological phenomenon not easily mobilized or manipulated to promote Israel's immediate political needs. Nevertheless, it should not be dismissed, since individual politicians holding philo-Semitic views occasionally appear in Washington, and since groups holding these views provide a favorable atmosphere for the activities of other pro-Israeli politicians. On the other hand, the influence of these groups can be expected to decline further as their members age. A perceived deterioration of Israel's moral standards and cultural achievements also serves to undermine the foundations of such groups, and their ability to influence the political process.

Fundamentalist Groups. Although the United States is a democratic and liberal country in which religious faith and institutions are formally separated from the state, it is at the same time a Christian society with a sizable Protestant majority. Protestant fundamentalist groups in the United States have gained in political strength in recent years, and as the 1984 presidential election has shown, relations between church and state are becoming an important political issue. Quite naturally, various religious groups display different attitudes vis-à-vis Israel. Some groups are influenced by a belief that the Old and New Testaments are the wellspring of ideas and inspiration for revival of the community of believers—fundamentalist groups in particular view the Holy Scriptures as a main source of guidance for coping with day-to-day problems.

Fundamentalist groups' views towards Israel are also influenced by Biblical concepts pertaining to the reunification of Jacob's offspring and the reestablishment of the Jewish state as an essential precondition for the second coming of Jesus. This is the major basis for what is a general Protestant commitment to and support of renascent Israel.

The "Bible Belt" in the South and Midwest is home to a number of pro-Israeli Protestant groups, and various politicians—most notably Jimmy Carter in the late 1970s—have been motivated at least in part by ethical-religious factors. The right-wing "Moral Majority" movement founded by Jerry Falwell is also supportive of Israel (see Friedman 1981, 7–34). This movement wielded certain influence in the 1980 and 1984 elections, and will probably maintain political influence and clout as long as conservative tendencies in the United States do not weaken.

The Israeli problem in this sphere is how to transform fundamentalist sympathy into political influence. This is an organizationally complex and morally difficult question, since sizable segments of the pro-Israeli liberal American Jewish community strongly object to movements such as the Moral Majority and to Israeli cooperation with leaders such as Falwell. During the second Likud government (1981–1984) however, contacts were made with right-wing fundamentalist groups that resulted in these groups' mobilization on behalf of Israel on a number of occasions, including the campaign against the U.S.-Saudi Arabia AWACS deal (see Rafiah 1983, 25).

The Democratic Party. This party has historically derived its strength from a coalition of organized labor, liberal factions (mostly from the Northeast), Southerners, blacks, and Jews—most of whom have maintained relatively stable pro-Israeli attitudes. Until the 1980 presidential elections, a majority of American Jews voted for the Democratic Party, and many individual Jews were active in fundraising and organizing Democratic Party campaigns. Since then, however, increasing numbers of American Jews have crossed party lines to vote for Republican candidates, such as Ronald Reagan, who have demonstrated a strong commitment to Israel. As a result, a number of Democratic leaders have begun to reconsider their attitude vis-à-vis Israel and to refrain from supporting it too explicitly. Further, there has been a general decline in support among blacks, trade union members, Southerners and liberal groups. In part, the traditional Democratic sympathy for Israel had been directed towards Israeli governments led by the Israeli labor movement, whose political and social views were in tune with most of those within the broad Democratic Party spectrum. Objections to the Likud government focused on the Palestinian issue and attitudes displayed by the Likud towards such issues as human rights and the regional arms race.

Should the decline of blacks, trade unions, liberal and Southern support for Israel continue, the pro-Israeli attitude within the Democratic Party may erode still further. However, such erosion, if it occurs, is expected to unfold only slowly. In the foreseeable future, Democrats are expected to continue to support reasonable Israeli policies vis-à-vis the Middle East conflict and other international politics.

Factors and Perceptions Influencing Pro-Israeli Attitudes

Israel as a pioneering democracy. In general, pro-Israeli attitudes in the United States are based on perceived ideological similarities between the two countries. One of these similarities concerns the pioneering ethic upon which generations of young Americans have been raised. Upon its establishment, and for a number of years thereafter, the most widespread image of Israel was that of a frontier state struggling to establish its borders and develop its newly acquired territory. This image had a positive influence on the attitudes of a number of American political leaders—President Lyndon Johnson, for one, citing it as one of the justifications for a pro-Israeli policy. By the late 1960s, however, Israel's pioneering image had begun to undergo a change. One reason for this change was a very real transformation in Israeli society: materialistic attitudes had begun to take hold, and there was a feeling that the old pioneering spirit had in fact evaporated. Second was the Six Day War of 1967. Until this war, most Americans had viewed Israel as the underdog in the Arab-Israeli conflict, constantly struggling for its existence against powerful enemies out to destroy it. This underdog image was weakened when Israel occupied the West Bank, the Gaza Strip and the Golan Heights in 1967, and has been further undermined since then by Israel's refusal to negotiate with the Palestinians, its military government in the occupied territories and military involvement in Lebanon, and the growth of its reliance on military power to achieve political goals. Thus, Israel no longer appears as the underdog in the Middle Eastern conflict; nor is it perceived as pursuing just wars against its opponents. Rather, the newer view of Israel is that of a regional power losing its democratic values, guided by expansionist policies and not loath to take strong actions against other countries in the Middle East or the Palestinians.

Until recently another closely related image of Israel has persisted without major change—that of a democracy with a stable government. Together with the continuous support of the American Jewish community, this particular image, common in wide social circles in the United States, has been largely responsible for continued substantial U.S. aid to Israel. Its influence is particularly great when pro-Israeli groups stress the contrast between Israel and the non-democratic Arab states. However, the new image of political instability in Israel created by the results of the 1981 and 1984 general elections may cast additional doubts about the desirability of supporting Israel.

Israel as a Jewish Refuge. Humanitarian considerations also influence U.S. attitudes towards Israel. In the United States there is a deep respect for individual liberty and the right to enjoy political and religious freedom from persecution. In this light, Israel enjoys U.S. sympathy for its role as a refuge for persecuted Jews. The best-known case involves Soviet Jewry, which became a joint U.S.-Israeli cause, although some action has also been taken on behalf of other Jewish communities, such as those in Syria and Iran.

In the short range, the perception of Israel as a Jewish refuge should continue to generate U.S. support. The long-term outlook, however, is more unclear. Policy shifts in oppressive countries—e.g., a more liberal Soviet policy on Jewish emigration, a drop in Jewish demand for emigration, or vague Israeli policy in this sphere—could cause such change, and in turn the sympathy enjoyed by Israel, to diminish or disappear. The case of Soviet Jewry is particularly interesting, since it illustrates a situation in which initial American Jewish-Israeli cooperation led to a certain amount of long-range conflict. In the late 1960s Israel had purposely adopted a vague policy concerning emigration of Soviet Jewry. In the 1970s and 1980s, however, both Israel and the American Jewish community succeeded in transforming the issue into a matter of general U.S. discussion and concern. The struggle launched by American Jewish groups and organizations, combined with U.S.-Israeli government cooperation, led to a series of actions in Congress (trade limitations, latent and public threats to hold up political negotiations, abstention from sports tournaments, etc.) that helped force a Soviet change in emigration policy for a short period.

In the longer run, however, Soviet Jewish emigration also had negative consequences both for relations between Israel and several large American Jewish organizations (mainly HIAS and the JDC) and for Israel's image among the American public. These consequences were the result of Israel's policy of directing all Soviet Jews to Israel, opposing their absorption into the United States through aid given by large Jewish organizations. Such a position ran counter to that of HIAS and the JDC, who were prepared to work for continued Soviet Jewish emigration to the United States as well as to Israel. These divergent attitudes contributed to a prolonged and sometimes heated debate between Israel and significant segments of the American Jewish community. Another negative result of Soviet Jewish emigration to the United States was the necessary reallocation of funds within the American Jewish community, to Israel's detriment (Edelman 1982, 155–161).

Accordingly, the question of whether and how Israel may gain in terms of American sympathy from its participation in political struggles on behalf of Jewish diasporas in distress—even when its actions are influenced by purely humanitarian considerations—is an open one. This is particularly the case when disagreements in policy jeopardize Israeli interests in terms of its ability to act vis-à-vis the administration. It should be noted here, however, that while the problem of Soviet Jewry has aroused great interest in recent years, the question of Jews in Arab countries has been neglected and nearly forgotten. Except for some diplomatic representations concerning the fate of Syrian and Iranian Jewry, Israel has not made substantial efforts directed at bringing about a more active American policy aimed at improving the situation of these Jews. Thus, Israel has neither fostered nor strained American-Israeli relations on this account.

Israel as a Scientific and Technological Partner. In recent years, a conscious effort has been made to promote Israel as a scientifically and technologically advanced state. For Americans who consider modern advanced technological systems crucial, such an image creates or strengthens pro-Israeli attitudes. On the other hand, Israel's scientific and technological image is strongly associated with intelligence and military achievements (e.g., the purported achievements of the Israeli intelligence agencies, the bombing of the Iraqi nuclear reactor in 1981, etc.). In recent years, U.S. society has become less sympathetic both to militarism and to covert or overt intelligence actions. Thus, the link between modernity and militarism does not always work to Israel's benefit.

In any case, the image of Israel as being scientifically and technologically advanced is both intangible and of short-range effect—especially if such an image does not directly influence any clearly defined American interest groups. Moreover, there is a certain danger associated with promoting Israel's scientific and technological prowess in a country that prides itself on its preeminence in the fields of science and technology. Israel's achievements may be interpreted as a possible threat since they may cause grave apprehensions about the possibility of Israeli competition in certain technological fields wherein the Americans hope to maintain their own predominance. Israel's development of various weapon systems and its achievements in the field of medical instrumentation, for example, caused a certain amount of apprehension and negative reaction in U.S. circles. With this in mind, a clear distinction must be made between promoting a general image of scientific and technological modernity—an intangible factor—and seeking actual scientific and technological ties, which are tangible and quantifiable factors. While Israel can benefit more directly from the promotion of the latter, there are clear risks involved in overselling its products

U.S.-Israeli Economic, Political, and Military Ties. Within the economic, political, and military spheres, Israel has made a concerted effort in the last decade to attain long-range formal U.S. commitments. This represents a change from the position of Israeli governments of the 1950s and 1960s—one that was based not only on Israel's growing dependence on the United States but on a growing sense of insecurity regarding future U.S. policies in the Middle East. Israel's hope is that cooperation anchored in formal agreements will create a set of dynamics that will result in American readiness to continue mutually beneficial connections.

Unlike some of the other factors described above, economic, political, and military ties are generally quantifiable: various types of aid extended to Israel can be compared with aid given to other Middle Eastern states. Experience has shown Israel that the more it learns to develop and exploit the latent potentialities of establishing joint projects and promoting trade relations, the more it will be able to reduce its dependence on shifting trends in American public opinion, changing definitions of American national interests, and changes in the leadership and senior personnel of the administration and Congress.

Israel as a Strategic and Military Partner. The basic outlook concerning future U.S.-Israeli strategic cooperation is positive, since there seem to be no significant ideological or emotional obstacles to block its implementation. In addition to the perceived ideological similarities described above, the present Israeli and United States governments have an important joint interest in preventing Soviet re-penetration into the Middle East. Israel has also shown itself capable of promoting American as well as Israeli interests in the region, the classic example being its intervention in the September 1970 Jordanian-Palestinian crisis (and to some extent, its actions against the PLO in the later stages of the 1982 Lebanon War).

Continued strategic cooperation, however, has important ramifications for both Israel and the United States. One possible area of Israeli concern is acquiring the image of an American proxy that automatically implements instructions issued by the White House. To avoid this danger, Israel must make it clear that it will offer its assistance in safeguarding U.S. interests only when such action is fully congruent with its own requirements and policies. As for the United States, strategic cooperation with Israel may at times conflict with other global and regional interests, particularly those concerning strengthened ties with moderate Arab states. Since the Arab states—including Egypt—are opposed to Israel's inclusion in any regional organization or strategic arrangements in which they themselves participate, American policymakers face a dilemma with regard to closer cooperation with Israel (see Kissinger 1982). U.S. policy thus has been based on an attempt to preserve balance and evenhandedness in supporting moderate Middle Eastern states within a general framework of checking Soviet influence and safeguarding vital American interests. At times, however, these considerations have introduced noticeable tensions in U.S.-Israeli relations.

Nonetheless, there are a number of long-range advantages to U.S.-Israeli strategic cooperation. (In the short range, Israel may benefit from substantive U.S. aid in times of acute military crises.) Even a partial framework of strategic cooperation may bring about a more permanent U.S. military commitment to Israel if such a framework succeeds in winning over skeptics or opponents of increased U.S. aid. Such a scenario seems possible, given the fact that Israel has important benefits to offer in return: its substantial military power; its highly developed military and defense infrastructure, which can provide a U.S. base in the event of an unusually acute regional conflict; high-quality military and defense products (such as ammunition and medical supplies); and reliable intelligence information during regional conflicts. This last point is particularly worth stressing, since important segments of the American intelligence community have long felt a need for closer cooperation with Israel. Cooperation up until now has been informal but mutually beneficial: Israeli warnings—which went unheeded—concerning the incipient fall of the Shah of Iran; information concerning outbreaks of terrorism in Lebanon and Europe and internal threats against pro-Western governments; intelligence cooperation during the 1982 Lebanon War; and U.S. intelligence obtained through satellites and surveillance devices passed on to Israel. For obvious reasons, such cooperation has not been publicized. However, it is clear that pro-Israeli segments of the American intelligence community will continue to serve as advocates for strengthened U.S.-Israeli cooperation in this sphere.

Another point favoring continued U.S.-Israeli strategic cooperation is the fact that Israel still enjoys a relatively stable political regime that can be relied upon to carry out its side of any bilateral agreement: since the early 1950s, Israel's governments and major political parties have been consistently pro-American in orientation. Finally, Israeli leaders stress that strategic cooperation is not meant to replace or supplant the country's own self-defense capability. Israel has always maintained that it has sufficient manpower to repel Arab attacks, so that American soldiers need never be called upon to defend its existence. This is an important consideration, given the U.S. public's sensitivity to the question of military intervention abroad.

Although tension occasionally characterizes U.S.-Israeli relations, it is difficult to foresee a long- or medium-range development in which the United States may disregard basic Israeli needs in planning its policies in the Middle East. On the other hand, an analysis of American policies in the late 1970s and early 1980s should show that concrete strategic understanding and cooperation are not easily attainable and perhaps may clash with Israeli interests. Overreliance on the United States and close strategic cooperation can have a high price tag manifested in the loss of freedom of political maneuverability, a potential for diplomatic tensions, threat of sanctions, etc.

Israel as a Leading Opponent of Terrorism. An additional focus of U.S.-Israeli concern is terrorism, which in the late 1970s and early 1980s has struck both Israeli and American facilities and interests. There is a growing awareness that the nerve centers of American society are exposed and vulnerable to terrorist strikes. Accordingly, the administration has introduced a number of anti-terrorist measures, many of which are modeled on Israeli policies and methods. Thus, there continues to be great deal of respect for the ways in which Israel has combated terrorism in the past; the raid at Entebbe, for example, is still favorably recalled by many Americans. Israel's policy of swift and sometimes brutal reprisals, however, has to some extent offset its positive image. The bombing of terrorist command positions in the midst of Lebanese civilian concentrations, for instance, has been critically regarded by a large segment of the U.S. public. In brief, while there is considerable professional appreciation and sympathy for Israeli successes in the war against terrorism, uncontrolled use of Israeli military force detracts from this sympathy. Nonetheless, for the short and medium ranges, further U.S.-Israeli cooperation in anti-terrorist activities is expected to remain a positive factor in relations between the two countries. The continued existence of this factor depends, however, on how long terrorism remains a central problem in the international arena. Should it become confined to the Middle East, sympathy for Israel may wane, since Middle East terrorist activities are usually identified with the Palestinian struggle for self-determination, a struggle viewed as justified by some U.S. groups. If, however, terrorism continues to strike at U.S. targets abroad, sympathy for Israel may increase.

Israel as a Trade Partner. Continued Israeli economic and technological development, along with the recent agreement concerning a U.S.-Israeli free trade zone, may cause a strengthening of the trade factor as a positive influence on U.S.-Israeli relations. Technological and scientific development has continued despite the severe crisis afflicting the Israeli economy in the late 1970s and early 1980s, with Israel experiencing a clear shift towards the production of sophisticated, high-technology products by various defense and civilian industries (e.g., Israel Air Industries, Rafael, Elsint, Elbit, and Tadiran). As a result, it has acquired a reputation as a technologically advanced country with proven scientific capability and a significant capacity for additional development in the fields of agriculture, electronics, computers, medical instrumentation, solar energy, and modern military equipment.[2] The question is how these achievements will affect the promotion of Israeli interests in the United States. The Pentagon, for example, persistently opposes full utilization of U.S.-Israeli trade potential in the field of military-related products, rejecting the Israeli argument that production of sophisticated items in Israel and their sale either in the United States or to pro-American governments serves to reduce Israeli economic dependence on the United States. The paradox is that the Pentagon and other groups generally hostile to Israel would very much like to see a lessening of Israel's economic dependence. One of Israel's objectives in the strategic dialogue conducted in 1983 was the attainment of better terms for Israel's defense-related exports, new markets for Israeli military and high-technology industries, and increased access to American markets for general Israeli exports.[3] In the meantime, however, the paradox remains, applying as well to non-military trade.

In the case of non-military exports, it is American industrial and commercial interests that are opposed to further Israeli penetration into U.S. markets. Israeli attempts to compete with characteristically American products such as medical instrumentation has already met with opposition, in some cases because U.S. companies either have established markets in Arab countries or would like to expand their activities there. The Arab boycott and Arab investments in the United States present two additional obstacles to increased U.S.-Israeli trade. (see Emerson 1982). Perhaps the best means of overcoming these factors is to penetrate markets in which Arab influence is slight, e.g., those in the high technology field—although here there is strong opposition from competing American firms.

In the final analysis, the Israeli goal of expanding exports to the United States depends mainly on continued technological development and the creation of an efficient export sector. The establishment of a free trade zone—one of whose purposes is to allow for U.S. products to be exported to Europe via Israeli firms—is also expected to alleviate Israel's balance of trade deficit with the United States. Increased economic ties, it should be pointed out, bring political benefits as well, since U.S. firms doing business with Israel can be expected to take a more active interest in Israel's security as well as its economic needs.

Groups and Factors Causing Ambivalence Toward Israel

While the groups and factors in the previous category generally work to promote Israel's interests, those discussed in this section may work either for or against Israel, depending both on the current American domestic arena and shifts in Israeli governments or policies. As such, they are highly significant "swing" factors capable of either tilting American policy in a direction more desirable to Israel or inflicting serious damage on U.S.-Israeli relations. For Israeli policymakers the implications are clear: if Israel develops realistic policies—especially in regard to the peace process in the Middle East—it may be able to exploit some of the following factors in promoting its interests in the United States; to the extent that it pursues unrealistic policies, opposition to Israel is likely to grow.

Ambivalent Groups

Non-Fundamentalist Protestants and Catholics. While America, as noted before, is basically a Protestant society, there are two opposing trends within the Protestant community regarding Israel (Friedman 1982, 101–110). Support of Israel is evinced mainly by fundamentalist movements in the South. Opposite tendencies, however, exist among groups such as the Council of Churches and the (Quaker) Society of Friends, the latter group exhibiting a continuous interest in Middle Eastern affairs. These groups are noted for their universalist, humanitarian tendencies, which in turn have produced strongly favorable feelings towards the Arabs, the Palestinians, and the PLO. There is a growing commitment to act on the Palestinians' behalf, coupled with a tendency to automatically criticize what are regarded as uncompromising Israeli policies vis-à-vis possible solutions to the Palestinian problem.

Fundamentalism is not characteristic of the American Catholic community, and American Catholics thus generally display moderate attitudes concerning the role of religion in American politics. Concerning Israel and the Palestinians, they tend to be in favor of Palestinian self-determination, but are influenced in the main by the attitude of the Vatican, which generally places more of a stress on questions pertaining to the holy places and the status of Jerusalem. With regard to these issues, the Church favors a solution other than full Israeli sovereignty.

From the Israeli point of view, the key to enhancing positive relations with the American Catholic community clearly lies in improved Israeli-Vatican relations. This, in turn, is dependent on Israeli sensitivity to the security and maintenance of Catholic holy places and the status of the Catholic community and its possessions in Israel. It is important to note that the American Catholic community is an important potential (and to some extent actual) source of tourism; friendly relations thus have economic as well as political implications. Within the political realm, the relaxation of tensions in the West Bank and progress in the peace process may also promote a greater concurrence of views between Israel and both the American Catholic (see Mendes 1983, 80–86) and Protestant communities.

The Black Community. Usually it is difficult to separate religious and ethnic factors; most Americans of Polish or Irish origins, for example, are Catholic, and most Swedes or Anglo-Saxons are Protestants. Nevertheless, there are a number of communities in which orientation, influence, and political actions are determined more by ethnic or racial composition. American blacks comprise such a community.

Until the late 1960s, the American black community was generally regarded as both pro-Jewish and pro-Israeli. Black-Jewish relations were favorably influenced by the traditional Jewish commitment towards humanitarian movements, concretely expressed in Jewish involvement in the civil rights movement and its various organizations, as well as in Jewish activities in the field of communal social work. For a long period there was an unofficial Jewish-black coalition in the area of social and political campaigns for the protection and advancement of civil rights. Jews and blacks were the most important ethnic groups in the Democratic coalition contributing to the election of presidents Kennedy and Carter. Moreover, there was a tacit political coalition and cooperation between black and Jewish leaders concerning the social, economic, and political demands of each community. Until the 1970s, black sympathies were translated into durable support for Israel—a tendency strengthened by the fact that many Southern blacks belonged to fundamentalist Protestant communities that pursued a clearly pro-Israeli policy (Friedman 1981, 121–134).

In recent years, however, new social and political developments have adversely affected Jewish-black relations. As the American Jewish community has become more bourgeois, it has shifted some of its support to the Republicans. It is also heavily engaged in its own internal affairs and more fully integrated into the American mainstream; whereas the blacks' social and economic position has in some respects worsened. Furthermore, a portion of the U.S. black leadership has drawn closer to the African and Arab states, and the influence of Black Muslim leaders has left an imprint on the behavior of the black community with regard to Israel. Progressively, the weight of these factors has undermined black support of Israel in recent years.

Nevertheless, a number of black leaders, notably Bayard Rustin and Benjamin Hooks, still display affinity for Israel. Although they do not refrain at times from criticizing its policies, these leaders are still willing to actively promote Israeli interests. On the other hand, strong pro-Arab and pro-Palestinian attitudes have been expressed by black leaders such as Andrew Young and Jesse Jackson, who in seeking to promote ties with black Africa have cultivated ties with Arab and Palestinian representatives in the United States. Israel's friendly relations with South Africa, along with the non-acceptance of the Black Hebrew community in Israel, have also not helped the cause of advancing Israeli interests among U.S. blacks. Moreover, since the 1973 Yom Kippur War, there has been increased identification with the Palestinian Arab cause. Israel has been portrayed to large black audiences as an imperialist conqueror of a repressed people's land, and black leaders have openly made comparisons between the exploited black community and the dispossessed Palestinian Arabs.

Thus, in place of the traditional identification with the Jews and with Israel as an underdog nation, the link between American blacks and the Palestinian Arabs has broadened. It seems that Israel is almost fighting a rearguard battle to neutralize hostile sentiments among a large segment of American blacks. Great efforts will be needed to restore the intimacy between both blacks and Jews and blacks and Israel, and to persuade black community leaders to exert a positive influence in the process of shaping U.S. policy towards the Middle East and Israel. As has been noted above, a slight potential for success in such efforts still exists because of the Protestant religious influence on large segments of the black community and the ties which still survive between some black and American Jewish leaders. The Israeli government, however, has apparently written off the black community as a potential source for sympathy, so that any positive future developments depend entirely on the Jewish-black relations within the United States.

Liberal Groups. As discussed earlier, perceived ideological similarites between the United States and Israel are an important factor influencing pro-Israeli attitudes. American academics, intellectuals, professionals, and teachers still preceive Israel as a sister "immigrant" society and fellow democracy associated with liberal activities and human and civil rights movements. Such sympathy was the basis for contacts between Israeli representatives and various liberal and progressive elements in the American society, with Israel making a case for itself as a stable democracy and a reliable U.S. partner in the Middle East, especially when compared with the capricious authoritarian or oligarchic regimes in the region.

During the past two decades, however, Israel has become a riddle—perhaps a kind of paradox—for American liberals and especially for

American leftists. Its image as a society in search of social justice has been marred by domestic problems, its policies in the occupied territories and its friendly relations with South Africa, South American dictatorships, and various autocratic regimes in Africa and Southeast Asia. All of these have led to lowered esteem in leftist and liberal American circles. The 1982 Lebanon War has caused further, and perhaps irreversible, deterioration in Israel's image among these groups. Only drastic changes in Israel's policies may alter these attitudes.

Organized Labor. Israel's ongoing decline in status and growing isolation have negatively influenced its relations with groups who had previously been consistently supportive. One such group is American organized labor, which has had a long-standing relationship with the Israeli trade union movement (the Histadrut). Until the mid 1970s, the Labor Party led Israel's government; this created a basis for close understanding between Israeli representatives and U.S. labor leaders, as did the belief that the two movements shared similar democratic values and a similar commitment to the improvement of workers' standard of living.

Some of these pro-Israeli sentiments did not abate in the course of the seven years of Likud-led government; between 1977 and 1984, the Histradrut diligently maintained contacts with U.S. organized labor in order to safeguard their continued relationship. The labor movement's traditionally conservative attitude in U.S. foreign policy matters—in particular, its hostility towards communism—has also helped sustain sympathy for Israel, since Israel is regarded as the chief obstacle to Soviet expansionism in the Middle East. Nonetheless, it would be a mistake to assume U.S. labor movement support for Israel as an unchanging given; in recent years, as a result of various Israeli policies towards the United States and the Middle East, signs of erosion have become apparent.

Ambivalent Factors

Israel as a Dependent State. Ever since the late 1960s, American economic aid has been an essential component of U.S.-Israeli relations. The "patron-client" relationship in which the dependent state strives for higher levels of support (supplied by the patron only in exchange for specific services or actions) has been exploited by each side since this time, becoming especially pronounced during periods of political negotiations between Israel and its regional neighbors. The pattern was highly evident, for example, during talks concerning the separation of forces and interim agreements following the Yom Kippur War; the Camp David talks and ensuing negotiations regarding a peace treaty with Egypt; and the 1984 talks concerning Israeli evacuation from Lebanon. In each of these instances, the United States undertook to increase its aid to Israel in exchange for Israeli readiness to agree to political, military, and sometimes economic concessions to the Arab countries (such as the Israeli withdrawal from the oil fields and air bases in the Sinai). Recently, an increased sophistication could be discerned in the American position: in return for its aid, the administration now attempts to impose certain policies to ensure that Israel will not act against U.S. interests, or at the very least, will coordinate its actions with the United States. An example of this pattern was provided during the evacuation of Yassir Arafat and his men from Tripoli late in 1983. Israel's economic dependence on the United States—more specifically, the fact that the two countries were in the final stages of negotiations concerning increased economic aid— played a clear role in Israel's allowing Arafat to leave Tripoli.

U.S. military and economic aid has contributed to Israel's development and has prevented its suffering an even more massive and severe economic crisis; it has also given Israel a number of strategic political advantages, since such aid is interpreted as evidence both of American willingness to support Israel at crucial periods and a long-term commitment to Israel. As the amount of aid grows, so too does the U.S. stake in protecting its previous investments. Put in more abstract terms, one of the dependent state's interests is to lead the superpower into an "investment trap." The United States appears to be entangled in such a trap: between 1970 and 1984, U.S. economic aid to Israel totaled a staggering $32 billion, including $11 billion in grants. In view of its continuing economic crisis, Israel is presently demanding a further dramatic increase in American economic and military aid. It appears that the United States will maintain high levels of aid—the current level of both economic and military aid is about $3 billion per annum (Gazit 1983)—for the next several years.

As a result of this massive military and economic assistance, however, Israel is confronted by a number of difficult questions concerning its policies vis-à-vis the United States which in turn determines, to some extent, U.S. reciprocal policy. It has been argued that extremely high levels of assistance gravely hinder any prospect of Israeli economic self-sufficiency and place a political millstone around the country's neck. Moreover, within the United States, economic aid to Israel has led to a certain amount of resentment. Black leader Jesse Jackson, for example, has charged that Israel receives more U.S. financial aid than all the nations of black Africa combined, an argument that has generated anger against Israel in various segments of the American public, particularly among the black community. Against the background of slow and uncertain economic recovery coupled with lingering unemployment, it is not difficult to generate public debate in the United States on the question of America's obligations to Israel. An additional, related question being asked more often in recent times is why U.S. citizens should be obligated to bear the burden of such high levels of aid to Israel—especially when Americans visiting Israel are impressed by what in many ways seems to be a flourishing economy.

In summary, U.S. economic aid to Israel is both an expression of genuine commitment and a factor liable, under certain circumstances, to boomerang against Israel's interests. While a reduction in aid would be a short-term blow both to its economy and prestige, Israel might actually benefit in the long run, since its economy would be forced to adjust to difficult conditions. This in turn could promote Israeli economic independence and help prevent further erosion in U.S. public opinion.

Israel's Stance in Peace Negotiations. One of the cornerstones of U.S. policy in the Middle East is to press for continuation of the peace process even when the outlook seems uncertain. The long-range goal here is to minimize the need for continued U.S. involvement in the region's recurrent crises. Israel's stance in peace negotiations thus has direct effects on U.S. interests—as well as on Israel's image, whether positive or negative, within the United States.

On the whole, Israel's image has not been particularly positive in recent years, despite the fact that since the mid-1970s, U.S. aid to Israel has been closely linked to the continuation of the peace process. Israel's perceived inflexibility on what are regarded as marginal or symbolic issues (e.g., objection to a Jordanian-Palestinian delegation) had led to its image in the United States as an intransigent nation both with regard to its ultimate objectives and its general attitude towards peace. Other issues of conflict include Israel's settlement policy in the West Bank and Gaza, its negative position regarding autonomy talks, its rejection of the Reagan initiative, and its refusal on several occasions to respond positively to political signals emanating from Arab states and/or Palestinian organizations viewed by the United States as moderate in orientation. Most serious of all is the incompatibility of U.S. and Israeli long-range objectives with regard to the Palestinian problem, the U.S. view favoring some form of Palestinian right to self-determination being in conflict with Israel's flat rejection of such a solution.

The recent war in Lebanon has had both positive and negative effects on Israel's image. U.S.-Israeli coordinated operations in Lebanon in the latter half of 1983 somewhat ameliorated earlier criticisms of the Israel invasion; although there are no guarantees that such criticisms will not be resumed with even greater vehemence should current circumstances undergo an alteration. If the peace talks resume, and if a solution is found for the West Bank and Gaza, Israel's position will improve both in the eyes of the administration and the U.S. public. If, however, Israel does not change its operative policy with regard to the occupied territories—especially with regard to Jewish settlements in the West Bank—many U.S. groups are likely to hold it responsible for continued deadlock in peace negotiations.

The Issue of Jerusalem. Once the question of the occupied territories and the Palestinians' rights to self-determination has been examined, there is no way to ignore the highly complex problem of Jerusalem. Judging from the great interest it arouses in large segments of American public opinion, the question of Jerusalem's ultimate status may turn out to be a stumbling block in future U.S.-Israeli relations. For now, Israel's annexation of East Jerusalem and the various proposals it has made for access of Christians and Moslems to the holy places has worked both for and against it; while the actual annexation is criticized, the access allowed to the holy places and the liberal administration of the Old City has brought a good deal of praise.

Long- and short-term factors play an active role in determining the attitudes of various groups to the Jerusalem problem, and these attitudes in turn are capable of influencing other groups and factors. The American public is interested in such issues as Jerusalem's unification, the sovereignty question, international supervision, and status and administration of the holy places, while Israel has two goals that enjoy a nearly full national consensus: ensuring Jerusalem's continued unification and its recognition as Israel's capital. On the whole the Israeli goals have been endorsed by the American Jewish community, various Protestant groups, and philo-Semitic groups. The open question is whether other groups—especially U.S. policymakers—can be influenced through these groups to change the official U.S. policy of opposing the annexation of the Old City and, consequently, not recognizing Jerusalem as Israel's capital. As has been mentioned above, the American Catholic community has not been targeted as a group likely to change its views, in light of the fact that it generally accepts the Vatican policy of pressing for internationalization of the city.

Influence of the UN and Other International Organizations. Although the United States has shown consistent support of Israel within the UN and related international agencies, it appears that the fiercely anti-Israel propaganda emanating from these bodies has had a cumulatively negative effect on U.S. public opinion. From Israel's point of view, the Reagan administration is an improvement over the Carter administration, which attributed great importance to the UN in the context of its human rights campaign. The Reagan administration, in contrast, is generally suspicious and even hostile to the UN, and has adopted an even more sympathetic position in support of Israel. Occasionally the administration (under both Carter and Reagan) has refrained from voting in support of Israeli positions as a reaction against Israeli actions undertaken without prior consultation with Washington. On the whole, however, Israel has been successful in influencing the administration to adopt pro-Israeli positions and veto anti-Israeli resolutions; this, to a large extent, reduces the damage done to Israel's image.

Groups and Factors Influencing Anti-Israel Policies

Anti-Israeli Groups

The Arab Lobby and Arab-Americans. Beginning in the late 1970s, an active and increasingly powerful Arab lobby began to emerge in the United States. Its first big triumph occurred in 1978, when the Carter administration announced plans to sell planes to Egypt and Saudi Arabia. Despite a strenuous campaign conducted by pro-Israeli and Jewish lobbying groups, Congress eventually approved the sale. Three years later, over similar opposition, the sale of AWACS to Saudi Arabia was approved. The Saudi lobby was especially prominent among those groups working in concert with American business interests to promote and ensure this deal (Rafiah 1983).

Based on their control of oil reserves, petrodollars, and strategic routes, Arab influence in international organizations has not diminished. Pro-Arab lobbies now reach centers of power to which they had no access until the late 1970s. In the United States, Arab influence in the black, academic and business communities is growing. Massive investments (though dwindling in recent years) in economic projects and large American corporations have engendered political power and influence: large oil companies, investment companies, and various consultant firms all extend support to the Arab cause.

As long as Arab lobbying activities are conducted according to accepted norms of American politics, there is little Israel can do to stop them. On occasion, Israel has attempted to stress the negative consequences of Arab influence and the Arab boycott. However, these attempts have led to countercharges concerning Jewish economic power and its purportedly harmful effects on the American society (see, for example, Mathias 1981, 993). Stronger and closer U.S.-Israeli economic relations may bring this factor into a somewhat better balance.

The Arab community in the United States essentially plays the role of countering and offsetting Jewish influence on public opinion and on the administration's policies. The Arab community consists of two large groups—Christian Lebanese and Palestinian Arabs—and a number of smaller groups associated with other Arab countries. Judging by the administration's behavior during the 1982 Lebanon War, the influence of the Christian Lebanese community is not significant. On the other hand, there is evidence of growing strength and influence within the Palestinian Arab community. As a whole, the Arab-American community is still inferior to American Jewry in organization, power, and direct political influence. However, it compensates in part for these shortcomings by high levels of activity and extensive access to resources, advice and organizational help originating in the Arab states and channelled through Arab embassies in the United States. There is little doubt that this group will continue to gain in sophistication and exposure: its voice will be heard even more in the media, from platforms of international organizations such as the UN, in Congressional subcommittees, and on campuses. It is hard to expect that the Arab lobby's activities in countering and offsetting Jewish influence on public opinion and administration policy will diminish in the near future. However, if the Israeli government decides to forge contacts or open serious negotiations with the Palestinians, a number of Palestinians residing in the United States may be among the first to extend their public blessing and participate actively in peace negotiations. This is likely since various Palestinian figures have openly expressed views that are less extreme than those voiced by their associates in the PLO or organizations sponsored by the rejectionist states.

The "Arabists". Career State Department and Pentagon officials known as the "Arabists" (since most have held posts in Arab countries) are among those responsible for the U.S. policy of "evenhandedness" in the Middle East. The administration's recurrent attempts to maintain such a policy has had negative implications for Israel, since considerations that place Israel and Arab states on opposite poles of the spectrum— disregarding the Arab states' greater economic power, size, and resources— almost necessarily lead to decisions unfavorable for Israel. Israel can reduce the weight of Arab influence if it succeeds in mobilizing and activating the pro-Israeli factors and groups in the American system. An increase in open U.S.-Israeli cooperation, or a clear Israeli demand for open, explicit agreements with the United States as either part of the peace process itself or a consequence of a final settlement may weaken the influence of the Arabists and others who advocate an evenhanded policy. However, there may be high costs in terms of a drop in public support for Israel, a loss of political and military maneuverability, or the abolition of fixed levels of economic and military aid. An alternative method of combating the evenhanded policy is to appeal directly to the American public. Israeli policymakers have in fact been doing this for many years, although there has been a certain amount of erosion recently in their ability to communicate the message that America's moral obligation to Israel should take precedence over cold calculations concerning the possible economic, political, or strategic benefits of an evenhanded policy.

Anti-Semitic Groups. Anti-Jewish tendencies manifested in some American communities are nourished partly by anti-Semitism, a phenomenon better known within white groups. Though anti-Semitism is not strong in the United States, there are small neo-Nazi and anti-Semitic groups whose pronouncements and activities contribute to an atmosphere hostile to general Jewish goals and to Israeli interests. Whether this anti-Semitism is directed only against Jews or against Israel as well, its influence is clearly felt in the political attitudes of certain wider groups in the United States; attempts to separate anti-Semitism from anti-Zionism have not been totally successful. On the other hand, anti-Semitic outbursts have in the past led other groups to sympathize both with the American Jewish community and more indirectly, with Israel as well (Raab 1976, 65–71).

Factors and Perceptions Influencing Anti-Israeli Attitudes

Israel as an Occupying Power. The issue of Israeli settlements in the occupied territories has created a good deal of tension in U.S.-Israeli relations, as has the larger issue of the status of the Palestinians. There is a growing tendency among large American social groups to sympathize with the Palestinians' arguments, a tendency fortified in part by Israel's sometimes harsh military and administrative measures (e.g., land expropriations, deportations, arrests and blowing up of houses of suspected terrorists) and general settlement policy. Various public declarations such as the Begin government's immediate rejection of the Reagan initiative and unilateral steps such as the application of Israeli law on the Golan Heights have also contributed to the growing distance between Israel and groups in the United States which in the past offered it massive support, not only among liberals but among conservatives. Similarly, it is difficult to justify Israeli stances that seem by their hawkishness to be aimed at obstructing the peace process, or to justify Israeli policies of discrimination against the Palestinians.

A shift in Israeli policy on these issues could well change the general atmosphere concerning U.S.-Israeli relations. A halt in settlement activity and land expropriations, for example, would expose Israel to criticism from a small segment of the American Jewish community (as well as a larger group within Israel), but would gain positive reactions from substantial segments of the Jewish and non-Jewish American population.

Israel as a Supporter of Reactionary Regimes. In recent years Israel has been linked with arms sales and military aid to right-wing dictatorial regimes, especially in Latin and South America. Disclosure of information concerning Israeli aid to the Somoza regime in Nicaragua, the former military junta in Argentina, the South African government, and others have contributed to a negative image in the eyes of liberal groups and individuals supporting human and civil rights in foreign countries. There is a paradox here, however: while Israel's aid to these regimes has been condemned by the media and American public opinion, it has been carried out with the administration's tacit blessing.

Conclusions

In view of Israel's isolation in the international arena and its economic, political, and moral dependence on the United States, there is no doubt that intimate U.S.-Israeli relations constitute a major objective in Israeli foreign policy. By safeguarding this objective, it is felt, other Israeli strategic and tactical interests will also be guaranteed. On the basis of this assumption, it is important to determine the major groups and factors in the American system that both display interest in Israel and that influence U.S. policymakers' attitudes—for these, in turn, lead to U.S. commitments and military and economic aid.

It is difficult, however, to determine the size of these groups, in large part because their strength is constantly changing. Whenever the Middle East or Israel are in the midst of heightened military or political activities interest in the region increases, although in general it appears that interest is progressively waning, chiefly because of the fatigue involved in constantly trying to follow the volatile course of developments in a conflict whose permanent solution is not yet in sight. Nonetheless, the analysis in this article indicates that in the forseeable future, a small number of groups will still continue to support Israel. Even if their membership and active supporters are diminishing, their level of commitment and willingness to act is still high. Table 1.1 summarizes the composition of these pro-Israeli groups and factors.

The most consistent of these groups and factors is, of course, the American Jewish community. Some of the other pro-Israeli groups and individuals are influenced in part by intangible factors such as Israel's image as a democratic state and a modern nation that produces sophisticated and technologically advanced goods. Other groups support Israel for tangible reasons such as its capability for military, intelligence, and economic cooperation with the United States. As previously noted, the number of members in these groups is not high, but their influence is a definite one because of their relatively high level of commitment. The most noticeable recent development within these groups, however,

Table 1.1
Pro-Israeli Groups and Factors

Group/Factor	Nature of Commitment/Influence		Time Range		Ease of Manipulation	
	Tangible	Intangible	Short	Long	High	Low
American Jewry	X	X		X	X	
Philo-Semites		X		X	X	
Fundamentalists		X	X			X
Democratic Party	X	X	X			X
Israel as a pioneering democracy		X		X	X	
Israel as Jewish refuge		X	X			X
Israel as scientific, technological partner	X	X		X	X	
U.S.-Israeli economic, political, military ties	X		X		X	
Israel as strategic/ military partner	X			X	X	
Israel as opponent of terrorism	X	X	X		X	
Israel as trade partner	X		X			X

is a steadily increasing degree of criticism of Israel; Israel, in fact, may lose some of these groups' support in the near future.

Groups with larger memberships and supporting circles have mainly entered the second category—i.e., they support Israel at times, refrain from supporting it on other occasions, and at times oppose increased U.S.-Israeli cooperation. These are the main targets for Israeli persuasion efforts.

Finally, more groups show a growing degree of opposition to Israel. In this group one finds the pro-Arab lobbies, large corporations which maintain close trade relations or involvement in the oil industry, the State Department and Pentagon Arabists, and chiefly groups which oppose Israeli policy concerning the Palestinians for moral or ideological reasons. Table 1.3 summarizes this category.

In summary, Israeli policymakers have the option of selecting several groups and acting to strengthen them and their relations with Israel so that they will promote or strengthen Israeli interests. This is an easy solution which has guided the efforts of Israeli representatives to coordinate various activities, mainly those of pro-Israeli groups. A more

Table 1.2
Ambivalent Groups and Factors

Group/Factor	Nature of Commitment/Influence		Time Range		Ease of Manipulation	
	Tangible	Intangible	Short	Long	High	Low
Non-fundamentalist religious groups		X		X	X	
The black community	X	X		X		X
Liberal groups		X		X		X
Organized labor	X			X	X	
Israel as dependent state		X		X		X
Israel's stance in peace negotiations		X	X		X	
The issue of Jerusalem		X		X		X
Influence of UN and other international bodies		X		X		X

Table 1.3
Anti-Israeli Groups and Factors

Group/Factor	Nature of Commitment/Influence		Time Range		Ease of Manipulation	
	Tangible	Intangible	Short	Long	High	Low
Arab lobbies		X		X		X
"Arabists"	X	X		X		X
Anti-Semitic groups		X		X		X
Israel as occupying power		X		X	X	
Israeli aid to reactionary regimes		X	X		X	

difficult route is that of regarding all of the various groups inventoried here as a system in which the various members interact and influence U.S.-Israeli relations. Any attempt to manipulate such a system will be successful only if guided by clear political notions and attitudes. Furthermore, the analysis here clearly demonstrates that Israel's adoption of realistic views and policies would lead to increased support for its own political and economic interests. A better presentation of Israeli objectives is not possible at present because of the hawkish attitudes of the Israeli government in regard to the future of the occupied territories, the nature of the borders on Israel's eastern front, the way in which the peace process is to be revived, and the administration of the occupied territories. If Israel takes no clear-cut realistic initiatives, other initiatives will inevitably emerge, with negative implications for Israel's image in the United States and subsequent U.S. policy.

Notes

1. Since 1937, the Jewish rate of population growth in the United States has not kept apace with that of the general American population: the percentage of Jews has gradually fallen from a peak of 3.7 in 1937 to 2.7 in 1979. See Goldstein 1980, 9–65.
2. The value of Israeli electrical and electronics exports, for example, rose from $287 million (1980), to $397 million (1981), to $465 million (1982). Most of the increase occurred in a specific category, that of electronic instruments for surveillance, science, and medicine, with exports in this category increasing from $98.6 million (1980), to $146.3 million (1981), to $177.9 million (1982). See the *Statistical Quarterly of Foreign Trade*, Vol. 34 (1) 1983.
3. In 1983, Israeli exports to the United States totaled $1.119 billion; forecasts for 1983 indicated a 10 percent increase. See the *Statistical Quarterly of Foreign Trade*, Vol. 34 (3) 1983, 22.

Bibliography

Books

Elazar, Daniel J. *Community and Polity: The Organizational Dynamics of American Jewry*. Philadelphia: Jewish Publication Society, 1976.

Evron, Yair. *The Middle East: Nations, Superpowers and Wars*. New York: Praeger, 1973.

Feuerwerger, Marvin C. *Congress and Israel—Foreign Aid Decision-Making in the House of Representatives 1969–1976*. Westport, Conn.: Greenwood Press, 1979.

Hertzberg, Arthur. *To Be Jewish in the American Diaspora*. (Heb.) Jerusalem: Zionist Library, 1981.

Kissinger, Henry. *Years of Upheaval*. Boston: Little Brown and Co., 1982.

────── . *White House Years*. Boston: Little Brown and Co., 1979.

Quandt, William. *A Decade of Decisions*. Berkeley and Los Angeles: University of California Press, 1977.

———. "United States Policy in the Middle East: Constraints and Choices," in Hammond and Alexander (ed.) *Political Dynamics in the Middle East.* New York: American Elsevier, 1972.

Rubin, Jakob. *Partners in State Building: American Jewry and Israel.* New York: Diplomatic Press, 1969.

Safran, Nadav. *Israel—The Embattled Ally.* Cambridge, Mass.: Harvard University Press, 1978.

Snetsinger, John. *Truman, the Jewish Vote and the Creation of Israel.* Stanford, Calif.: Hoover Institution Press, 1974.

Articles and Publications

Avidan, Meir. "Main Aspects of U.S.-Israeli Relations During the 1950s." Jerusalem: The Leonard Davis Institute for International Relations, 1982.

Cohen, Steven. "Attitudes of American Jews Towards Israel and Israelis." New York: Institute on American Jewish-Israeli Relations, American Jewish Committee, 1983.

Edelman, Joseph. "Soviet Jews in the United States: An Update." *American Jewish Yearbook* 1982, 155–161.

Emerson, Steve. "The Petrodollar Connection." *The New Republic*, February 17, 1982.

Feldman, Shai. "Reagan's Administration and Israel: the Second Term." (Heb.) Tel Aviv: The Jaffe Center for Strategic Studies, No. 14 (March 1985).

Friedman, Murray. "Intergroup Relations." *American Jewish Yearbook* 1982, 101–110. 1981, 121–134.

———. "Religion and Politics in the Age of Pluralism: The Last Generation in an Ethno-Cultural View." *Tefutzot Yisrael* (Heb.) Summer-Autumn 1981, 7–34.

Gazit, Mordechai. "Israeli Military Procurement from the United States." (see Chapter 3 in this volume).

Goldstein, Sidney. "The Jews in the United States—The Demographic Aspect." *Tefutzot Yisrael* (Heb.) Spring 1980, 9–85.

Laufer, Leopold Y. "U.S. Aid to Israel—Problems and Perspectives." (see Chapter 4 in this volume).

Maslow, William. "The Structure and Functioning of the American Jewish Community." New York: American Jewish Congress, 1974.

Mathias, Charles. "Ethnic Groups and Foreign Policy." *Foreign Affairs.* Summer 1981, 993.

Mendes, Meir. "The Vatican and Israel." Jerusalem: The Leonard Davis Institute for International Relations 1983, 80–86.

Pomerance, Michla. "American Guarantees to Israel and the Law of American Foreign Relations." Jerusalem: The Leonard Davis Institute for International Relations, 1974.

Raab, Earl. "Agreement and Reservations in the Relations between American Jewry and the State of Israel." *Gesher* (Heb.) Winter-Spring 5742, 46–97.

———. "On Those Emotionless and Apathetic to Anti-Semitism." *Tefutzot Yisrael* (Heb.) Spring 1976, 65–71.

Rafiah, Zvi. "Domestic Factors and their Influence on Shaping Mideast Foreign Policy." Jerusalem: The Leonard Davis Institute for International Relations, 1983, 25.

Sheffer, Gabriel. "A Shift in the Relations between American Jewry and Israel." *Gesher* (Heb.) Winter-Spring 5743, 30–37.

Slonim, Shlomo. "United States-Israel Relations, 1967–1973: A Study in the Convergence and Divergence of Interests." Jerusalem: The Leonard Davis Institute for International Relations, 1982. *Jerusalem Papers on Peace Problems*. Summer-Autumn 1981, 7–34.

TWO

Trends in American
Attitudes Toward Israel

EYTAN GILBOA

Introduction

In democracies the people elect their leaders for a prescribed period of
time. Election of particular politicians usually indicates preferences for
values, personalities, policies, and programs. However, since voting is
usually decided by a number of other variables as well, it cannot serve
as a reliable index for policy-making on a particular issue. Therefore,
opinions of the public on specific issues must be obtained through other
means, one of which is public opinion polls.

This study deals with public opinion polls on a specific foreign issue—
Israel and the Arab-Israeli conflict. According to a number of polls
(Rielly 1983, 8–10; Dawson 1973, 29–33; Erikson and Luttbeg 1973),
Americans are not usually interested in foreign affairs. Yet they are most
interested in Israel and the Arab-Israeli conflict; in the course of the
last two decades, Israel has received almost as much attention in the
American media and in political and public circles as any domestic issue.
This interest is probably due to the special relationship that has been
forged between the two countries, the values and traditions they have
in common, and the presence of a large American-Jewish community.

This work presents a critical analysis of polls that have measured
American attitudes towards Israel and the Arab-Israeli conflict from the

This article represents the initial phase of a comprehensive project on American public
opinion toward Israel and the Arab-Israeli conflict. The author thanks Ms. Yael Nachmias
for her research assistance and the Leonard Davis Institute for International Relations for
research grants which made this study possible.

end of World War II and the establishment of Israel until 1984. The main goal of the study is to identify and explain basic trends in American opinions towards Israeli issues. Any trend analysis of this kind presents several difficulties. First, research on past public opinion is inherently limited by the availability of data. Pollsters do not usually conduct polls with a view to the future, and on many occasions the researcher is both perplexed and frustrated to discover that no polls were conducted on specific important issues at specific critical times. Moreover, in order to be valid, trend analysis must be "based upon the same question being asked of completely comparable samples" (Roll and Cantril 1972, 109). In this work, only one question was found that met this vital criterion for the entire period under study; other questions were valid only for shorter periods of time.

An added difficulty lies in the fact that fluctuations and changes in opinions must be seen first and foremost in the context of ongoing events. As Charles Roll and Albert Cantril (1972, 117) explained, "there is nothing immutable about the results of a poll . . . what a poll provides is a picture of the public's view at only one point of time and only on questions being asked." Thus, it was necessary to structure the polls within the contexts of major events and processes.

Finally, various elements of polls such as wording of questions, the wording of possible answers, and the order and context of questions and answers, are liable to cause the same person being polled to give radically different responses (Robinson and Meadow 1982, Ch. 6 and Bishop, *et al.* 1978, 81–92). This phenomenon has invited manipulation of polling; the researcher must always be aware of the pitfalls inherent in such manipulation.

The structure and methodology of this study were designed in ways that were intended to minimize the inevitable hazards of research on public opinion polls. A special effort, the first of its kind, was made to examine the results of many polls within the context of significant events that occurred in Israel, the Middle East, and the United States. Each section of this study presents most of the available data in a chronological order structured around major events. The first section deals with the period from the creation of Israel until the 1967 Six Day War. The second section focuses on the period between the Six Day War and the Sadat visit to Jerusalem, an event that represented a major turning point in the Arab-Israeli conflict. The third section deals with the peace-making process started by the Sadat visit and completed in April 1982; while the fourth and final section examines the outbreak of the highly controversial 1982 Israeli war in Lebanon and the effects of this war on basic American attitudes towards Israel.

While this work does not pretend to offer a comprehensive review of the Arab-Israeli conflict, it does describe each major event in the periods under study. Such description is necessary in order to provide a context for the analysis of the polling data. It is important to add that the data itself does not cover all of the various aspects of American attitudes towards Israel. Although issues such as U.S. economic aid and the Palestinian question have sometimes been raised in polls, space limitations did not allow for the inclusion of these and other specific issues (see, however, Gilboa 1985).

Only national polls of reliable polling agencies such as Gallup, Harris, and Yankelovich, Skelly, and White were used in this study. The results of the polls were collected from periodicals, newspapers, and official publications of polling agencies, as well as from organizations such as the Council on Foreign Relations, the Foreign Policy Association and the American Jewish Congress. Results of polls that did not provide complete information on sampling techniques, questions, answers, and other technical issues were omitted.

A considerable effort has been made to identify all existing data and integrate it into patterns and frameworks. In several areas this integration exposes both the weaknesses and the strengths of public opinion polls, at least as they were manifested in polls on American attitudes towards Israel and the Arab-Israeli conflict. It is hoped, however, that the comprehensive nature of the study will place the various issues in proper perspective.

The Establishment of Israel
Until the Six Day War, 1948-1967

Very few polls were taken during the first 20 years of the Arab-Israeli conflict, and most that were, were clustered around two major events: the establishment of Israel and the Sinai campaign of 1956. During this period the American Institute of Public Opinion (Gallup), the National Opinion Research Center in Chicago (NORC), and the Survey Research Center in Berkeley (SRC/C) took several polls that measured American sympathies towards Israel and the Arabs (see Table 2.1).

Such polls have been conducted throughout the Arab-Israeli conflict from 1947 to the present, and they provide interesting comparisons about the relative popularity of Israel and the Arabs among the American public. Table 2.1 shows a 2 to 1 margin in favor of Israel in the late 1940s and 3 to 1 by the mid-1960s. The majority of the respondents, however, did not take a position, either having no opinion or expressing sympathy with neither side. Polls on specific issues, in contrast, yielded much more conclusive results.

Table 2.1
Sympathy with Jews or Arabs, 1947–1949, 1964

Questions
a. If war breaks out between the Arabs and Jews in Palestine, which side would you sympathize with?
b. The United Nations has recommended that Palestine be divided between the Jews and the Arabs. The Arabs say they will not agree to have Palestine divided, and fighting has broken out between the Jews and Arabs. Do you sympathize with the Jews in this matter?
c. In the conflict in Palestine, do you sympathize with the Arabs or with the Jews?
d. Suppose there were a war between the Arab nations and Israel. Which side do you think you would probably sympathize with?

Q	Date	Poll	Jews/Israel	Arabs	Both, Neither Don't Know
		Partition Resolution Before the U.N.			
a	Nov. '47	G	24%	12%	64%
b	Feb. '48	NORC	35	16	49
		Israel's War of Independence			
c	June '84	NORC	34	12	54
c	July '48	NORC	36	14	50
c	Oct. '48	NORC	33	11	56
		Armistice Agreements			
c	Mar. '49	NORC	32	13	55
d	Nov. '64	SRC-C	25	7	68

Sources: Charles H. Stember, et al., *Jews in the Minds of America*, (N.Y.: Basic Books, 1966), p. 179; and Hazel Erskine, "The Polls: Western Partisanship in the Middle East," *Public Opinion Quarterly* 33 (Winter 1969–1970), p. 628.

U.S. policy towards the establishment of Israel was a subject of considerable controversy within the Truman administration, and has become a fascinating subject for research and academic debate. Truman's principal advisors, (including the secretaries of state and defense) opposed the idea. Truman, however, overruled them and decided to support the UN partition resolution that called for the partition of Palestine into two states, one Jewish and one Arab (Harry Truman 1955, Chs. 10–12 and Margaret Truman 1973). He also issued a de facto recognition of Israel immediately after its establishment on May 14, 1948. Several senior officials of the Truman administration, along with many scholars, have argued that Truman supported the creation of Israel because he needed the "Jewish vote" in the 1948 presidential elections (see Snetsinger 1974; Divine 1974, Vol. 2; but for a different perspective see Feis 1969; and Safran 1978, 37–42). It is true that Truman trailed his Republican opponent, Governor Thomas Dewey, in many polls. However, regarding his support of Israel, Truman maintained on several occasions that he was representing the will of the American people. On October 4, 1946, for example, Truman stated:

> This proposal (a viable Jewish state in Palestine) received widespread attention in the U.S., both in the press and in public forums. From the discussion which has ensued, it is my belief that a solution along these lines would command the support of public opinion in the U.S. (U.S. Department of State, FRUS, 1946, III: 703).

Was Truman right? What were the American opinions regarding the establishment of a Jewish state during the crucial period immediately after World War II?

At the close of hostilities in 1945, thousands of Jewish refugees—survivors of the war and the Holocaust—had gathered in camps in Europe. They wished to immigrate to Palestine, but Britain, who ruled the area under a mandate from the League of Nations, denied them visas. Truman was affected by the plight of the Jewish refugees and asked Britain to lift the restrictions on their immigration to Palestine (see Sykes 1965, Ch. 12 and Bain 1979). Between 1946 and 1947, Gallup conducted polls on this critical issue. All of them revealed an overwhelming support for Jewish immigration to Palestine. At the beginning of December 1945, for example, Gallup conducted a survey to find out how many Americans had followed the discussions about permitting Jews to settle in Palestine. Those who answered in the affirmative (55 percent) were then asked to express their opinions on the issue itself. These opinions are presented in Table 2.2.

Table 2.2 shows that about three fourths of the American public in December 1945 supported Jewish immigration to Palestine. A similar result was obtained in May 1946 in response to the query, "do you think it is a good or a poor idea to admit 100,000 Jews to settle in Palestine?" Of those responding, 78 percent thought it was a good idea, 14 percent thought it was a poor idea, and only 8 percent had no opinion (Gallup 1946, 584).

In February 1947, Britain decided to bring the Palestine problem before the United Nations. The General Assembly discussed the problem

Table 2.2
Jewish Immigration to Palestine, 1945

Question		
a. Have you followed the discussion about permitting Jews to settle in Palestine? (Yes - 55% No - 45%) IF YES: What is your opinion on the issue? (Gallup)		

Answer	U.S. National Total	American Jews
Favor the idea	76%	90%
Favor if Jews do	4	-
Against the idea	7	10
Favor leaving the question up to British	1	-
Favor leaving the question up to Arabs	1	-
Do not know	8	-
Miscellaneous	3	-
Total	100%	100%

Source: The *Gallup Poll*, December 7–12, 1945, p. 554.

in April and appointed a special committee, the United Nations Special Committee on Palestine (UNSCOP), to suggest solutions. (UN Special Committee on Palestine, 1947). UNSCOP unanimously recommended terminating the British mandate. A majority of its members (7 out of 11) also recommended partition of the area into independent Arab and Jewish states, while the minority (3 members) recommended one binational state. A regular session of the General Assembly was about to decide on these recommendations at the time when officials of the Truman administration were discussing American options. Although many of them opposed the partition recommendation (Wilson 1979, Ch. 8; and Ganin 1979), U.S. public opinion was supportive of the idea. In October 1947, Gallup asked the following question: "The U.N. has recommended that Palestine be divided into two states—one for the Arabs and one for the Jews—and that 150,000 Jews be permitted now to enter the Jewish state. Do you favor or oppose this idea?" Of those responding, 65 percent supported the idea, 10 percent were against it, and 25 percent had no opinion. (Gallup, October 24–29, 1947, 686).

While an overwhelming majority of the American people supported Jewish immigration to Palestine and the creation of Israel, only a minority supported active U.S. participation in the implementation of those goals. In May 1946, Gallup formulated this question in connection with the

Jewish immigration issue: "England has suggested that we send troops to Palestine to help keep order there if the Arabs oppose letting 100,000 Jews enter Palestine. Do you approve or disapprove of our sending troops to Palestine to help England keep order there?" Only 21 percent of the respondents approved of such a suggestion, about three quarters disapproved and 5 percent had no opinion—the lowest figure, so far, for the "no opinion" column. This result was to be expected since only a year and a half had passed since the end of World War II and the United States was not yet prepared to assume any new military commitments overseas.

In his October 1947 poll Gallup repeated the question about possible U.S. intervention in the Arab-Jewish dispute. This time, however, he added another option—UN intervention. The question read as follows: "If England pulls her troops out of Palestine and war breaks out between the Arabs and the Jews, do you think the U.S. should send troops to keep the peace or should this be done by a United Nations volunteer army?" Only 3 percent of the respondents supported the sending of U.S. troops to Palestine, 65 percent thought that the UN should perform this mission, 18 percent rejected both options, and 14 percent had no opinion. Thus, the American public demonstrated that while it supported the idea of an independent Jewish state, it was not ready to directly participate in the translation of the idea into reality.

Israel was born on May 14, 1948, and was immediately attacked by armies of several Arab countries. The war lasted until January 1949, when the first in a series of cease-fire agreements was signed (see Kurzman 1970; Kimche and Kimche 1960; and Lorch 1961). Israel and many other countries saw the cease-fire agreements as a stage towards peace, but events turned the process in the opposite direction. The Arabs undermined several conciliation efforts and organized and sponsored acts of terrorism across the Israeli border that caused Israeli retaliations. They also imposed an economic embargo on Israel and barred the passage of Israeli ships in the Suez Canal (see Stock 1967; Eytan 1958; and Lorch 1976, Ch. 3).

These developments were clearly reflected in polls that examined responsibility for the conflict. (see Table 2.3).

Table 2.3 shows that in all the polls that were taken on this issue from 1953 to 1957, Americans assigned the Arabs the greater share of the blame for the Middle East conflict. The ratio of blame against the Arabs rose in September and November 1955 following an announcement by Nasser that Egypt had signed a major arms deal with Czechoslovakia (see Ra'anan 1969, Part 1 and Glassman 1975, Ch. 2). Along with increasing Arab terrorism, this deal sealed Israel's decision to launch a preemptive attack on Egypt in October 1956. The attack was carried

Table 2.3
Blame for the Arab-Israeli Conflict, 1953–1957

Question
a. Have you heard or read about the recent conflict between Israel and the Arab countries? IF YES: Which side do you feel is more to blame in this dispute—Israel or the Arabs/Egypt? (NORC)

Date	Israel	Arabs/Egypt	Neither	No Opinion
Nov. 25, 1953	9%	11%	13%	67%
Egyptian-Czechoslovakian (USSR) Arms Deal				
Sept. 29, 1955	6	12*	14	68
Nov. 23, 1955	5	15	18	62
Apr. 20, 1956	7	18	18	57
Suez-Sinai Crisis and War				
Nov. 15, 1956	19	29*	14	38
Israeli Withdrawal from Sinai (1957)				
Apr. 26, 1957	12	40*	18	30

*Egypt only
Source: Erskine, op. cit., pp. 633–634.

out in cooperation with France and Britain, whose prestige and economic interests had been badly hurt by Nasser's nationalization of the Suez Canal (see Cooper 1978 and Thomas 1966).

The Sinai Campaign began on October 29, 1956 when Israeli paratroopers were parachuted deep into Sinai to capture the strategic Mitla pass. This action was followed by quick land operations that brought Israeli forces to the Suez Canal. The Anglo-French military moves began on October 31 with air raids on Egyptian airfields and strategic bases along the Suez Canal. These actions were followed by paratroop landings at key points of the Canal. At the United Nations, both the United States and the Soviet Union denounced the military operations of Israel, France, and Britain, calling for an immediate cease-fire and withdrawal of all the participating forces (see Hoopes 1973, Chs. 23–24 and Bowie 1974). The American position was somewhat surprising: Washington was siding both with Moscow (its major foe in the Cold War) and Egypt (which had recently become a Soviet ally) against France and Britain, its European allies, and Israel, its Middle Eastern ally.

One explanation of the American stand is that the 1956 presidential elections were scheduled to take place just a few days after the outbreak of the war. President Eisenhower had promised the American public an "era of peace"; the Anglo-French-Israeli attack had obviously embarrassed him (see Eisenhower 1965 and Divine 1974, Chs. 3–4). There may also have been reasons rooted in U.S. policy regarding international conduct. Eisenhower and Secretary of State Dulles both claimed that the military operation against Egypt had no justification. On October 31, for example, Eisenhower told the American public that, "There can be no peace without law. And there can be no law if we work to invoke one code of international conduct for those who we oppose and another for our friends" (cited in Donovan 1972, 255–256). Regardless of Dulles' and Eisenhower's real reasons for opposing the Sinai Campaign, the American public tended to agree with their basic positions. Most Americans, even those who sympathized more with Israel, did not justify the Israeli action. At the beginning of November 1956, the National Opinion Research Center of Chicago (NORC) asked the American public whether, "Israel was justified or not in sending armed forces into Egyptian territory." Of those responding, 43 percent replied that Israel was not justified, and 26 percent said that it was (Lipset 1978, 24). Toward the end of the same month Gallup found an even lower rate of approval for the Israeli action: in a national sample, only 10 percent now said that they approved of "Israel's action in Egypt," while 47 percent disapproved (the figures in three large cities—New York, Chicago, and Washington—were somewhat different—23 percent approved of the Israeli action and 47 percent were opposed). The same poll also revealed a much higher rate of disapproval (62 percent) of the British and the French operation (Gallup November 13, 1956, 1454). It should be noted as well that in both the NORC and the Gallup polls, significant segments (31 percent and 43 percent respectively) held no opinion.

Under tremendous American pressure Israel finally agreed to withdraw from Sinai. Although Israel wished to link its withdrawal with a peace agreement, Eisenhower insisted on an unconditional withdrawal, threatening economic sanctions if Israel did not comply. When Americans were asked whether they were satisfied or dissatisfied with the way President Eisenhower and Secretary of State Dulles had handled the Israel-Egypt problem, 50 percent expressed satisfaction with Eisenhower's policies and actions, 23 percent were dissatisfied, and 27 percent had no opinion (Gallup April 6–11, 1956, 1484).

Despite these results, Table 2.3 shows that even after the Sinai Campaign, Arabs were still assigned the greater share of the blame for the conflict. This share rose substantially—to 40 percent (while the Israeli share dropped to 12 percent)—after the Israeli withdrawal from

Table 2.4
Favorability Rating Toward Israel, 1956

Question				
a. How would you rate your feelings toward the following countries? (Gallup)				

	Highly Favorable	Mildly Favorable	Neutral	Mildly Unfavorable	Highly Unfavorable
England	23%	34%	27%	7%	9%
France	16	36	34	9	5
Israel	12	21	53	8	6
Egypt	4	13	52	17	14

Source: The Gallup Poll, December 14–19, 1956, pp.1464–5.

Sinai. A poll on American attitudes towards foreign nations that was taken during the Sinai crisis also gave Israel a more favorable rating than Egypt (see Table 2.4). These results reflect a basic negative attitude towards Egypt and other Arab countries that threatened Israel, attacked American and Western interests, and aligned themselves with the Soviet Union.

In the wake of the Sinai Campaign, Eisenhower adopted a new American doctrine for the Middle East that was utilized in May 1958, when the United States intervened militarily in a civil war in Lebanon (see Campbell 1960, Ch. 9 and Bryson 1977, Ch. 15). The Arab-Israeli conflict at this time assumed a relatively low profile. Israel's superior military performance in Sinai had convinced Nasser and the Arabs that they would not easily be able to defeat Israel. Moreover, UN forces entered Sinai as part of the agreement to end the Israeli occupation of that area and thus effectively kept the peace along the Israeli-Egyptian border (see Laqueur 1970, Part 3; and Bell 1969). Israel also enjoyed free navigation to Eilat, its southernmost port. Judging by poll-taking, the Arab-Israeli conflict did not generate much U.S. interest in the years following the Sinai Campaign; the one poll on the issue during the entire decade of 1957 to 1967, taken by SRC-C in November 1964, showed that about 40 percent of the respondents held no opinion and 28 percent felt sympathy for neither side (see Table 2.1). This indifference, however, underwent a radical change in June 1967 when another major war broke out between Israel and its neighbors.

The Six Day War Until
Sadat's Breakthrough, 1967–1977

The Six Day War marked a watershed both in the history of the Arab-Israeli conflict and the history of poll-taking on American attitudes towards this conflict. From now on polls were conducted more frequently by more polling agencies and focused on a number of different aspects of the conflict. Opinions of elite groups—those in leadership positions in various public and private sectors—were also solicited, and several attempts were made to measure the sources and depth of opinions.

The Six Day War broke out on June 5, 1967 when Israel launched a preemptive attack against Egypt, Syria, and Jordan (see Draper 1968; Laqueur 1969; for an Arab perspective, Abu-Lughod 1970; see also Kimche and Bawley 1971; and Khouri 1968). As its name suggests, the war lasted six days, during which time Israel destroyed most of the armies that had challenged it. In the course of hostilities Israel also captured and occupied the entire area of Sinai, the West Bank, and the Golan Heights. The war had been preceded by a serious crisis that had begun on May 15 when Nasser had ordered his troops to move across the Suez Canal into Sinai. During the next two weeks the Egyptian president ordered the removal of the UN peace-keeping force from Sinai, closed the Straits of Tiran (which controlled the sea route to Eilat) to Israeli ships, and deployed most of his armed forces in Sinai and along the Egyptian-Israeli border. Nasser also concluded a military agreement with Jordan and made several inflammatory speeches warning of the upcoming conflict (see Safran 1969, Ch. 6 and Yost 1968, 305–320). Syria, for its part, had already been involved in frequent clashes with Israel, firing shells into Israeli settlements and towns in the northern part of the country.

The threats from three of its fronts forced Israel to mobilize its armed forces. However, with the bitter lessons of the Sinai Campaign in mind, Israel decided to give the United States and other Western countries a chance to diffuse the crisis through diplomatic means. When these were exhausted, war became inevitable.

The outbreak of the war led to an unprecedented wave of sympathy towards Israel (see Laqueur 1967, 49–59). On June 7, Gallup found 56 percent of those responding expressing support for Israel, while only 4 percent were sympathetic to the Arab nations. A Harris poll taken on June 10 revealed a pro-Israeli margin of 41 to 1 percent. Public support for Israel in the United States rose to its highest level since the nation's independence, while the percentage of those favoring the Arab nations shrank to its lowest level in the history of the conflict (see Tables 2.1 and 2.5).

The reasons for this dramatic shift in favor of Israel are easily discernible. First, Israel was seen as a victim of Arab aggression. On June 10, Harris asked, "Who do you think has more right on its side—the Arabs or Israel?" Of those responding, 46 percent said that Israel had more right on its side; only 4 percent sided with the Arabs. Harris also asked, "Do you agree or disagree that the Arabs have wanted to start a war with

Table 2.5
Sympathies Toward Israel and the Arabs, 1967–1977

Questions
a. Have you heard or read about the situation in the Middle East? IF YES: In the Middle East situation are your sympathies more with Israel or more with the Arab nations? (Gallup)
b. In the latest war between Israel and the Arab states, do you feel more sympathetic to the Israelis, the Arabs, or don't you have any strong feelings either way? (Harris)
c. In terms of the Mideast trouble, if war should break out between Israel and the Arabs, with whom would you probably identify most—Israel or the Arab nations? (Yankelovich)
d. In the dispute between Israel and the Arabs, which side do you sympathize with more—Israel or the Arabs? (Harris)

Q	Date	Poll	Israel	Arab Nations	Neither	DK*NO**	Both
	Six Day War (June 5–10, 1967)						
a	June 7, 1967	G	56%	4%	25%	15%	
b	June 10, 1967	H	41	1	40	18	
a	Feb. 1969	G	50	5	28	17	
	War of Attrition (April 1969–August 1970)						
a	Mar. 1970	G	44	3	32	21	
	Yom Kippur War (October 6–25, 1973)						
a	Oct. 6–8, 1973	G	47	6	22	25	
a	Oct. 19–22, 1973	G	48	6	21	25	
a	Dec. 7–10, 1973	G	54	8	24	14	
a	Dec. 1973	G	50	7	25	18	

Israel for a long time?" An overwhelming majority of 63 percent agreed with this statement, only 5 percent disagreed, and 32 percent were not sure. The comparable results for an identical question about Israel were 45 percent in disagreement, 16 percent in agreement, and 39 percent unsure (Erskine 1969–1970, 630–635).

The "underdog" image of Israel during the pre-war crisis was the second reason behind the pro-Israeli shift in American sympathies. Arab armies substantially outnumbered the Israel Defense Forces, and during most of the crisis that had preceded the war there was real fear—both in Israel and abroad—that the Arabs might succeed this time in their attempt to annihilate the Jewish state. Israel's swift and decisive defeat of three Arab armies was seen not only as a dramatic victory but an

Table 2.5 Cont.

Q	Date	Poll	Israel	Arab Nations	Neither	DK*NO**	Both
c	Nov. 1974	Y	55	9	17	14	5
d	Dec. 1974	H	52	7	24	11	6
a	Jan. 1975	G	44	8	22	26	

American Reassessment After Breakdown in Israeli-Egyptian Talks
(March–August 1970)

a	Apr. 1975	G	37	8	24	31	

Israel-Egypt Interim Agreement (September 1975)

c	Jan. 1976	Y	56	9	22	11	2

Begin Wins Israeli Elections (May 1977)

a	June 1977	G	44	8	28	20	
a	Oct. 1977	G	46	11	21	22	

Sadat Visits Jerusalem (November 1977)

a	Dec. 1977	G	44	10	27	19	

*Do not Know
**No Opinion

Sources: The Gallup Poll, 1935–1971, Vol. 3, pp. 2068, 2071–72, 2149, 2181, 2242, *1972–1977* Vols. 1, 2, pp. 196, 220, 408, 458, 1221, 1220, 1222. Harris: Erksine op. cit., p. 630. Louis Harris, "Oil or Israel?" *New York Times Magazine,* April 6, 1975. Yankelovich: Geraldine Rosenfield, *Attitudes of the American Public Toward Israel and American Jews: The Yankelovich Findings,* N.Y.: American Jewish Committee, December 1974; and *Supplement,* April 1975.

American gain as well, since both Egypt and Syria were close allies of the Soviet Union and their defeat was interpreted as a major blow to the Kremlin's prestige in the region. This blow was all the more important in view of the concomitant American failures in Vietnam and the psychological need of Americans to identify with a winning cause (see Lewis 1968, 321–335 and 1969, 642–652; and Mangold 1978).

From the Six Day War until the Yom Kippur War of October 1973, Israel enjoyed a wide margin of sympathy over the Arabs (see Table 2.5). In February 1969, for example, the margin was 50 to 5 percent, or a ratio of 10 to 1. In April 1969, Egypt began a war of attrition against Israel. Nasser hoped that constant shelling of Israeli troops across the Suez Canal would force Israel to withdraw from Sinai without obtaining any concessions from Egypt in return (see Bulloch 1974 and Whetten 1974). The "War of Attrition" lasted until August 1970. During this war the Soviet Union dispatched approximately 200 pilots to Egypt, along with more than 10,000 officers and military advisers (see Rubinstein 1977). The Arab refusal to negotiate peace with Israel, the War of Attrition, and the deepening Soviet involvement in Egypt were reflected in a poll conducted by Gallup in March 1970 on the topic of American sympathies towards the Middle East. At that time 44 percent expressed sympathy towards Israel, while only 3 percent sympathized with the Arab countries. This was the lowest figure ever recorded for the Arab side—a ratio of almost 15 to 1 in favor of Israel.

Many diplomatic initiatives were made during 1971 and 1972 towards resolution of the Arab-Israeli conflict (see Quandt 1977, Ch. 3 and Pranger 1971). All of these failed because of conditions presented by each side that were unacceptable to the other. Finally, in 1973, Egypt and Syria conspired to impose their conditions on Israel through means of war. In October 1973, on Yom Kippur—the holiest day in the Jewish calendar—they launched a full-scale surprise attack on Israel. This time the war lasted about three weeks. After suffering initial losses in Sinai and the Golan Heights, Israeli forces mounted a counterattack that drove across the Suez Canal, capturing Egyptian territory and reaching a point just 60 miles from Cairo (see Laqueur 1974; Monroe and Farrar-Hockley 1975; Herzog 1975; and Heikal 1975). On the Syrian front, Israel drove Syrian forces back from the Golan and captured additional Syrian territory.

But although Israel won a military victory, the costs of the war were very high. In psychological terms, it was the Arabs—especially Egypt— who emerged as the victors. Several months before the outbreak of the war, Egyptian president Anwar Sadat had persuaded King Feisal of Saudi Arabia to use the "oil weapon" against the United States. During the war Saudi Arabia and other Arab oil-producing countries in fact imposed an oil embargo on the United States and western Europe (see Sherbiny and Tessler 1976; Stookey 1975; and Feith 1981, 19–39). Polls now showed that 48 to 47 percent of the American public expressed sympathy towards Israel, while only 6 percent expressed sympathy towards the Arabs. About a month after the war the pro-Israeli margin was, respectively, 54 to 8 percent and 50 to 7 percent. More than half of the American public supported Israel, while only 6 to 8 percent supported the Arabs. However, in comparison to the favorable ratios of the Six Day War and the War of Attrition (14 to 1), the ratio of sympathy for Israel was now 8 or 7 to 1.

Although the oil embargo created long lines in American gas stations and substantially increased oil prices, it had very little effect on American opinions concerning the Arab-Israeli conflict. Polls conducted after the

Yom Kippur War revealed that Americans tended to blame the energy crisis on (in descending order of importance) the oil companies, wasteful consumption, the federal government, and the Arab nations (see Gruen 1975–1976, 33–39). Gallup found in December 1973 that only 1 percent of the public blamed Israel for the energy crisis, while Harris found that three out of four Americans blamed the 1973–1974 oil shortage on the Arab embargo and two out of three blamed the Arabs for the rise in the price of oil.

In January 1974, Secretary of State Henry Kissinger mediated an agreement between Israel and Egypt to disengage their forces along the Suez Canal. This agreement was not only seen as a first vital step on the road to resolution of the conflict, but also led to the lifting of the oil embargo. In May, a similar agreement was concluded between Israel and Syria (see Reich 1977 and Quandt 1977, Ch. 7). "The sympathy index" for this period shows that the margin between Israel and the Arabs remained stable. The Yankelovich organization found a pro-Israeli margin of 55 to 9 percent in October 1974, while a similar margin, 52 to 7 percent, was found by Harris in November–December 1974. Harris also found a higher ratio of sympathy (56 to 5 percent) among a national leadership group drawn from government and politics, business, labor, communications, education, religion, and voluntary organizations (Harris 1975, 21). In January 1975, Gallup identified a 44 to 8 percent margin in favor of Israel.

While the figures for the Arabs in the three polls are similar, there is a significant difference in the margin of sympathy for Israel in the Gallup poll as opposed to those of Harris and Yankelovich. This difference may be due to the fact that Gallup measured the opinions of an "aware" group—those who had heard or read about the situation in the Middle East—while Yankelovich and Harris did not. It is interesting to note that Yankelovich's question was somewhat different from those of Harris and Gallup. Yankelovich asked, "In terms of the Mideast trouble, if war should break out, with whom would you probably identify most?" This question presented a possible situation of war in the future, while the Gallup and Harris poll asked for opinions on the current American situation. As can be seen from Table 2.5, the Yankelovich question always received a higher margin in favor of Israel—notwithstanding, the Yankelovich results were quite similar to those of Harris.

Kissinger believed that the Arab-Israeli conflict should be resolved in step-by-step stages with the disengagement agreements (dealing primarily with military issues) followed by a series of agreements on selected political-strategic issues (see Kissinger 1982 and Perlmutter 1975, 39–49). Accordingly, in January 1975, he revived his famous shuttle diplomacy and began an effort to achieve an interim agreement between Israel and

Egypt. In March 1975 this step failed: the differences between the two sides were too wide for Kissinger to bridge (see Safran 1978, Chs. 25–26). Kissinger, however, implied that his failure was due primarily to Israeli intransigence and thus persuaded President Ford to call for a reassessment of U.S. policy in the Middle East. This "reassessment" was essentially a code word for pressure and sanctions against Israel (see Sheehan 1976 and Golan 1976). Among other things, Israeli requests for military supplies were either delayed or frozen.

All these developments were reflected in the "sympathy index." A poll taken by Gallup in April 1975 revealed that in comparison to his previous poll of January 1975, the ratio of sympathy towards Israel dropped by 7 percent. The Arabs, however, did not pick up the points, their rate remaining the same as in the earlier poll. The points lost by Israel moved instead into the "do not know" column, indicating that there was confusion among the American public concerning the real reasons for Kissinger's failure to produce an agreement.

In August 1975 Kissinger renewed his shuttle diplomacy. This time he was much more successful: on September 1, Israel and Egypt signed an agreement that provided for an Israeli withdrawal from strategic passes in Sinai and the oil fields of Abu-Rudeis in return for a number of Egyptian political concessions and U.S. political and economic commitments (see Reich 1977, Ch. 5). Yankelovich conducted a poll on American sympathies towards the Middle East after the conclusion of the interim agreement, and even he did so only in January 1976, several months after the event. Yankelovich found that 56 percent of those responding sympathized more with Israel and 9 percent with the Arabs. This result is almost identical to that of his earlier poll of October 1974, which showed a 55 to 9 percent margin of sympathy in favor of Israel (see Table 2.5). The fact that both those polls were conducted several months after Israel reached agreements with Arab countries may account for the close similarity of their results.

The interim agreement of September 1975 contributed to an atmosphere of optimism and stability in Arab-Israeli affairs. Within the United States, the 1976 presidential campaign went into gear, producing a new president, Jimmy Carter, a new administration, a new perception of the Arab-Israeli conflict, and new plans to resolve it. Carter adopted the recommendations of a study group at the Brookings Institution that called for a comprehensive resolution of the Arab-Israeli conflict with the participation of the Soviet Union and the Palestinians (Brookings Institution 1975). On March 16, 1977, Carter outlined three principles for peace in the Middle East: (1) Recognition of Israel and its right to exist in peace by its Arab neighbors, which would entail open borders, tourism, cultural exchange, and trade; (2) Establishment of permanent borders through negotiations; and (3) Establishment of a homeland for Palestinian refugees that would be contingent on Palestinian recognition of Israel's right to exist (see U.S. Department of State Bulletin, April 11, 1977 and Carter 1982, 273–318).

These principles stemmed from Carter's perception of the Arab-Israeli conflict as the most destabilizing factor in the entire international system, and of the Palestinian issue as the central problem of the Arab-Israeli conflict. This perception was shaped to a large extent by Zbigniew Brzezinski who later became Carter's national security adviser (see Brzezinski 1975, 3–17 and 1983). Carter tried to organize an international conference in Geneva with all parties of the conflict participating under the co-chairmanship of the United States and Soviet Union (see Spiegel in Shaked and Rabinovich 1980, 93–120; and Sicherman 1978). However, neither Egypt nor Israel reacted favorably to the idea.

In the meantime, in May 1977, elections were held in Israel that produced a revolutionary change in Israeli politics. Israel had been governed since its establishment by a coalition under the leadership of the Labor Party. In 1977, this party lost to Menachem Begin and his opposition Likud (Union) party (see Arian 1980 and Peretz 1977, 254–255). Begin, known for his staunchly nationalistic outlook, was described both by his Israeli political opponents and by most of the American and Western media as a politician who at best was likely to block any further steps towards peace, and at worst, to cause another major war (see, for example, The New York Times and Le Monde, May 19, 1977; and Time and Newsweek, May 20, 1977).

For a while the "hysteria" over Begin and the future of Israel did not affect Israel's general standing in American public opinion. A short while after Begin's victory, Gallup found a 44 to 8 percent ratio of sympathy in favor of Israel. This ratio was identical to the Gallup ratio of January 1975 (see Table 2.5).

In November 1977, Sadat made his historic trip to Jerusalem and started a peace-making process that culminated in a peace treaty between Israel and Egypt (see Shamir 1978; Dayan 1981; and Fahmy 1983). Sadat and Begin now stood on the center stage of Middle Eastern politics, and it was clear that they were about to negotiate historic changes in the traditional patterns of the Arab-Israeli conflict. Carter, in common with almost everyone else, was taken totally by surprise by Sadat's bold move, which ran counter to Carter's own grand design for a comprehensive resolution of the Arab-Israeli conflict through the mechanism of the Geneva conference. Significantly, Sadat's decision to go to Jerusalem came about in large part because he opposed Carter's strategy of courting both the Soviet Union and radical elements such as the PLO and Syria.

Sadat's initiative transformed him into a well-known and popular figure in America. He was certainly more popular than Begin and almost as popular as Carter. Among other things, he succeeded in changing Egypt's image in the United States, as well as contributing to the shaping of more favorable attitudes towards the Arabs in general (*The Gallup Opinion Index*, February 27, 1978; also see Bagnied and Schneider in Adams 1981, 53–66).

Table 2.5 shows that sympathy for the Arabs first climbed into a double-digit figure in October 1977, after the Begin victory in Israel, but before the Sadat visit to Jerusalem. A poll taken after the Sadat visit showed a marginal slip in the Arab column. Since October 1977, however, the Gallup sympathy rate for the Arabs has never declined to a single-digit figure. Moreover, the ratio of sympathy for Israel—which between 1967 and 1977 had generally been more than 5 to 1—dropped after November 1977 to about 4 to 1. It can be argued that the combination of two historic events within a six-month period—Begin's election and the Sadat visit to Jerusalem—caused a shift in the relative strength of Israel and the Arabs in American public opinion. It is important to stress, however, that despite this shift, Israel has continued to enjoy a substantial margin of sympathy over the Arabs in American public opinion polls.

Israeli-Egyptian Peace-Making, 1977–1982

As previously noted, Sadat's visit to Jerusalem was a breakthrough in the Arab-Israeli conflict. For the first time in the history of this conflict, the head of a leading Arab country was ready to extend recognition to Israel. However, the conclusion of an actual peace agreement was still far away. The complexity of the conflict and its long, bitter history precluded any easy or quick resolution. Indeed, negotiations between Israel and Egypt lasted almost a year and a half, (from November 1977 until March 1979), while implementation of the actual peace agreement took another three years, concluding in April 1982 (see Sachar 1981 and Friedlander 1983).

Back in November 1977, however, most American politicians, policy-makers, and journalists expected a much faster peace-making process. The return of Sinai and the removal of the Israeli settlements there in exchange for a turnabout in Egyptian-Israeli relations was seen as a fair deal, and when expectations of an obstacle-free process were not fulfilled, the blame was quickly assigned to Israel in general and Begin in particular.

Sadat, for his part, proved to be a master at manipulating U.S. public opinion on Egypt's behalf. In January 1978, for example, the Egyptian leader ordered his minister of foreign affairs to walk out of a meeting of the Israeli-Egyptian Political Committee being held in Jerusalem. Negotiations between the two countries broke down. At about this time, however, Sadat visited the United States amid overwhelmingly favorable media coverage. When negotiations broke down, the media accordingly was far more critical of Israel than of Egypt. A telephone poll conducted by Gallup after these events also demonstrated Sadat's public relations victory: results of this poll showed a substantial slip in the pro-Israeli margin of sympathy, from 44 percent to 33 percent, and a slight increase for the Arab side, from 10 percent to 14 percent. (see Table 2.6).

The 33 percent figure represented the lowest support registered for Israel since 1964, while the 14 percent figure for the Arabs represented the highest support registered for them since 1948. However, it should be noted that most of the decline in pro-Israeli sentiment manifested itself in an increased percentage of those taking a more neutral, rather than pro-Arab, position.

A number of changes in American attitudes towards the Arab-Israeli conflict were also found in a series of specific questions about the Israeli-Egyptian negotiations. In January 1978, Harris found that the American public blamed Israel and Egypt equally (22 percent each) for the breakdown in negotiations. But in answer to the question concerning "who really wants peace in the Middle East," Egypt received a better rating than Israel (see Table 2.7).

Table 2.7 shows how Sadat's visit changed the U.S. assessment of the Egyptian interest in peace. In November 1977, only 37 percent of the public thought that Egypt really wanted peace, while a majority of 55 percent held the same opinion about Israel. About two months later Israel and Egypt scored similar results, and after this point Egypt received a higher score. Further comparison of the 1977 and the 1978 results shows that Sadat succeeded in changing Egypt's image only. Those of Saudi Arabia and Jordan, if affected at all, were affected in the opposite direction: in January 1978, for example, their scores were lower than those of 1977.

During 1978, several polls evaluated the performance of Begin and Sadat in the peace effort. On several occasions NBC, CBS, and other organizations asked Americans to evaluate the handling of peace negotiations by Sadat and Begin. The results of these polls are presented in the following table.

Table 2.8 shows that Sadat outscored Begin on this issue from the beginning of the process. After the January 1978 breakdown in the talks both leaders received lower marks, but Begin suffered a larger drop.

Polls on two additional specific issues revealed an interesting phenomenon: that evaluations of leaders differed from those of their countries. In January and April 1978, Harris asked Americans which leader (Sadat

Table 2.6
Sympathies Toward Israel and the Arab Nations, 1978–1982

Questions

a. Have you heard or read about the situation in the Middle East? IF YES: In the
   Middle East situation are your sympathies more with Israel or more with the
   Arab nations? (Gallup)[†]
b. In terms of the Mideast trouble, if war should break out between Israel and the
   Arabs, with whom would your sympathies lie—Israel or the Arab nations?
   (Yankelovich)
c. In the Middle East situation, are your sympathies more with Israel or more with
   the Arab nations? (WP/ABC)

Q	Date	Poll	Israel	Arab Nations	Neither	DK*NO**
	Breakdown in Israeli-Egyptian Talks (January 1978)					
	Sadat Visits U.S.					
a	Feb. 1978	G	33%	14%	28%	25%
a	Mar. 1978	G	38	11	33	18
	PLO Terrorist Attack on an Israeli Bus, 35 Killed (March 1978)					
	Litani Operation					
a	Apr.–May 1978	G	44	10	33	13
a	Sept. 1978 (early)	G	41	12	29	18
	Camp David (September 1978)					
a	Sept. 1978 (late)	G	42	12	29	17
a	Nov. 1978	G	39	13	30	18
a	Jan. 1979	G	40	14	31	15

or Begin) they would trust more in a conflict between them. On both
occasions the results were tied: each leader received 32 percent of the
vote in January and 35 percent in April (Lipset 1978, 26–28). However,
when Sadat was replaced by Egypt and Begin by Israel in the same
questions, the results were different. In the January poll, 43 percent of
those responding said they would trust Israel more, as opposed to 20
percent in favor of Egypt. In the April poll, the figures were 43 and
24 percent respectively. In February 1978, NBC asked, "As of today,
who do you think has made more concessions towards a peace agreement
in the Middle East . . . President Sadat of Egypt or Prime Minister
Begin of Israel?" A majority of 55 percent said that Sadat had made
more concessions, while only 15 percent said the same of Begin. Again,
when a related question was asked about the countries ("Which country

Table 2.6 Cont.

Q	Date	Poll	Israel	Arab Nations	Neither	DK*NO**
	Israel-Egypt Peace Agreement (March 1979)					
b	Apr. 1979	Y	47	11	19	22
b	Dec. 1979	Y	49	6	16	29
a	Oct. 1980	G	45	13	24	18
	Clashes Between Israel, Syria and the PLO in Lebanon (June 1981)					
a	July 11–14, 1981	NG	49	10	20	21
a	July–Aug. 1981	G	44	11	34	11
a	Nov. 1981	G	49	12	20	19
a	Jan. 1982	G	49	14	23	14
c	Mar. 3–9, 1982	WP/ABC	55	18	13	14
	Return of Sinai to Egypt					
a	Apr.–May 1982	G	51	12	26	11

†Until December 1973, Gallup used the word "troubles" instead of "situation."
*Do Not Know
**No Opinion

Sources: Gallup: Connie de Boer, "The Polls: Attitudes Toward the Arab-Israeli Conflict," *Public Opinion Quarterly* 47 (Spring 1983) p. 123 and *Gallup Report,* August 1981, p. 2; Yankelovich: Geraldine Rosenfield, *Attitudes of the American Public Toward American Jews and Israel: December 1979* N.Y.: (American Jewish Committee, Information and Research Services, March 1980, publication 80/180/1) p. 9. WP/ABC Poll: *Washington Post,* August 20, 1982.

has been most willing to compromise?"), the results were different: 45 percent of those responding said that Egypt was most willing to compromise, while 26 percent held that view regarding Israel.

The slide in American sympathy towards Israel as recorded in the February 1978 Gallup poll and the polls described above was temporary, however (and not as suggested by Kohut 1978). Table 2.6 shows that as early as March 1978, Israel had already gained back 5 percent in the polls, while the Arabs had slipped by 3 percent. During the next few months, the margin of sympathy in favor of Israel remained in the vicinity of 4 to 1. A number of significant events occurred during this period. On March 11, Palestinian terrorists landed on the Israeli shore of Kibbutz Ma'agan Michael, killed a noted American photographer, Gail Rubin, and then proceeded to the Haifa-Tel Aviv highway where

Table 2.7
Peace Intentions, 1977–1979

Question			
a. Do you feel that (Read list) really wants a just peace in the Middle East, only reluctantly wants a just peace, or really does not want peace? (Harris percentage indicates "really wants peace.")			

	November 1977	January 1978	August 1979
Israel	55%	51%	59%
Egypt	37	52	63
Jordan	34	28	-
Saudia Arabia	29	26	-
PLO	-	13	18

Sources: Harris-CBS (Nov. 1977): *New York Times*, November 2, 1977; Harris (Jan. 1978): William C. Adams, "Middle East Meets West: Surveying American Attitudes," *Public Opinion* (April-May 1982), p. 52; Harris-ABC (Aug. 1979): Louis Harris, "Americans Sympathize with Israel in its Dispute with PLO," *ABC News-Harris Survey*, August 27, 1979.

they attacked a bus, killing 35 persons and wounding 82. On March 14, Israel responded with a large-scale land operation in Southern Lebanon (Operation Litani) driving out PLO forces and destroying its bases in the entire area south of the Litani river (Inbar 1983, 47–58). On April 11, the Israel Defense Forces withdrew from southern Lebanon, following the formation of a UN force to prevent any use of southern Lebanon as a PLO terrorist base against Israel. A few days later, the film "Holocaust" was broadcast over four consecutive nights of American television. All these events contributed to the increase in American sympathies towards Israel. As can be seen in Table 2.6, in comparison to the February 1978 figures, Israel gained 11 percent in the April–May 1978 polls, while sympathy for the Arabs dropped by 4 percent.

Israel's basic strength in American public opinion can also be seen in results of the following polls measuring the degree of favorable feelings towards Israel. The results of these polls appear in Table 2.9.

In Table 2.9, it can be seen that Israel suffered a drop of 3 percent in the favorable column in 1978—the period after Begin's election and Sadat's visit—while its unfavorable rating climbed 3 percent. By 1979, however, the trend had been reversed in both columns. An additional survey conducted by the Chicago Council on Foreign Relations in November 1978 revealed similarly high marks for Israel. In this survey—which was conducted in the form of a thermometer reading for each country—Israel was given a reading of 61°, a reading bettered only by

Table 2.8
Sadat and Begin: Handling of Peace Negotiations, 1977–1978

"Doing an excellent or good job in handling peace negotiations."

	Date and Poll							
	Nov. 1977 NBC	Jan. 1978 NBC	Feb. 1978 NBC	Mar. 1978 NBC	Apr. 1978 NYT/CBS	Aug. 1978 NBC	Sept. 1978 NBC	Mar. 1979 NYT/CBS
Sadat	66%	65%	56%	46%	57%	40%	64%	60%
Begin	49	49	29	25	34	21	53	53

Sources: NBC (Nov. 1977; Feb. 1978), Seymour Martin Lipset, "The Polls on the Middle East," *Middle East Review*, (Fall 1978), pp. 26–28; NBC-Poll, April 2, 1978; NYT/CBS Poll, April 14, 1978, March 26–27, 1979; NBC-AP Poll, September 26, 1978.

Table 2.9
Israeli Favorability Rating, 1976–1981

Question

a. You will notice that the 10 boxes on this card go from the highest position of plus five—for someone or something you have a *very favorable* opinion of—all the way down to the lowest position of minus five—for someone or something you have a very *unfavorable* opinion of. How far up the scale or how far down the scale would you rate Israel? (Gallup)

	1976	1977	1978	1979	1980	1981
Favorable	60%	62%	59%	68%	74%	75%
Unfavorable	24	25	28	24	21	19
No Opinion	16	13	13	8	5	6

Source: Scalometer Ratings, *Gallup Report*, September 1982, p. 21.

Canada with 72°, Britain with 67°, and France with 62°. The Egyptian rate was 53°, and that of Saudi Arabia only 48° (Rielly 1979, 18). These results are probably directly related to the agreements signed by Israel and Egypt in September 1978 at Camp David.

In July 1978, negotiations between Israel and Egypt reached another impasse. This time President Carter decided to use all of his influence to achieve a breakthrough. He invited Sadat and Begin to a summit conference at the presidential resort of Camp David to break the deadlock and devise a formula for a peace agreement. The Camp David summit was a unique event in the history of the U.S. presidency, with Carter transferring most of his regular duties to Vice President Walter Mondale while he moved to a secluded location to mediate between two stubborn and determined leaders (see relevant chapters in Dayan 1981; Carter 1982; Brzezinski 1983; Weizman 1981; and Vance 1983). Carter's stakes in the conference were high: in the event of failure, he risked suffering a devastating blow to his prestige and political future, while the chances for a peace agreement between Israel and Egypt would be all but doomed. In light of these dangers, Carter decided to minimize external pressures and interference by isolating the Israeli and Egyptian delegations. In an even more unusual move, the mass media were also barred from Camp David and were left in the dark for the better part of the conference (see Spragens and Terwood in Adams 1982, 117–127).

The Camp David summit yielded two important frameworks: one for a peace agreement between Israel and Egypt, and one for the resolution of the Palestinian issue and the areas of the West Bank and Gaza (see International Communication Agency 1978). Interestingly, two polls measuring sympathy towards Israel and the Arabs—one taken before and one after Camp David—yielded almost identical results (see Table 2.6). Americans apparently differentiated between Egypt and other Arab countries that had denounced Sadat for his willingness to sign a peace agreement with Israel. In contrast to Gallup's finding, however, an NBC/AP poll in September 1978 showed that the U.S. perception of both Begin and Sadat had improved following Camp David, with Begin's favorable rating finally exceeding 50 percent (see Table 2.8).

After several more months of hard bargaining that were probably reflected in the "sympathy index" for November 1978 and January 1979 (see Table 2.6), Israel and Egypt finally signed a comprehensive peace agreement, the first of its kind in the history of the Arab-Israeli conflict (see *The Middle East Journal* 1979, 327–347; *Washington Quarterly* 1979; Kedourie 1979, 17–18; Tucker 1978, 25–33; and Jureidini, McLaurin and Price 1979). Unfortunately, Gallup did not conduct polls on American sympathies towards Israel and the Arabs until October 1980. Yankelovich did conduct such polls in April and December 1979. But as mentioned earlier in this study, his question was different from the one used by Gallup, and had most recently been employed in January 1976, three and a half years earlier. In comparison to his 1976 results, Israel lost 9 percent in April 1979, while the Arabs gained 2 percent. By December 1979, however, Israel had gained 2 percent, while the Arabs had slipped 5 percent (see Table 2.6).

It is important to note that Israel's gain in both the Yankelovich and Gallup polls of late 1979 (see Table 2.9) were probably connected with events in other parts of the Middle East. At the beginning of 1979, for example, the Shah had left Iran and an anti-American regime headed by Ayatollah Khomeini had taken over. In November 1979, Iranians seized American diplomats at the U.S. embassy and precipitated a crisis that lasted more than a year (see Legum 1981). These events probably contributed to Israel's enhanced image in the United States as a stable and strong democracy. Implementation of the first stages of the peace agreement with Egypt also strengthened U.S. recognition of Israel's commitment to peace.

In November 1980, Ronald Reagan defeated Jimmy Carter in the presidential elections. Upon his inauguration in January 1981, Reagan adopted a new global strategy (see Kegley, Jr. and Wittkopf 1982, 223–244 and Ikle 1982, 11–18). Concerning the Middle East, this strategy called for the containment of Soviet threats, especially in the Persian Gulf, by a pro-Western alliance of Arab countries and Israel (see *Orbis* 1982, 5–34; Campbell 1981, 593–628; and Tucker 1981, 27–36). Within this new strategy the Arab-Israeli conflict was relegated to a lower position on the list of U.S. priorities. Reagan apparently assumed that Soviet threats—as so devastatingly and brutally demonstrated in the invasion of Afghanistan—would be sufficient to unite rival Arab countries and Israel under the American flag. Consequently, he ignored the Camp David accords and did not appoint a special representative to the autonomy talks.

Within a few months, however, Reagan discovered how wrong were his basic assumptions on the Arab-Israeli conflict and its place in the politics of the Middle East (see Inbar 1983, 58–71 and Mendelsohn 1982, Ch. 7). The southern front of the Arab-Israeli conflict was moving closer to a state of peace, but the northern front was moving towards war. A fragile 1976 cease-fire agreement between various Lebanese factions collapsed in April 1981. Syrian forces attacked Lebanese Christians, and Israel—arguing that this attack violated a tacit agreement with Damascus—sent warplanes to defend the Christians. The PLO also joined the warfare, shelling Israeli towns and villages in the northern part of the country. Israel responded to these attacks with air strikes against PLO bases in Lebanon. On a different front, Israel also raided and destroyed the Iraqi nuclear reactor near Baghdad on June 7, 1981 (see Snyder 1983, 565–593 and Perlmutter 1982, 34–43).

Neither the PLO nor Iraq were popular in the United States. Unlike Carter, Reagan identified the PLO as a terrorist organization in close collaboration with the Soviet Union. Iraq was also considered a Soviet puppet whose acquisition of nuclear weapons could threaten U.S. allies in the Persian Gulf. Despite this assessment, the Reagan administration strongly criticized the Israeli battle with the PLO and Syria in Lebanon and the raid on the Iraqi nuclear reactor (see the following in *The New York Times:* June 11, 1981; June 12; July 2; July 18; July 20; and July 28). Reagan even decided to withhold a delivery of F-16 combat aircraft to Israel pending a review of alleged Israeli violations of the U.S. law regarding limitations on the use of U.S. weapons. Reagan's real concern, however, was not so much with legal points as with the effects of the battles in Lebanon and Iraq on its grand strategy. From Reagan's perspective, the violence in the Arab-Israeli conflict hindered U.S. efforts to build an anti-Soviet alliance: it diverted the attention of U.S. allies from the Soviet threat and created disputes both in American-Arab and American-Israeli relations.

From April until June 1981, Israel was involved in an election campaign in which the Labor party unsuccessfully attempted to unseat Begin (see Arian 1983). In December, Begin once again surprised the world with a sudden move to gain Knesset approval for a law effectively annexing the Golan Heights. The law when passed led to severe U.S. criticism (see *The New York Times* of December 15 and 28, 1981). This time, the criticism was coupled with action against the Begin government: the United States suspended an agreement for strategic cooperation that had been signed by the two countries just a few months earlier (see *The New York Times* of December 19 and 28, 1981).

A crisis of confidence now existed between Israel and the United States. American policymakers complained that Begin was unpredictable and that by taking action without consulting the United States, he was harming interests in the Middle East. However, polls taken during the summer and autumn of 1981 did not reveal any significant change in the American sympathies towards the Middle East. In July 1981, Gallup found a ratio of 49 to 10 percent in favor of Israel. In comparison to the earlier poll of October 1980, Israel gained by 4 percent while the Arabs slipped 3 percent (see Table 2.6). A poll taken in January 1982 after the assassination of Sadat (October 6, 1981) and the annexation of the Golan Heights shows a ratio of 49 to 14 percent in favor of Israel. It could be that Sadat's murder demonstrated the vulnerability of Arab leaders and regimes in contrast with Israel's stability, and that this mitigated the criticism leveled against Israel for its decision to annex the Golan Heights.

By the beginning of 1982, Reagan felt obliged to revise his basic approach towards the Arab-Israeli conflict. He now perceived this conflict as an obstacle to his design for an anti-Soviet alliance in the Middle East, and as a result priority was assigned to the formation of a program that would propel other issues of the Arab-Israeli conflict, including the Palestinian problem, closer to resolution. No actual steps were taken, however, because Israel had not yet completed the withdrawal from Sinai, and implementation of the remaining provisions of the Israeli-Egyptian peace agreement had not yet been carried out. On April 25, Israel completed the withdrawal from Sinai and the long and difficult implementation of the peace agreement reached its successful end. With this, Israel's popularity in the United States reached a level that had earlier been achieved only immediately after the Yom Kippur War. Gallup found in April and May 1982 that a majority of Americans, 51 percent, now sympathized with Israel, while only 12 percent sympathized with the Arabs. With the punctual completion of the Sinai withdrawal, Israel's credibility was restored and its image in the United States once again enhanced.

The War in Lebanon and Its Effects on U.S. Public Opinion

On June 6, 1982—exactly 15 years and a day after the outbreak of the Six Day War—hostilities once again erupted in the Middle East (see the following, though they lack historical depth and perspective: Jansen

1982 and Randal 1983). This time the battlefield was in Lebanon. The immediate cause of the Israeli invasion was an attack by Palestinian terrorists on the Israeli ambassador in London. Portents of the war, however, had been in the air for quite some time. On a number of occasions Israel had warned that it could not tolerate the threat of the semi-independent PLO mini-state in Lebanon (see Yaniv and Lieber 1983, 117–142). The PLO had been increasing its military power in Lebanon, and Israel feared a situation in which the PLO would incite an all-out Arab war against Israel. Israeli leaders were also concerned with the accumulation of PLO terrorism both in Israel and abroad.

The war began with Israeli forces crossing the northern Lebanese border to destroy PLO bases. But the aims of Ariel Sharon, Israeli minister of defense and architect of the campaign, were far more ambitious: Sharon was calculating on a total PLO and Syrian withdrawal from Lebanon that would lead to the formation of a pro-Israeli Christian government—one that might even be willing to sign a peace treaty. Within a few weeks, Sharon and other Israeli leaders discovered how wrong these assumptions had been. In retrospect, they probably underestimated as well the degree of opposition to the war that emerged in Israeli society.

The war in Lebanon was unique in many respects. First, every previous Arab-Israeli war—with the possible exception of the Sinai Campaign—had been forced on Israel by the Arabs, while this one had been initiated by Israel. Moreover, all of the earlier wars had erupted during the period of Labor party rule in Israel, when nationalist groups were in the opposition. Since the latter had always favored a hard-line policy vis-à-vis the Arabs, they had always supported the government in times of war. In 1982, however, the Likud party was in power and the more dovish Labor party was in the opposition. As a result, the Lebanese action was controversial from the start in Israel as well as abroad.

Adding to the complexity of the situation was the fact that Israeli targets in Lebanon were the PLO and the Syrians, not the indigenous population. Indeed, most native Lebanese initially welcomed the Israeli operation as liberation from more than a decade's worth of Palestinian terrorism and harassment. From the purely military point of view the war in Lebanon was also unusual in that most of its battles were fought in highly populated urban areas, including the capital city of Beirut: a tragic consequence of this situation was the high number of civilian casualties that resulted. Finally—and this proved significant in terms of American public opinion—the Lebanese war was the first in history to be televised from both warring ends.

There were several stages to the actual fighting. The first drive was completed by June 14, when Israeli forces reached the outskirts of Beirut.

Another drive occurred in the eastern front between June 22 and 25, when Israeli troops fought Syrian forces. On June 10, President Reagan demanded an immediate cease fire and withdrawal of Israeli forces from Lebanon. On June 22, the President met Begin in Washington and the two reached an agreement concerning a desired settlement in Lebanon. Nonetheless, many of Reagan's officials remained highly critical of the Israeli operation (see *The New York Times*, June 22, 1982).

As mentioned earlier, the mass media played a special role in this war. During most of June, the American public was saturated daily with extensive reports from the battlegrounds. Not all of the reports were accurate or objective; many were grossly distorted (see Muravchik 1983, 11–66; Podhoretz 1982, 21–31; Gervasi 1982; Miller 1982, 26–33; for a rather dismal defense of the press, Morris 1982, 23–33; for additional studies see Landau 1984). A striking case in point were the casualty reports bandied about for several weeks by much of the U.S. media. According to these reports, 10,000 Lebanese civilians had been killed during the initial phase of the war, 40,000 wounded, and 600,000 left homeless. In fact, the *total* population of Southern Lebanon—the area in question—was approximately 500,000.

During the second week of the war, Gallup measured American sympathies towards the Arab-Israeli conflict. His results were very similar to those of April-May 1982 (see Table 2.10 and compare with the relevant results in Table 2.6). But the results exactly a month later showed a dramatic shift: sympathy for Israel had declined by 11 percent, while sympathy for the Arabs was up 2 percent. The media coverage of the war and the emerging siege of West Beirut were probably responsible for the considerable decline in the pro-Israeli rating.

The siege of West Beirut represented a new phase in the war. Israel demanded the withdrawal of the PLO leadership and their troops from Beirut. When PLO head Yassir Arafat refused, Israel decided to tighten the noose around him with daily air raids and shellings. Living conditions in West Beirut seriously deteriorated as a result. During the siege, the American media was particularly critical of Israel; Arafat, in contrast, was accorded unusually sympathetic coverage as he went about his daily activities. During this period only ABC and the *Washington Post* took a poll on American sympathies towards Israel and the Arabs. In comparison to the June Gallup poll, the WP/ABC poll showed a much higher degree of sympathy for both sides (52 percent for Israel, 18 percent for the Arabs). One explanation for this may be that the Gallup poll dealt only with those who had heard or read about the situation in the Middle East, while WP/ABC did not make such a distinction. It is also interesting to note that WP/ABC had conducted a similar poll in March 1982,

Table 2.10
Sympathies Toward Israel and the Arab Nations, 1982–1984

Questions
a. Have you heard or read about the situation in the Middle East? IF YES: In the Middle East situation are your sympathies more with Israel or more with the Arab nations? (Gallup)
b. At the present time, do you find yourself more in sympathy with Israel or more in sympathy with the Arab nations? (L.A. Times)
c. In the Middle East situation, are your sympathies more with Israel or more with the Arab nations? (WP/ABC)
d. With regard to the situation in the Middle East, at the present time do you find yourself more in sympathy with Israel, or more in sympathy with the Arab nations? (Roper)

Q	Date	Poll	Israel	Arab Nations	Neither/Both	DK*NO**
		War in Lebanon (June–September 1982)				
a	June 11–14, 1982	G	52%	10%	29%	9%
b	June 4–8, 1982	LA Times	48	17	22	13
a	July 11–14, 1982	G	41	12	31	16
c	Aug. 17, 1982	WP/ABC	52	18	16	14
		Sabra and Shatila Massacre (September 16–17, 1982)				
a	Sept. 22–23, 1982	NG	32	28	21	19
c	Sept. 24–26, 1982	WP/ABC	48	27	12	13
a	Jan. 1983	G	49	12	22	17
c	Jan. 1983	WP/ABC	47	17	15	21
		Sharon Resignation—Following Kahan Report (February 1983)				
c	Feb.–Mar. 1983	WP/ABC	52	16	13	19
a	July 1983	G	48	12	26	14
d	Jan. 1984	R	64	8	35	13

Sources: Geraldine Rosenfield, "U.S. Public Opinion Polls and the Lebanon War," American Jewish Year Book 84 (1984), p. 109; Washington Post, August 20, 1982 and March 9, 1983; Los Angeles Times, February 25, 1983; Gallup, January and July 1983, Gallup Report International, Vol. 1, no. 6, August 1983, pp. 6–7; Newsweek, October 4, 1982; Steven J. Rosen and Yosef I. Abramowitz, How Americans feel about Israel (Washington, D.C.: AIPAC Papers on U.S.-Israel Relations: 10, 1984) p. 6.

before the outbreak of the war (see Table 6), that yielded virtually identical results.

On August 19, American mediator and special ambassador to the Middle East Philip Habib achieved an agreement concerning the evacuation of the entire PLO apparatus and Syrian forces from Beirut. One significant provision in this agreement required the establishment of a multinational force of French, Italian, and U.S. troops to supervise the evacuation. The force arrived in Beirut, and the evacuation of the PLO and the Syrian troops was completed by September 1, 1982. A Harris poll revealed that a majority of Americans, 54 to 40 percent, disapproved of the decision to dispatch U.S. forces as part of the original three-nation peace-keeping force (see *Washington Post*, July 19, 1982). On September 8, the multinational force left Beirut. However, two tragic and dramatic events soon brought it back. The first event was the assassination of Lebanese president-elect Bashir Gemayel, a Maronite Christian and Phalangist leader, on September 14. As tension flared, Israeli troops entered the predominantly Moslem area of West Beirut on September 15 in order to prevent the resumption of the civil war. Three days later, Christian Phalangists attacked the Palestinian refugee camps of Sabra and Shatila—located in an area controlled by Israeli troops—and murdered about 500 persons. In comparison to other Middle East massacres, the number of casualties in Sabra and Shatila was relatively low (see, for example, Hirst 1982 for an account of a large-scale—and virtually unreported—massacre in Hama, Syria). Nonetheless, because of Israel's alleged involvement in the case, a tremendous wave of criticism was triggered both in Israel and abroad.

Two polls were conducted immediately after the Sabra and Shatila massacres. Gallup took a poll between September 22 and 23 and found a substantial drop in the rate of sympathy for Israel. Only 32 percent of those responding sympathized with Israel, the lowest rate since 1967. This represented a drop of 9 percent in comparison to the July 1982 results, and 20 percent in comparison to the June 1982 results. The number of those who sympathized with the Arabs grew in the September poll by 10 percent to a record level of 28 percent. These results obviously reflected anger at the alleged Israeli involvement in the massacre. In the same poll, Gallup also asked for the views of Americans about the Israeli involvement. The results show that only 8 percent of the respondents believed that Israel could not be held at all responsible for the massacre; the vast majority said that Israel was either partially or very much responsible (see Table 2.11).

A WP/ABC poll conducted between September 24 and 26 showed a smaller decline in the amount of sympathy for Israel—only 4 percent in comparison with the August 1982 poll—along with a 9 percent

Table 2.11
Beirut Massacre

Question
a. Which of the following comes closest to your view? (Asked only of those who
   had heard about the massacre in Beirut September 22–23, 1982, *Newsweek-*
   Gallup)

Statement	Percentage
Israel cannot be held responsible for the massacre because it was carried out by Lebanese Christian militia.	8%
Israel must bear partial responsibility because its troops had taken control of the area where the massacre occurred.	49
Israel is very much responsible because it let Christian militia soliders into the Palestinian camps.	32
Don't know.	11
Total	100%

Source: *Newsweek*, October 4, 1982, p. 23.

---

increase in the number of those sympathetic to the Arabs (see Table
2.11). Thus, although both Gallup and WP/ABC found an identical
rise in the Arab rate, they differed on the decline in the Israeli rate (see
Adams 1982, 51–55 for an analysis of the Gallup results).

The Gallup ratio of 32 to 28 percent did not last long, however. In
face of mounting public pressure, the Israeli government appointed on
September 28, 1982 a special commission headed by Chief Justice Itzhak
Kahan to investigate the massacre. In January 1983, Gallup found a
ratio of 49 to 12 percent in favor of Israel. This ratio was very similar
to the one of January 1982 (49 to 14 percent). The Kahan Commission
issued its report on February 8; subsequently, Israeli minister of defense
Ariel Sharon was forced to resign from his position. At the end of
February and the beginning of March 1983, WP/ABC took another
sympathy poll. Their results were now 52 to 16 percent in favor of
Israel, a result very similar to that of March 1982 (55 to 18 percent).
A Gallup poll of July 1983 yielded a ratio of 48 to 12 percent in favor
of Israel. All these results show that by the beginning of 1983, American
sympathies towards Israel and the Arabs had returned to their pre-war
levels.

Nonetheless, the Lebanon War was clearly a controversial one, in Israel as well as abroad (see Rabin 1983). Israeli opposition parties and extra-parliamentary movements such as "Peace Now" criticized the war, especially its more advanced stages. The internal debate in Israel was widely reported in the United States, and it probably affected American views towards the war. One measure of the war's controversy was the number and frequency of polls conducted on its legitimacy. No less than ten polls were taken on this issue between June and September 1982. The results of all these polls are presented in Table 2.12.

Table 2.12 shows that pollsters used three sets of terms in their questions about the war: approve/disapprove; justified/unjustified; and right/wrong. These sets of terms are not identical; the words "justify" and "right" carry more moral content than "approve", and it is possible for a policy to be justified but mistaken or correct but unjustified. At least one leading and experienced pollster, however, used these terms interchangeably. Between July 9 and 14, 1982, Harris asked whether the Israeli move into Lebanon was justified or not (question d), but in a subsequent interpretation of this question published in the *Washington Post* on July 19, 1982 he wrote that "A 44 to 36 percent plurality would grant its *approval* of that invasion . . . " (emphasis added). A second discrepancy in wording was Harris' use of the phrase "move into Lebanon" in his question, and the term "invasion" in his interpretation.

Table 2.12 shows how these and other terms were used in the various questions. It seems evident that the phrase could lead respondents to a particular answer. Not only did most of the questions about the war seek to solicit moral judgments, they often contained their own bias in one direction or another. Accordingly, results varied considerably from one question to another. The question, "do you approve or disapprove of the Israeli invasion of southern Lebanon?" (b), for example, yielded a 41–24 ratio of disapproval in June 1982. Gallup asked a similar question (g) in August and received a 60–30 ratio of disapproval. A simple question pertaining to the justification of the war (i), however, yielded a much narrower difference: 41 percent of those responding on August 18 thought the Israeli action was unjustified and 37 percent took the opposite position. A month later, the results were 46 percent and 37 percent. A much more substantial difference in results occurred when respondents were classified as either "aware" or "unaware." Of the aware group, 52 percent felt that the Israeli action was justified and 38 percent felt it was unjustified; corresponding figures for the unaware group were 28 and 43 percent.

A number of other questions in Table 2.12 included information or statements liable to create biases. A question that included a statement

Table 2.12
Attitudes Toward the War in Lebanon, June–September 1982

Questions

a. Israel recently began military operations in southern Lebanon to stop Palestinian artillery attacks on settlements in Israel. Do you approve or disapprove of this action?

b. Do you approve or disapprove of the Israeli invasion of southern Lebanon?

c. Some people say Israel is right to fight in Lebanon in order to stop the PLO. Others say Israel is wrong to go into Lebanese territory. Do you think that Israel is right or wrong to fight in Lebanon?

d. As you know, Israel moved into Lebanon to try to eliminate the PLO and Syrian military bases there which had been used to shell northern Israel. If the conflict ends with all foreign military powers—Israeli, Syrian and the PLO—finally getting out of Lebanon, do you think the Israeli move into Lebanon was justified or not?

e. "Israel was right to take defensive action by moving into Lebanon, since the PLO bases there were regularly shelling Israel." Agree or disagree.

f. "Israel was wrong to go to war and kill thousands of Lebanese civilians." Agree or disagree.

g. The Israelis sent their military forces into Lebanon. Do you approve or disapprove of this action?

h. The Israelis have given the following reasons for sending troops into Lebanon: to stop the rocket attacks on Israeli settlements and to remove PLO military forces from Lebanon. Do you think the Israelis were justified in sending troops into Lebanon for these reasons or not?

i. Some people say Israel was justified in invading Lebanon. Others say Israel was not justified. What do you think?

Table 2.12 Cont.

Q	Date	Poll	Approve	Justified	Right	Disapprove	Not Justified	Wrong	Other/Don't Know
a	June 11–14	G	40%			35%			25%
b	June	NBC	24			41			35
		(aware grp)	32			54			14
c	June 26–27	CBS			34			38	28
d	July 9–14	H		44			36		20
e	July 9–14	H			57			28	15
f	July 9–14	H			35			52	13
b	Aug.	NBC	25			51			24
g	Aug. 4–5	NG	30			60			10
h	Aug. 4–5	NG		47			41		12
d	Aug. 5–10	H		43			42		15
b	Aug. 9–10	NBC	25			51			24
i	Aug. 18	WP/ABC		37			41		21
	Aug. 18	(aware)		52			38		10
	Aug. 18	(unaware)		28			43		29
i	Sept. 24–26	WP/ABC		37			46		17

Sources: George Gallup, "Americans' Pro-Israel Sentiments Unaffected by Lebanon Incursion," *The Gallup Poll* July 4, 1982; G. Rosenfield, "U.S. Public Opinion and the Lebanon War," *American Jewish Year Book* 84 (1984), pp. 112–113; C. de Boer, "The Polls: Attitudes Toward The Arab-Israeli Conflict," *Public Opinion Quarterly* 47 (Spring 1983), p. 130; *Washington Post*, July 19, 1982, Boer, op cit., p. 131; *Newsweek*, August 16, 1982; *Washington Post*, August 20, 1982, September 28, 1982.

Table 2.13
Opinions on Israeli Uses of Force

Date	Poll	Subject	Justified	Not Justified	No Opinion
Nov. 1956	NORC	Sending armed forces into Egyptian territory	26%	43%	31%
Apr. 1978	NYT/CBS	Reprisals in Lebanon to PLO attacks	29	57	14
July 1981	NYT/CBS (aware grp)	Attack on the Iraqi Nuclear Reactor	39	39	22
July 1981	NG	Bombing of PLO positions in Beirut	31	50	19
Aug. 1982	WP/ABC	Invading Lebanon	37	41	22

Sources: Seymour M. Lipset, "The Polls On The Middle East," *Middle East Review* 11 (Fall 1978), p. 24; *New York Times*, April 14, 1978; NYT/CBS Poll, June 22–27, 1981; *Newsweek*, August 3, 1981; Table 2.12, question i.

of Israeli interests (e.g., a or h) yielded results that tended to justify the war, while others that included negative information (e.g., f) yielded a higher rate of opposition to the war.

In general, it seems that the Israeli war in Lebanon was not popular in American public opinion, and that many Americans questioned its legitimacy (see, however, Tucker 1982, 19–30). On the other hand, analysis of earlier polls shows that the percent of respondents expressing a belief that the war was justified was not much different from percentages found in polls concerning previous Israeli uses of force (see Table 2.13). Table 2.13 demonstrates that the sending of the Israeli army into Egyptian territory in 1956 was seen as unjustified by a 43 to 26 percent plurality. In April 1978, only 29 percent justified the Israeli reprisals in Lebanon against the PLO, while 57 percent thought these actions unjustified. In 1981, opinion was equally divided about the justification for the Israeli raid on the Iraqi nuclear reactor. Seen in this context, American views regarding the legitimacy of the Israeli operation in Lebanon were not different from those concerning earlier actions in which Israel took the initiative.

Conclusions

The first public opinion polls on Israel were conducted even before its establishment. Until the 1967 Six Day War, however, they appeared infrequently and only during times of crisis and war. Since 1967, polls have been conducted on a more regular basis and have encompassed a wide variety of subjects and issues. Understandably, the most substantial polling is still undertaken during periods immediately following dramatic events in Israel or in the Arab world.

Because this study sought to reveal trends in American opinions on Israel, it made extensive use of what was termed the "sympathy index" (Tables 2.1, 2.5, 2.6, and 2.10). Close examination of the data reveals that the U.S. public has regularly supported Israel by a margin of at least 4 to 1. In times of crisis and wars such as the Six Day War and the War of Attrition, this ratio has risen to 14 to 1. The lowest level of sympathy recorded for Israel—32 percent—was noted in a poll taken immediately after the tragic events in Sabra and Shatila. This finding indicates that at least one third of the American people supports Israel even under the most adverse circumstances. In comparison, the lowest figure of sympathy for the Arabs, 3 percent, was recorded during the War of Attrition. The Arabs achieved much higher ratios of sympathy on two occasions, in February 1978 after a major breakdown in the negotiations between Israel and Egypt, and in September 1982, immediately after the massacre in Sabra and Shatila.

Another measure of Israel's popularity in American public opinion was found in a series of polls that posed a situation where U.S. support for Israel meant antagonizing the Arabs, and vice versa (see Table 2.14).

In these polls as well Israel was supported by wide margins, the pattern of support holding firm even during the controversial 1982 war in Lebanon.

Results of the "sympathy index" and Table 2.14 provide only a partial view of American opinions on Israel. By symbolically pitting Israel against the Arab world, they shed light on basic attitudes alone; the Arab world, as this study shows, is not homogeneous, and Egypt under Sadat's peace policy was able to win considerable sympathy in the U.S. Furthermore, general support does not mean automatic support for every Israeli policy or action. Since 1977, for example, the public has on a number of occasions criticized Israeli positions in the peace negotiations with Egypt, as well as certain Israeli uses of force in the region. Despite this, however, there is abundant evidence pointing to a basic and strongly favorable American attitude towards Israel.

What factors account for this phenomenon? While a complete explanation is obviously beyond the scope of this study, several brief points seem worthy of mention. It is clear, for example, that there are many forces shaping U.S. public opinion: the president and other political leaders, the mass media, intellectuals, and various interest groups (see Welch and Comer 1975; Cantril 1980, and Bennet 1980). Ralph Levering suggested that "most Americans, having limited knowledge about foreign

Table 2.14
U.S. Support to Israel or the Arabs? 1977–1982

Question

a. Some people think the United States should pay more attention to the
   demands of the Arabs, even if it means antagonizing Israel, while other
   people think the U.S. should give its strongest support to Israel, even if it
   means antagonizing the Arabs. If these were the only two choices, what
   should the U.S. do—pay more attention to the Arabs, or give our strongest
   support to Israel?

Date	Poll	Israel	Arabs	Both/ Neither	No Opinion
Oct. 1977	NYT/CBS (aware grp)	54%	27%	19%*	
Apr. 1978	NYT/CBS (aware grp)	43	29	28*	
Aug. 1979	G	38	25	18	19
Mar.–Apr. 1980	G	37	27	21	15
June 1980	NYT/CBS	43	23	9	25
Aug. 1981	PS	47	11	26	16
May 1982	PS	50	9	26	16
June 1982	NYT/CBS	41	21	12	26

*Both, neither and no opinion.

Sources: New York Times, April 14, 1978 and Nov. 2, 1979; Geraldine
Rosenfield, *Attitudes of the American Public Toward American Jews and Israel:
August 1979; March–April 1980*, (N.Y.: The American Jewish Committee
Information and Research Services, June 1980, mimeo), p. 5; C. de Boer, "The
Polls: Attitudes Toward the Arab-Israeli Conflict," op. cit., p. 123; P. & S.: Garth-
Furst, International Inc., Memorandum, May 17, 1982.

affairs, usually have looked to their president and other officials for
guidance in foreign affairs" (Levering 1978, 31). The problems of Israel
and the Arab-Israeli conflict have been extremely complex, and the U.S.
public has in general had limited knowledge of them. This study found
that the positions of the president on Israel and the Arab-Israeli conflict
were significantly correlated with public opinion on Israel. Since the
end of World War II, most American presidents have supported Israel.
The public has followed them in their support—and when Presidents
Eisenhower and Carter voiced criticism of general or specific Israeli
policies, it seems that the public has followed them as well. In 1956,
for instance, President Eisenhower criticized the Israeli military operation

in Sinai, while in 1977–1978 President Carter criticized several Israeli positions in the course of negotiations with Egypt. In both instances, the U.S. public adopted similarly critical views of Israel.

The role of the mass media in the shaping of public opinion has yet to be fully measured and explored (for conflicting views see Lemert 1981; Graber 1980 Ch. 5; and Paletz and Entman 1981 Ch. 13). At least one study found a correlation between coverage of Israel and the Arab-Israeli conflict in the American prestige press from 1966 until 1974, and rates of sympathy towards Israel (Belkaoui 1978, 732–738). On the other hand, the American media, especially the prestige press, was very critical of Israel during the 1982 war in Lebanon. Despite this, as this study shows, the American public did not alter its basic positive attitudes towards Israel.

In the final analysis it could well be that U.S. public opinion regarding Israel is tied to a number of fundamental elements shared by the two countries: common values, similar political and social systems, and joint strategic interests. American-Israeli relations have passed through periods of close collaboration and tense disagreements, and in both cases, American public opinion has played a significant role. In the first case it has encouraged presidents to support and cooperate with Israel, while in the second case, it has prevented serious ruptures. From this perspective it seems that American-Israeli relations are based on solid foundations, and that this situation will prevail as long as the forces shaping those foundations remain in power.

Abbreviations

CBS—CBS News Poll
G—American Institute of Public Opinion, The Gallup Organization
GA—Gannett News Service Poll
H—Louis Harris and Associates
NBC—NBC News Poll
NG—Newsweek Poll-Gallup
NORC—National Opinion Research Center, Chicago
NYT/CBS—New York Times/CBS News Poll
PS—Penn and Shoen Associates
R—Roper
SRC/C—Survey Research Center, Berkeley
WP/ABC—The Washington Post/ABC News Poll
Y—Yankelovich, Skelly and White Inc.

Bibliography

Books

Abu-Lughod, Ibrahim (ed.) *The Arab-Israeli Confrontation of June 1967: An Arab Perspective.* Evanston, Ill.: Northwestern University Press, 1970.

Arian, Asher. (ed.) *Elections in Israel–1981.* Tel-Aviv: Ramot, 1983.

Arian, Asher (ed.) *The Elections in Israel, 1977.* Jerusalem: Academic Press, 1980.

Bagnied, Magda and Schneider, Steven. "Sadat Goes to Jerusalem: Televised Images, Themes and Agenda." Pp. 53–66 in Adams, William C. (ed.) *Television Coverage of The Middle East.* Norwood, N.J.: Ablex, 1981.

Bain, Kenneth R. *The March to Zion: U.S. Policy and the Founding of Israel.* College Station, Texas: Texas A & M University Press, 1979.

Bell, J. Bowyer. *The Long War: Israel and the Arabs Since 1946.* Englewood Cliffs: Prentice-Hall, 1969.

Bennet, W. Lance. *Public Opinion in American Politics.* New York: Harcourt, Brace, Jovanovich, 1980.

Bowie, Robert R. *Suez 1956.* New York: Oxford University Press, 1974.

Bryson, Thomas. *American Diplomatic Relations with the Middle East 1784–1975.* Metuchen: Scarecrow Press, 1977.

Brzezinski, Zbigniew. *Power and Principle: Memoirs of the National Security Adviser, 1977–1981.* New York: Farrar, Straus, Giroux, 1983.

Bulloch, John. *The Making of a War: The Middle East from 1967 to 1973.* London: Longman, 1974.

Campbell, John. *Defense of The Middle East: Problems of American Policy.* New York: Praeger, 1960.

Cantril, Albert H. (ed.) *Polling on The Issues.* Washington, D.C.: Seven Locks Press, 1980.

Carter, Jimmy. *Keeping Faith: Memoirs of a President.* New York: Bantam Books, 1982.

Cooper, Chester. *The Lion's Last Roar: Suez 1956.* New York: Harper and Row, 1978.

Dawson, Richard. *Public Opinion and Contemporary Disarray.* New York: Harper and Row, 1973.

Dayan, Moshe. *Breakthrough: A Personal Account of the Egypt-Israel Peace Negotiations.* New York: Knopf, 1981.

Divine, Robert A. *Foreign Policy and U.S. Presidential Elections 1952–1960.* vol. II. New York: Newview Points, (a division of Franklin Watts), 1974.

Donovan, John (ed.) *U.S.-Soviet Policy in The Middle East 1945–56.* New York: Facts on File, 1972.

Draper, Theodore. *Israel and World Politics: Roots of the Third Arab-Israeli War.* New York: Viking Press, 1968.

Eisenhower, Dwight D. *The White House Years: Waging Peace 1956–1961.* Garden City, N.Y.: Doubleday, 1965.

Erikson, Robert S. and Luttbeg, Norman R. *American Public Opinion: Its Origins, Content and Impact.* New York: John Wiley, 1973.

Eytan, Walter. *The First Ten Years: A Diplomatic History of Israel*. New York: Simon and Schuster, 1958.

Fahmy, Ismail. *Negotiating for Peace in the Middle East*. Baltimore: Johns Hopkins University Press, 1983.

Feis, Herbert. *The Birth of Israel: The Tousled Diplomatic Bed*. New York: Norton, 1969.

Friedlander, Melvin A. *Sadat and Begin: The Domestic Politics of Peacemaking*. Boulder: Westview Press, 1983.

Gabriel, Richard A. *Operation Peace for Galilee: The Israeli-P.L.O. War in Lebanon*. New York: Hill and Wang, 1984.

Gallup, George H. *The Gallup Poll: Public Opinion, 1935-1971*. Vol. I 1935–1948; Vol. II 1949-1958; Vol. III 1959-1971. New York: Random House, 1972.

Gallup, George H. *The Gallup Poll, Public Opinion, 1972-1977*. Vol. I: 1972–1975; Vol. II: 1976-1977. Wilmington: Scholarly Resources, 1978.

Ganin, Zvi. *Truman, American Jewry and Israel 1945-1948*. New York: Holmes and Meier, 1979.

Gervasi, Frank. *Media Coverage of the War in Lebanon*. Washington, D.C.: The Center for International Security, 1982.

Glassman, John. *Arms for the Arabs: The Soviet Union and the War in the Middle East*. Baltimore: Johns Hopkins University Press, 1975.

Golan, Matti. *The Secret Conversations of Henry Kissinger: Step-by-Step Diplomacy in the Middle East*. New York: Quadrangle, 1976.

Graber, Doris. *Mass Media and American Politics*. Washington, D.C.: Congressional Quarterly, 1980.

Heikal, Mohamed. *The Road to Ramadan*. New York: Quadrangle, 1975.

Herzog, Chaim. *The War of Atonement: October 1973*. Boston: Little Brown, 1975.

Hoopes, Townsend. *The Devil and John Foster Dulles*. Boston: Little Brown, 1973.

Jansen, Michael. *The Battle of Beirut: Why Israel Invaded Lebanon*. London: Zed Press, 1982.

Khouri, Fred J. *The Arab-Israeli Dilemma*. Syracuse: Syracuse University Press, 1968.

Kimche, David and Bawly, Dan. *The Six Day War: Prologue and Aftermath*. New York: Stein and Day, 1971.

Kimche, Jon and Kimche, David. *A Clash of Destinies: The Arab-Jewish War and the Founding of the State of Israel*. New York: Praeger, 1960.

Kissinger, Henry A. *Years of Upheaval*. Boston: Little, Brown, 1982.

Kurzman, Dan. *Genesis 1948: The First Arab-Israeli War*. New York: World Publishing Co., 1970.

Landau, Julian J. (ed.) *The Media: Freedom or Responsibility, The War in Lebanon 1982, A Case Study*. Jerusalem: B.A.L. Mass Communications, 1984.

Laqueur, Walter. *Confrontation: The Middle East War and World Politics*. London: Abacus, 1974.

Laqueur, Walter. ed *The Israel-Arab Reader*. New York: Bantam, Part 3. 1970.

Laqueur, Walter. *The Road to War: The Origin and Aftermath of the Arab-Israeli Conflict.* Baltimore: Penguin, 1967-1968.

Legum, Collin. *Crisis and Conflicts in the Middle East: The Changing Strategy from Iran to Afghanistan.* New York: Holmes and Meier, 1981.

Lemert, James B. *Does Mass Communication Change Public Opinion After All?* Chicago: Nelson Hall, 1981.

Levering, Ralph B. *The Public and American Foreign Policy 1918-1978.* New York: William Morrow and Co., 1978.

Lorch, Netanel. *One Long War.* Jerusalem: Keter, 1976.

Lorch, Netanel. *The Edge of the Sword: Israel's War of Independence 1947-49.* New York: Putnam, 1961.

Mangold, Peter. *Superpower Intervention in the Middle East.* New York: St. Martins Press, 1978.

Mendelsohn, Everett. *A Compassionate Peace: A Future for the Middle East.* New York: Hill and Wang, 1982.

Monroe, Elizabeth and Farrar-Hockley, A.H. *The Arab-Israel War, October 1973.* London: International Institute for Strategic Studies, 1975.

Paletz, David and Entman, Robert. *Media Power Politics.* New York: Free Press, 1981.

Pranger, Robert J. *American Policy for Peace in The Middle East, 1969-1971: Problems of Principle, Maneuver and Time.* Washington, D.C.: American Enterprise Institute for Public Policy Research, 1971.

Quandt, William B. *Decade of Decisions: American Policy Toward the Arab-Israeli Conflict 1967-1976.* Berkeley: University of California Press, 1977.

Ra'anan, Uri. *The USSR Arms The Third World: Case Studies in Soviet Foreign Policy.* Cambridge: M.I.T. Press, 1969.

Rabin, Yitzhak. *The War in Lebanon.* Tel-Aviv: Am Oved, 1983.

Randal, Jonathan C. *Going All The Way: Christian Warlords, Israeli Adventurers and The War in Lebanon.* New York: Viking Press, 1983.

Reich, Bernard. *Quest for Peace: United States-Israel Relations and the Arab-Israeli Conflict.* New Brunswick: Transaction, 1977.

Rielly, John E. (ed.) *American Public Opinion and U.S. Foreign Policy, 1983.* Chicago: The Chicago Council on Foreign Relations, 1983.

Robinson, J. and Meadow, R. *Polls Apart.* Washington, D.C.: Seven Locks Press, 1982.

Roll, Charles W. and Cantril, Albert H. *Polls: Their Use and Misuse in Politics.* New York: Basic Books, 1972.

Rosen, Steven J. and Abramowitz, Yosef I. *How Americans Feel About Israel.* Washington, D.C.: AIPAC Papers on U.S.-Israel Relations: 10, 1984.

Rubinstein, Alvin Z. *Red Star on the Nile: The Soviet-Egyptian Influence Relationship Since the June War.* Princeton: Princeton University Press, 1977.

Sachar, Howard M. *Egypt and Israel.* New York: Marek, 1981.

Safran, Nadav. *Israel: The Embattled Ally.* Cambridge: Harvard University Press, 1978.

Safran, Nadav. *From War to War: The Arab-Israeli Confrontation, 1948-1967.* New York: Pegasus, 1969.

Shamir, Shimon. *Egypt Under Sadat: The Search for a New Orientation* (Hebrew). Tel-Aviv: Dvir, 1978.

Sheehan, Edward R.F. *The Arabs, Israelis, and Kissinger: A Secret History of American Diplomacy in the Middle East.* New York: Crowell, 1976.

Sherbiny, Naiem A. and Tessler, Mark A. (eds.) *Arab Oil, Impact on The Arab Countries and Global Implications.* New York: Praeger, 1976.

Snetsinger, John. *Truman, The Jewish Vote, and the Creation of Israel.* Stanford: Stanford University Press, 1974.

Spiegel, Steven L. "The Carter Approach to the Arab-Israeli Dispute." Pp. 93–120 in Shaked H. and Rabinovich, I. (eds.), *The Middle East and the United States.* New Brunswick: Transaction, 1980.

Spragens, William C. and Terwood, Carole Ann. "Camp David and The Networks: Reflections on Coverage of the 1978 Summit." Pp. 117–127 in Adams, William C. (ed.) *Television Coverage of International Affairs.* Norwood: Ablex, 1982.

Stock, Ernest. *Israel on the Road to Sinai 1949–1956.* Ithaca: Cornell University Press, 1967.

Stookey, Robert W. *America and The Arab States.* New York: John Wiley, 1975.

Sykes, Christopher. *Crossroads to Israel 1917–1948.* Bloomington: Indiana University Press, 1965.

Thomas, Hugh. *Suez.* New York: Harper and Row, 1966, 1967.

Truman, Harry. *Memoirs: Years of Trial and Hope 1946–1952.* Garden City, N.Y.: Doubleday, 1955.

Truman, Margaret. *Harry S Truman.* New York: Morrow, 1973.

Vance, Cyrus. *Hard Choices: Critical Years in America's Foreign Policy.* New York: Simon and Schuster, 1983.

Weizman, Ezer. *The Battle for Peace.* New York: Bantam, 1981.

Welch, Susan and Comer, John (eds.) *Public Opinion: Its Formation, Measurement and Impact.* Palo Alto: Mayfield, 1975.

Wilson, Evan M. *Decision on Palestine: How the U.S. Came to Recognize Israel.* Stanford: Hoover Institution Press, 1979.

Whetten, Lawrence L. *The Canal War: Four Power Conflict in The Middle East.* Cambridge: M.I.T. Press, 1979.

Articles and Publications

Adams, William C. "Blaming Israel for Begin". *Public Opinion.* October/November 1982: 51–55.

Belkaoui, Janice M. "Images of Arabs and Israelis in The Prestige Press 1966–74". *Journalism Quarterly.* 55: 732–738, 799, 1978.

Benni, M. "Operation Peace for Galilee: The Crucial Military Steps" (Hebrew). *Ma'arachot.* 284: 24–48, 1982.

Bishop, George *et al.* "Effects of Question Wording and Format in Political Attitude Consistency". *Public Opinion Quarterly.* 42: 81–92, 1978.

Brookings Institution. *Toward Peace In The Middle East.* Report of a Study Group. Washington, D.C.: Brookings, 1975.

Brzezinski, Zbigniew. "Beyond Step-by-Step: Action Proposals". *Foreign Policy*. 19:3–17, 1975.

Campbell, John. "The Middle East: A House of Containment Built on Shifting Sands". *Foreign Affairs*. Vol. 60, No. 3: 593–628, 1981.

DeBoer, Connie. "The Polls: Attitudes Toward The Arab-Israeli Conflict". *Public Opinion Quarterly*. 47: 121–131, 1983.

Erskine, Hazel. "The Polls: Western Partisanship in the Middle East". *Public Opinion Quarterly*. 33: 627–640, 1969–70.

Feith, Douglas J. "The Oil Weapon De-Mystified". *Policy Review*. 15: 19–39, 1981.

Gilboa, Eytan. "Trends in American Attitudes Toward the PLO and the Palestinians". *Political Communication and Persuasion*. Vol. 3, No. 1: 45–67, 1985.

Gruen, George E. "Arab Petro-Power and American Public Opinion". *Middle East Review*. Winter 33–39, 1975–6.

Harris, Louis. "Oil or Israel". *New York Times Magazine*. April 16, 1975: 21.

Hirst, David. "A Hole at the Heart of Hama". *The Guardian*. December 9, 1982.

Ikle, Fred Charles. "The Reagan Defense Program: A Focus on The Strategic Imperatives". /*Strategic Review*. Vol. 10, No. 2, 11–18, 1982.

Inbar, Efraim. "Israel and Lebanon: 1975–1982". *Crossroads, An International Socio-Political Journal*. 10: 47–58, 1983.

Jureidini, Paul A. *et al.* *Arab Reactions to The Egyptian-Israeli Peace Treaty*. Abbott Associates SR 46 (March 26, 1979) 1979.

Kedourie, Elie. "After The Treaty". *The New Republic*. April 7, 1979: 17–18.

Kegley Jr., Charles W. and Wittkopf, Eugene R. "The Reagan Administration's World View". *Orbis*. 26: 223–244, 1982.

Kohut, Andrew. "American Opinion on Shifting Sands". *Public Opinion*. 1: 15–18, 1978.

Laqueur, Walter. "Israel, The Arabs and World Opinion". *Commentary*. 44: 49–59, 1967.

Lewis, Bernard. "The Great Powers, The Arabs, and The Israelis". *Foreign Affairs*. 47: 642–652, 1969.

Lewis, Bernard. "The Consequences of Defeat". *Foreign Affairs*. 46: 321–335, 1968.

Lipset, Seymour Martin. "The Polls on the Middle East". *Middle East Review*. Fall 1978.

Miller, Mark Crispin. "How TV Covers War". *The New Republic*. Nov. 29, 1982: 26–33.

Morris, Roger. "Beirut—and the Press—Under Siege". *Columbia Journalism Review*. November-December 1982.

Muravchik, Joshua. "Misreporting Lebanon". *Policy Review*. 23: 11–66, 1983.

Orbis. "U.S. Policy Toward The Middle East". Spring 1982: 5–34, 1982.

Peretz, Don. "The Earthquake: Israel's Ninth Knesset Elections". *The Middle East Journal*. Vol. 31, No. 3: 251–266, Summer 1977.

Perlmutter, Amos. "The Israeli Raid on Iraq: A New Proliferation Landscape". *Strategic Review*. 34–43, Winter 1982.

Perlmutter, Amos. "Crisis Management: Kissinger's Middle East Negotiation (October 1973–June 1974)". *International Studies Quarterly*. 19: 316–343, 1975.

Podhoretz, Norman. "J'Accuse". *Commentary*. 74: 21–31, 1982.

Rosenfield, Geraldine. "U.S. Public Opinion Polls and The Lebanon War". *American Jewish Year Book*. 84: 105–116, 1984.

Sicherman, Harvey. "Broker or Advocate? The U.S. Role in the Arab-Israeli Dispute 1973–1978". Philadelphia: Foreign Policy Research Institute. Monograph No. 25, 1978.

Snyder, Jed C. "The Road to Osirak: Baghdad's Quest for The Bomb". *The Middle East Journal*. 37: 565–593, 1983.

Tucker, Robert W. "Lebanon: The Case for the War". *Commentary*. Vol. 74, No. 4: 19–30, 1982.

Tucker, Robert W. "The Middle East: Carterism Without Carter?". *Commentary*. Vol. 72, No. 3: 27–36, 1981.

Tucker, Robert W. "Behind Camp David". *Commentary*. Vol. 66, No. 5: 25–33, 1978.

United Nations Special Committee on Palestine. *Working Documentation Prepared by The Secretariat*. 5 Vols. New York, 1947.

U.S. Department of State. *Bulletin*, April 11, 1977. U.S. Department of State. *Foreign Relations of the United States*. (FRUS) 1946, Vol. III.

U.S. International Communication Agency. Policy Statement Series. *A Framework for Peace in the Middle East*. 1978.

Washington Quarterly. "Egypt and Israel: Prospects for a New Era". Special Issue, Georgetown University, 1979.

Yaniv, Avner and Lieber, Robert J. "Personal Whim or Strategic Imperative? The Israeli Invasion of Lebanon". *International Security*. Vol. 8, No. 2 , 117–142, Fall 1983.

Yost, Charles W. "The Arab-Israeli War: How it Began". *Foreign Affairs*. 46: 305–320, 1968.

Newspapers and Periodicals

Le Monde
Newsweek
The New York Times
Time
Washington Post

THREE

Israeli Military Procurement from the United States

MORDECHAI GAZIT

Introduction

Since Israel's establishment in 1948, the issue of U.S. arms supply has been one of the most sensitive issues affecting relations between the two countries. For more than a decade following Israel's establishment, the United States adhered to a policy of not selling major military items to Israel. With one exception in 1958, these restrictions remained in force for approximately 14 years, even during periods in which Israel suffered from a marked inferiority in arms. Such was the case, for example, during the first months of the Israel War of Independence and during much of the 1950s, in particular the period immediately following announcement of the Czech-Egyptian arms deal in September 1955.

As will be seen, the United States raised several arguments to justify its policy during the time that arms restrictions were in effect. One argument was that U.S. economic aid, coupled with funds raised by American Jewry through the UJA and Israel Bonds, enabled Israel not only to consolidate its economy but to purchase arms in western Europe, notably in France after 1956. Another argument was that, by providing economic aid only, the United States was free to nurture its relations with Arab nations in the region.

During the period between 1948 and 1982, there were four distinct phases in U.S. arms policy towards Israel:

The first phase (1948–1961)—During this period, strict limitations on the export of American arms to Israel were in force. Until August 1949,

there was an absolute embargo; after this date, licenses were granted
for the export of military items on the open market, especially if these
could be defined as "items of low military potential" (U.S. Department
of State 1950, V:914). The Eisenhower administration approved the sale
of 100 recoilless guns to Israel in 1958, a year after the United States
had begun delivering arms—including M-47 tanks and artillery—to
Jordan. In 1960, Israel was sold an advanced radar system by the United
States.

The second phase (1962–1965)—During the Kennedy and Johnson
administrations, the United States began to publicly proclaim its readiness
of preserving a balance of arms in the Middle East. The change was
gradual and cautious. President Kennedy approved a deal for the sale
of advanced surface-to-air Hawk missiles to Israel in 1962 and agreed
to hold two meetings with Israeli officials to assess the Middle East
balance of arms. In 1965, President Johnson approved a U.S.-Israeli tank
deal, which marked the first time the U.S. administration had not restricted
its sales to strictly defensive items. Nonetheless, the United States
continued to emphasize its opposition to becoming the chief supplier
of arms for Middle East countries.

The third phase (1966–1969)—In 1966, the Johnson administration
approved the sale of Skyhawk planes to Israel. Following the Six Day
War, in 1968, the sale of Phantom planes was also approved.

The fourth phase (1969–1982)—Although the Nixon administration
openly advocated the principle of preserving the Middle East balance
of arms, it demonstrated extreme caution before finally negotiating a
new aircraft deal at the beginning of 1972. In 1974, President Nixon
gave the government of Golda Meir the first U.S. commitment concerning
ongoing long-term military supplies. This promise was reconfirmed in
a memorandum of agreement signed by the Ford administration and
the Rabin government in 1975, and once again affirmed in a similar
memorandum signed by the Carter administration and the Begin government in 1979.

Between 1974 and 1980, U.S. military aid to Israel averaged approximately $1.6 billion a year, of which $636 million was in the form
of grants. During the same period, Israel's average annual defense imports
amounted to $1.9 billion, one third of which was covered by grants,
and 85 percent of which was covered by U.S. military aid (grants and
loans combined). According to economist Eitan Berglas, U.S. military
grants failed to cover the increase in Israel's defense expenditures in the
years 1968 to 1972 and 1974 to 1980. However, if U.S. economic aid
to Israel is also taken into account (assuming that this aid eases the
burden imposed by security needs), the overall aid package did in fact

cover Israel's increased expenditures during these periods (Berglas 1983, 28–30).

U.S. economic and military aid to Israel in the period of 1951 to 1982 totaled more than $24 billion—$11 billion in grants and $13 billion in loans. Approximately 65 percent of this sum ($16 billion) was military aid, most of which, as described above, was supplied during the latter part of the period.

It should be noted that although the first encouraging changes in U.S. arms policy occurred during the presidencies of Kennedy and Johnson—both Democrats—party affiliation had nothing to do with the changes. It will be recalled that another Democratic president, Harry Truman, imposed a total arms embargo on Israel. Moreover, total U.S. military aid during the Kennedy and Johnson administrations amounted to approximately $250 million, in contrast to $4 billion in the Nixon administration and $2.7 billion in the Ford administration. U.S. military aid to Israel reached its peak ($7.4 billion) during the administration of Democrat Jimmy Carter. In this case, as in the others, developments in the Middle East, rather than domestic considerations, determined the size of the aid program. The Egyptian-Israeli peace treaty, for example, carried a huge price tag in the form of the need to redeploy troops and construct new airbases. During the Nixon administration, the vast increase in U.S. military aid was due to the War of Attrition of 1969–1970, the Jordanian civil war of 1970, and the airlift of supplies during the Yom Kippur War of 1973.

The Truman Administration

American restrictions on the export of arms to the Middle East, including Palestine, were initiated just prior to the adoption of the UN partition plan of November 29, 1947. Loy Henderson, director of the Office for Near Eastern and African Affairs in the State Department, initiated the partition decision on November 10, 1947, three weeks prior to the UN resolution. The U.S. embargo was made public on December 5, 1947. The reason given for the embargo was "the tense situation in Palestine and on its frontiers" and the danger that "Arabs might use arms of U.S. origin against the Jews, or Jews might use them against the Arabs. In either case we would be subject to bitter recrimination" (FRUS 1947, V:1249).

Despite the embargo, Zionist leaders in the United States and leaders of the Jewish community in Palestine went ahead with their requests for permits to purchase U.S. arms. On December 8, 1947, for example, Jewish Agency political head Moshe Shertok (Sharett) met with Henderson to request U.S. assistance in preparing the Jewish community to gradually take control from the British. Shertok requested U.S. military advisers and supplies, promising that the supplies would not be used prior to the British withdrawal (FRUS 1947, V:1303). This request, like all others, was denied. That the Jewish community in Palestine urgently needed military support was indicated by Senator Warren Austin, the U.S. delegate to the Security Council, when he reported on February 2, 1948 that, "the Palestine Commission's Special Report to the Security Council [noted that] some sort of international force [would] be necessary in Palestine as soon as the British leave in order to preserve law and order to defend the Jewish state." (FRUS 1948, V:614ff). Even more explicit was a CIA memorandum submitted at the end of February which argued that, "The Jewish effort . . . will not be sufficient to enable the U.N. Commission to carry out partition as envisaged by the U.N. General Assembly . . . a Jewish state can be established only in the event that the U.N. Commission is given a police force sufficiently strong to withstand Arab aggression or that the Jews of Palestine are provided with enough military support from outside to overcome opposition" (FRUS 1948, V:666, 672).

A similarly pessimistic assessment prevailed among leaders of the Jewish community. On December 9, 1947, Chaim Weizmann sent Truman a letter in which he emphasized that the community's gravest concern was the shortage of arms. Weizmann expressed hope that, "In our effort to correct this dangerous position, we shall have cause to rely on the goodwill of your Administration" (Central Zionist Archives, December 1947–May 1948, 40; FRUS 1947, V:1300). In his reply to Weizmann on December 12, Truman counseled restraint and tolerance, ignoring completely the question of arms. Weizmann reverted to the topic in a conversation with Truman on March 18, 1948, in which he requested that the embargo be lifted. Truman apparently did not reject the possibility out of hand; the Jewish Agency representative in Washington, Eliahu Epstein (Elath), reported that the president had led Weizmann to believe that favorable changes were about to occur in U.S. policy, especially with regard to the embargo (Central Zionist Archives, December 1947–May 1948, editorial note 474).

However, no such changes took place. Despite the recent and painful memory of the Holocaust, the attitude of the Truman administration seems to have been one of indifference. A State Department memorandum prepared in January 1948 stated simply ". . . that it was against American interests to supply arms to the Jews while . . . embargoing arms to the Arabs or to accept unilateral responsibility for carrying out the U.N. decision" (Forrestal 1951, 360). During July and August the argument was developed more fully in memoranda prepared by the State Department and the CIA. The main points of these memoranda were as follows:

(a) Arms deliveries to Israel would enable it to land a serious defeat on the Arab armies with which it was now at war. This could lead to the collapse of various Arab regimes and the rise of communism.

(b) The Arab states were liable to retaliate by holding back petroleum from the West, causing a fall in U.S. oil reserves and the disruption of economic reconstruction in western Europe.

(c) Britain, which had cut back on arms deliveries to the Arab states, would consider itself at liberty to renew them. A split between Britain and the United States could result, which would have serious implications for Western policy in Europe.

(d) Lives of American citizens in the Arab states could be jeopardized by the fury of the masses. American property could be damaged or confiscated, and concessions could be cancelled.

(e) The fate of 700,000 Jews in Arab states could hang in the balance (FRUS 1948, V:1217–1218 and 1279–1285).

In March 1948, Israel began receiving arms from Czechoslovakia, and by the latter part of the year the tide of battle turned in Israel's favor. The Czech-Israeli arms deal removed some of the urgency for a change in U.S. policy regarding its arms embargo. At the same time, however, the administration was disturbed by the Czech-Israeli link, preoccupied as it was with the Cold War. Adding to the administration's displeasure was the fact that a number of American Jewish volunteers were involved in the transportation of planes loaded with Czech arms to Israel. President Truman was personally disturbed by this development, so much so that his administration unsuccessfully approached the Prague regime on several occasions with the demand that it change its policy (FRUS 1948, V:588 and 1248).

The U.S. embargo was finally eased somewhat after the Security Council adopted a resolution on August 11, 1949 announcing the conclusion of the 14-month "truce era" and the beginning of what it termed an "armistice regime" period. At this time the U.S. government stated that it had no intention of permitting the sale of large quantities of sophisticated arms to the Middle East, since this could initiate an arms race in the region. Exports were to be limited "to such arms as are within the scope of legitimate security requirements" (FRUS 1949, V. 5:1341). This restriction remained in force for many years.

Prevented from purchasing arms in the U.S., Israel had great difficulty in the years that followed in obtaining the arms it needed elsewhere. This situation lasted seven years, until in 1956 France became Israel's main source of its military procurements. Throughout this period Egypt, Jordan and Iraq continued to turn to Britain for major arms supplies, relying on arms treaties that were still in force. Moreover, both Britain and the United States were attempting to set up a Middle East defense organization during the early 1950s. Egypt was to be the key member, and with this in mind, Britain adopted a policy in 1950 of strengthening the Egyptian army (FRUS 1950, V:132). Israel's objection to this policy was only partially successful. However, it was one of the factors behind the issuing of the Tripartate Declaration of May 25, 1950, in which Britain, France, and the United States declared the following:

(1) The three Governments recognize that the Arab states and Israel all need to maintain a certain level of armed forces for the purpose of assuring their internal security and their legitimate self-defense and to permit them to play their part in the defense of the area as a whole. All applications for arms or war material for these countries will be considered in the light of these principles. In this connection the three Governments wish to recall and reaffirm the terms of the statements made by their representatives to the Security Council on August 4, 1949, in which they declared their opposition to the development of an arms race between the Arab states and Israel.

(2) The three Governments declare that assurances have been received from all the states in question, to which they permit arms to be supplied from their countries, that the purchasing state does not intend to undertake any act of aggression against any other state. Similar assurances will be requested from any other state in the area to which they permit arms to be supplied in the future.

(3) The three Governments take this opportunity of declaring their deep interest in and their desire to promote the establishment and maintenance of peace and stability in the area and their unalterable opposition to the use of force or threat of force between any of the states in that area. The three Governments, should they find that any of these states was preparing to violate frontiers or armistice lines, would, consistently with their obligations as members of the United Nations, immediately take action, both within and outside the United Nations, to prevent such violation (FRUS 1950, V:167–168).

Although this declaration was meant in part to reassure Israel, it did not solve Israel's problem of where to obtain arms. The U.S. administration continued to place strict restrictions on the sale of arms. According to a 1950 State Department memorandum, the administration was willing to approve sales of "limited quantities of equipment at intervals." Purchases were to be limited to items on the open market, and even these "would be treated in the same way as the items which are being requested from Government stocks" (FRUS 1950, V:792–793).

During the remainder of the Truman administration, the Israeli government made several unsuccessful attempts to strengthen U.S.-Israeli relations in the hope of softening the U.S. position on arms. Thus in

1950 and 1951, Israel made a number of offers regarding construction of U.S. bases in the Negev and integration of the Israel Defense Forces into a regional defense pact against the Soviet Union. Prime Minister David Ben-Gurion went so far as to announce that within three years Israel intended to increase its population through immigration to 2,000,000 inhabitants and, with U.S. assistance, would be able to maintain an army of 250,000 soldiers. Such an army would be "both able and eager" to assist the United States and its allies in resisting Soviet aggression (FRUS 1950, V:960–961). A second offer concerned the stockpiling of raw material and food in Israel to be used in the event of a naval blockade. These stockpiles would be made available to the United States as well in times of need. In requesting U.S. aid to help develop its infrastructure, Israel also pointed out the potential value of an Israeli arms industry and well-developed naval facilities.

The Eisenhower Administration

The story of Israel's efforts in the 1950s to convince the United States to sell it arms is a sad one. The figures illustrate this well: By 1961, the sum total of U.S. military aid to Israel was $0.9 million, compared with $137.1 million worth of arms supplied to the four Arab states that had participated in the 1948–1949 war against Israel (*Congressional Quarterly* 1979, 48–59). A number of factors, to be described below, were behind this disparity.

For several years after the lifting of its embargo, the United States avoided selling any arms to the Middle East. During the last few months of the Truman administration, a change began to take place in U.S. policy with regard to the Arab states. However, after Eygpt's rejection of a Western offer, made in 1951 by the United States, Britain, France and Turkey, to join a regional defense pact, the United States shifted its efforts towards Turkey, Iran, Iraq, and Pakistan. Together with Britain, these nations formed the Northern Tier, later known as the Baghdad Pact. Although the United States did not join, it fully supported the alliance.

Overriding fierce Israeli protests, the Eisenhower administration began to supply military aid to Iraq in 1956. At about the same time U.S. arms began to arrive in Saudi Arabia, the administration arguing that these were needed both to preserve internal security in the kingdom and to protect some 6,000 American citizens residing there. Arms were supplied to Jordan in 1957 on the grounds that Jordan's independence and territorial integrity were a vital concern to the United States; later that year, following Syria's rapprochement with the Soviet Union, U.S. military aid was also given to neighboring Lebanon.

There was no corresponding military aid given to Israel during this period. According to Abba Eban, then Israeli ambassador to the United States, the Eisenhower administration went to great lengths to convince the Arab states that it did not favor Israel, avoiding any moves that might be interpreted as an act of "intimacy" between itself and the Jewish state (Eban 1977, 173).

Egypt was a key U.S. concern during this period, and another factor in the U.S. refusal to sell Israel arms. By selling arms to Iraq at a time when Iraqi-Egyptian relations were strained, the United States had taken a calculated risk: the hope was that Egyptian president Gamal Nasser would either overlook the shipment or else become motivated to seek closer ties with the United States so that his own country could receive military aid. In 1955, there were a number of contacts between the two countries, and in retrospect it seems clear that an arms sale would in fact have materialized had not Egypt insisted on a number of special terms that would have essentially converted the sale into a military grant.

From the Israeli point of view, the arms situation appeared increasingly perilous. Following the lifting of the arms embargo in 1949, the British had opened their arsenals to the Arabs. Now it seemed that the United States was following suit. Moreover, both the United States and Britain had dropped hints concerning the need for Israeli territorial concessions. In a major declaration concerning the Middle East, Dulles stated on August 26, 1955 that there was "no simple criterion" in delineating Middle East borders. Since the Israeli government had made no claims on territories beyond the cease-fire lines, the clear implication was that Israel was expected to make territorial concessions. Dulles' comment that even "territory which is desolate has sentimental value" was taken to refer to the Negev. On November 9, 1955, British prime minister Anthony Eden called for a territorial compromise that would set the border somewhere between that of the 1947 partition plan and the 1949 cease-fire lines (Eban 1977, 182). Seeking to reverse what it perceived as a pro-Arab trend, Israel decided in 1955 to resubmit two demands to the U.S. administration, the first concerning the need for either a security guarantee or defense treaty and the second, a demand for a balance of arms between itself and the Arab states. Both of these demands were rejected, as was a renewed Israeli offer to house U.S. military bases on its soil (Bar-Zohar 1975, 1159). Discussions concerning the latter reached a dead end in October 1955, less than a month after Nasser's announcement of a major arms deal between Egypt and the Eastern bloc. Any Israeli illusions concerning the possibility of U.S. aid in the wake of this deal were soon dashed. Eban (1977, 185) noted, "The State Department thesis during our many stormy discussions was that the Soviet transaction was more promise than fulfillment and that if war broke out in the Middle East, Israel would win a crushing victory."

In the course of two meetings with Secretary of State Dulles in October and December, Israeli prime minister Moshe Sharett attempted in vain to influence a change in U.S. policy. Dulles continued to maintain that the Czech-Egyptian arms deal had not disrupted the balance of arms between Egypt and Israel, although he added that if it became apparent that it had, the United States would reconsider its policy. However, Dulles continued, even in such a case, European countries—rather than the United States—were to be considered the traditional arms suppliers to the Middle East (Eban 1977, 194). Sharett came away from both meetings convinced that U.S. arms policy was not about to change (Sharett 1978, V: 1253).

In December 1955, Israel launched a retaliatory attack (the Sea of Galilee Operation) against Syria. Sharett, who was expecting Dulles' reply on the arms question at that time, believed that the operation caused Dulles to reject the Israeli request for military aid. In retrospect, however, it appears that Dulles had never seriously considered a favorable reply, since the U.S. refusal persisted for months after the operation. At the beginning of 1956, for example, Ben-Gurion and Sharett failed to convince U.S. presidential emissary Robert Anderson that Israel urgently needed U.S. military supplies in order to balance the Soviet bloc's arms deliveries to Egypt. The following month, Ben-Gurion sent a letter to Eisenhower in which he stated that the arms being delivered by the Soviets to Egypt gave it superiority while "Israel lacks means to defend herself." Ben-Gurion urged the president "not to leave Israel without sufficient capabilities for self defense." Eisenhower's reply, however, was noncommittal: "your request is under careful consideration in light of two requirements: securing Israel and creating a situation which will encourage peace in the region" (Ben-Gurion, c. 1972). On March 7, Eisenhower stated at a press conference that, "We do not believe that it is possible to assure peace in that area merely by rushing some arms to a nation that at most can absorb only that amount that 1.7 million people can absorb, whereas on the other side, there are some 40 million people." The following week Eisenhower softened his statement somewhat: "I never said, and I am sure that the Secretary of State never said that we would not supply arms to Israel. We hope for a better solution" (Public Papers of the Presidents of the United States 1958, 286 and 306). A solution, however, did not appear, and arms were not sent.

During the Eisenhower administration, the Israeli government made repeated efforts to change this policy. Israel's basic argument was that a "balance of forces" was needed in the Middle East, i.e., that any major arms deliveries to the Arabs must be balanced by comparable sales to

Israel. A number of statements by Dulles seemed to indicate that while the United States rejected the concept of a balance, it would consider sending modest supplies of arms to Israel (see for example Sharett 1978, V: 1253). Until 1958, however, no arms of any kind were sent. It was not until 1956 that the administration softened its stand somewhat by withdrawing its opposition to sales of U.S. military equipment manufactured in other countries to Israel. The first deal of this sort involved the sale of 12 Mystere IV jets built in France with U.S. government funds; in the same year the administration also approved the sale of two dozen Sabre jets manufactured in Canada under American license. On the whole, however, the U.S. stance towards Israel during the first half of the Eisenhower administration was considered unsatisfactory by Israeli leaders. Eban comments that, "This was the only period in which America could be justly accused of having let Israel alone to the winds and storms." By the beginning of 1956, he notes British and U.S. tanks were reaching Saudi Arabia, British tanks and planes were reaching Iraq and Jordan, and U.S. arms were reaching Iraq—all this in addition to the Soviet bombers, fighters, tanks, and submarines that were being sent to Egypt (Eban 1977, 190).

France's decision in 1956 to sell Israel arms was uncoordinated with—and basically opposed to—U.S. policy. One indication was the French decision to stop cooperating with the Middle East Armament Committee of which France had been a member since 1950 together with the United States and Britain, and in which it was meant to have coordinated all of its arms sales to the Middle East. After Nasser nationalized the Suez Canal in July, the last French restrictions on the supply of arms to Israel disappeared. With Israel as an ally, France started to plan a military operation against Egypt. The Franco-Israeli connection continued for years, until 1967. Thoughout this period, however, Israel never lost hope that arms from the United States would someday become available.

Britain's position in the Middle East was significantly weakened following the 1956 Sinai Campaign. As a result, the United States stepped in to bolster the West's position in the Middle East. Just as Truman took action in 1947 to fill the void created by the British withdrawal from Greece and Turkey, Eisenhower felt obliged in 1957 to extend U.S. commitments in other parts of the region. On March 9, 1957, Congress approved a resolution (later known as the "Eisenhower Doctrine") that not only authorized the president to grant military or economic aid to any Middle East country whose independence was threatened, but allowed the president, at his discretion, to send U.S. armed forces into Middle East countries threatened by "international communism." The extension of the American commitment had already manifested itself in the previously mentioned arms deliveries to Jordan and Lebanon. Although the aid was relatively restricted, consisting mostly of guns and a number of tanks, it highlighted the fact that the administration was supplying arms to four neighboring Arab states while persisting in its policy of refusing arms to Israel.

It was only the following year, as a result of several events which severely shook the Middle East—the establishment of a union between Egypt and Syria in January 1958, a coup d'etat in Iraq that in July 1958 brought about the collapse of the pro-Western monarchy, the dispatch of American marines to Lebanon on July 15, the transportation of British paratroopers to Jordan over Israel's air space on July 18— that a change occurred in Dulles' views concerning Israel's role and weight in the region. One result of this change was that the United States finally consented to sell Israel 100 recoilless guns of the kind it had already supplied to Jordan. In effect, this did not constitute a basic change. It was no more than a modest delivery of defensive weapons at a time when Israel was surrounded by neighbors in possession of both Soviet and American tanks. Moreover, the U.S. decision was grounded in a rapprochement between the United States and Israel that had begun nearly a year earlier. According to John Campbell (1960, 202), it was decided not to go beyond small-scale shipments of arms, for fear that, "[providing] Israel with arms would risk losing what gains the United States had made in its relations with several Arab states." In March 1960, Prime Minister Ben-Gurion met with Eisenhower to once again press the question of U.S. arms supply, in particular the sale of Hawk anti-aircraft missiles. Eisenhower gave no clear answer regarding the missiles, although a later memorandum to Kennedy made it apparent that the request had been denied (Kennedy Library POF Box 119A, January 30, 1961). On the general issue of U.S. military aid, Eisenhower restated the standard U.S. reply: it was not interested in becoming a principal arms supplier to the Middle East, preferring to leave this role to the Europeans (Bar-Zohar 1975, 1367).

Thus, with the exception of the recoilless guns (and a radar system sold in 1960), the Eisenhower administration was consistent in its refusal to supply Israel with arms. Concerning Israel's repeated efforts to change U.S. policy, Bar-Zohar (1975, 1320) comments that, "There was something pathetic and shameful about the desire to hold on to the American apron while time and again the U.S. tried to shake off the embarrassing nuisance."

The Kennedy Administration

John F. Kennedy was the first U.S. president to acknowledge, even if only implicitly, the necessity of maintaining a balance of arms between

Israel and the Arab states. His key statement on the matter was made in a press conference held on April 3, 1963. Following an introduction in which he pointed out that while the United States had never directly supplied any military equipment to Israel, its economic aid had enabled Israel to purchase arms from France, Kennedy added a highly significant sentence: "We would be reluctant to see a military balance of power in the Middle East which was such to encourage aggression rather than discourage it. So this is a matter which we will have to continue to observe" (Public Papers of the President of the United States 1964, 267).

Compared to Eisenhower's statement about the impracticality of maintaining a balance of arms between Israel with its small population and the populous Arab states, the difference in approach is immediately apparent. In contrast to his predecessor, Kennedy called for examination of the Middle East arms situation—a clear shift in U.S. policy (see Safran 1981, 581).

Notwithstanding, Kennedy's statement was worded with extreme caution. For one thing, he intended to signal the Soviet Union that it was not too late for the two powers to reach an understanding concerning a slowdown of the Middle East arms race. He also wanted, if possible, to avoid a strongly negative Arab reaction. And finally, with one exception, Kennedy had not yet introduced any concrete changes in U.S. policy regarding arms sales to the Middle East.

The press conference of April 1963 took place approximately two years into Kennedy's administration. Before this, Kennedy had made a number of other statements regarding the Middle East. During the presidential campaign of 1960, for instance, he had spoken before the Zionist Organization of America (ZOA) and proposed "that an intensive effort be made to limit an arms race in the Middle East with a realization that if this is not accomplished we shall not permit an imbalance to exist" (*Near East Report* November 12, 1960, and *The New York Times* August 26, 1960). Such a proposal echoed the Democratic Party platform pledge to pursue a Middle East solution "by seeking to prevent an arms race while guarding against the dangers of a military imbalance resulting from Soviet arms shipments" (*Near East Report* November 12, 1960). The *Near East Report* article—whose sources were undoubtedly reliable— went on to note: "It is known that Senator Kennedy believes that in the absence of peace and disarmament, Israel must receive sufficient aid so as to be strong enough to defend itself and deter attack."

There was, of course, no guarantee that once elected Kennedy would act in accordance with his pre-election statements. In fact, one of the first papers handed to Kennedy by Secretary of State Dean Rusk was a memorandum detailing the handling of Israel's arms requests by the previous two administrations without recommending any deviations from this policy (Kennedy Library POF Box 119A, January 30, 1961). In Israel, however, there were expectations that the change in administration would translate into a change in policy. It is interesting to note that Israeli leaders had never given up their efforts to induce such change, despite the meager results in the past. By 1960, Israel's basic arms position was more secure, thanks to its arms relationship with France. As a result, Israeli requests for U.S. arms during the Kennedy administration were presented without the tension that had marked such requests in the previous two administrations.

Before leaving for Washington in September 1959, Israeli ambassador Avraham Harman had been charged with the task of trying to obtain certain military items for Israel. The Soviet Union at this time was sending its best arms to Egypt and other Arab states, and Israel knew that only the United States was capable of supplying certain technologically advanced equipment. One such item was the Hawk anti-aircraft missile—the best of its kind in the Western world—the sale of which was limited to allies of the United States. Eisenhower, as previously noted, made no clear commitment concerning sale of the missiles. However, on May 30, 1961, a meeting took place in New York between Kennedy and Prime Minister Ben-Gurion, in which the latter described the balance of arms picture between Israel and the Arab states, in particular Egypt. Ben-Gurion emphasized Israel's weakness in the area of anti-aircraft defense, pointing out that a U.S. commitment to supply Hawk missiles would prevent exclusive Israeli dependence on France. Kennedy noted in reply that the Hawk request had been inconclusively considered by the Eisenhower administration, and promised to reexamine the request.

The "reexamination" took slightly over a year, but on September 26, 1962, the government announced its decision to sell the missile. This decision marked the first real breach in the U.S. policy of not selling arms to Israel. Philip N. Kluznick, the U.S. ambassador to the UN during the Kennedy administration called it a "great reversal" in an interview on file in the oral history section of the Kennedy Library (p. 12), adding that, "Kennedy had the courage to do something in the Hawk missile [matter] but has never been given credit for it."

The importance of the Hawk missile sale was manifested in a number of ways. First was the magnitude of the actual sale, which totaled tens of millions of dollars (on extremely favorable terms of credit). Second was U.S. justification of the sale on the grounds that there was a need to stabilize the balance of arms that had been disrupted by the Soviet delivery of fighters and bombers to Egypt, Syria, Iraq, and Yemen. And not least in significance was the fact that the decision followed a detailed and thorough review by the administration that had resulted in approval being given by all relevant U.S. government agencies, including the Defense Department.

According to a Defense Department memorandum of May 1962, there "was a valid military basis for the Israeli selection of the Hawk as an item of key importance in their military posture" (quoted in Gazit 1983, 94). The State Department also had several reasons for not opposing the deal. Since the Hawk was considered a defensive weapon the State Department experts assumed that the Arab reaction to the decision would be restrained. Moreover, U.S.-Egyptian relations had substantially improved by 1962 as a result of Kennedy's assiduous wooing of Nasser. In light of this, an assessment was made that Nasser would not come out strongly against the deal. However, to be on the safe side, the administration gave Nasser advance warning of its decision. The State Department was also convinced that the military balance had in fact been disrupted to Israel's detriment, so that the Hawk request was fully justified. Finally, in view of the escalation of Soviet arms in the region, the State Department was interested in signaling both the Soviets and the Arabs that the United States was not about to sit back and allow the arms race to develop in a totally one-sided manner (Gazit 1983, 42–46).

In recounting the decision to sell Hawk missiles to Israel, it is important to note a meeting that took place in July 1962 between U.S. and Israeli officials. The purpose of the meeting, as described in a State Department memorandum, was "to discuss Israel's view of the Israel-Arab military balance in light of the UAR's new arms acquisitions" (Kennedy Library NCS Box 117–118, July 6, 1961). Among those at the meeting was Brigadier Aharon Yariv of Israeli military intelligence, who gave a detailed analysis of Israel's military situation.

Several months earlier, in February 1962, U.S. envoy Chester Bowles had been sent to Egypt to see if Nasser might be willing, either overtly or covertly, to limit his arms purchases in return for similar Israeli promises. Nasser turned down the proposal, explaining that the Egyptian army would probably overthrow him if he supported it (Bowles 1971, 372). Six months later, presidential envoy Meyer Feldman arrived in Israel to inform Ben-Gurion of the decision in principle to supply the missiles. Before making the decision public, Feldman said, the administration wished to inform Nasser; this courtesy, it was felt, might lead to a more restrained Egyptian response. Ben-Gurion replied that Israel would be happy to forgo the missiles altogether if Nasser would agree to a reciprocal arms limitation agreement (Kennedy Library NCS Box 118–119, August 20, 1962).

Ben-Gurion's position enabled the Americans to inform Nasser that the decision to sell the missiles to Israel was a direct result of his own rejection of any arms limitations. Nasser thanked the administration for having made him privy to its decision, and when the deal was made public approximately one month later, the reaction of the Egyptian media was in fact quite restrained.

An additional U.S. effort to bring about an arms limitation agreement between Egypt and Israel was made in June 1963. Several developments had occurred in the interim that were of concern both to Israel and the United States. First was the news that Egypt was developing surface-to-surface missiles and other offensive weapons with the assistance of German scientists. Second was the announcement of a tripartite union between Egypt, Syria, and Iraq in April 1963. Following this announcement, Ben-Gurion had approached Kennedy with proposals calling for either a joint Soviet-American guarantee concerning the territorial integrity and independence of all Middle East states or a defense agreement between the United States and Israel. Although neither proposal was taken up seriously, the administration was nonetheless concerned about the tripartite union. Moreover, disturbances had broken out in Jordan in April, and a war in Yemen with increasing Egyptian military involvement that had been going on since the beginning of October 1962 was still far from over. The United States was also concerned about Israeli nuclear activities, even though Ben-Gurion had allowed two American experts to visit the Dimona nuclear reactor (Bar-Zohar 1975, 1393).

John McCloy, the administration's coordinator on arms control, was chosen as the emissary. His mission was to try to convince Israel to agree to international supervision of the nuclear reactor in Dimona in return for cancellation or limitation of the Egyptian missile program. However, McCloy's mission in Egypt failed completely. As result, he saw no point in proceeding to Israel, especially since Ben-Gurion had just resigned from the premiership.

Following this unsuccessful effort, the administration agreed to hold a second joint meeting on the balance of arms in November 1963. It seemed as if the administration had started to view these meetings as a normal part of U.S.-Israeli relations. On this occasion, Yitzhak Rabin, the chief of staff, was Israel's chief delegate, emphasizing in his presentation the need for U.S. tanks. (At the time, the Israel Defense Forces were equipped mainly with renovated World War II and light French tanks.) The fact that Rabin was able to present what amounted to an arms request at the meeting was itself an important development, one that undoubtedly emanated from Kennedy's public declaration concerning U.S. interest in the preservation of an arms balance.

Approximately 10 days after this meeting, President Kennedy was assassinated. A decision on the sale of tanks was thus deferred to the Johnson administration. Had he lived, it is likely that Kennedy would have approved the sale, since the general thrust of his administration's policy was to examine Israel's security needs on their merits.

The Kennedy Library contains a fascinating memorandum supporting this view. Summarizing a conversation between Kennedy and Golda Meir, then Israeli foreign minister, the memorandum quotes the following statement by Kennedy:

> The U.S. has a special relationship with Israel in the Middle East, really comparable only to that which it has with Britain over a wide range of world affairs . . . We are in a position to make clear to the Arabs that we will maintain our friendship with Israel and our security guarantees. . . . I think it is quite clear that in case of an invasion the United States would come to the support of Israel. We have that capacity and it is growing (Kennedy Library NSC Box 117–118, December 27, 1962).

In examining this statement a number of points are noteworthy. First was the fact that Kennedy made the statement on his own initiative, without any prodding from Meir. Second was the use of the terms "special relationship" in describing U.S.-Israeli relations; considering the atmosphere of alienation that had characterized the U.S. attitude towards Israel in the 1950s, this phrase is especially striking. Finally, the actual thrust of the message, i.e., an explicit commitment to come to Israel's aid in the event of an attack. This commitment was repeated by Kennedy in a letter sent to Prime Minister Levi Eshkol the following year (*Yediot Aharonot* October 20, 1963, story by Erel Guinay).

Although Kennedy acted with great care on the Israel issue, making moves that in retrospect appear to be modest, he was the one who changed the course of U.S. policy towards Israel. The decisions to sell Hawk missiles, the first sophisticated and expensive military item approved for sale to Israel, and the authorization of U.S.-Israeli discussions concerning the balance of arms in the Middle East, constituted a clear shift in the administration's attitude on the issues of balance of arms and arms supply to Israel. Added to this was Kennedy's promise to come to Israel's aid in the event of attack and his emphasis on the "special relationship" between Israel and the United States. These statements— as much as the increased economic aid granted during the Kennedy administration—seem a harbinger of the close U.S.-Israeli ties that developed in the course of the 1960's.

The Johnson Administration

By the beginning of the Johnson administration, Prime Minister Levi Eshkol was searching for new ways to strengthen defense ties between the United States and Israel. In his former position as minister of finance, Eshkol had learned to appreciate the importance of U.S. economic assistance. U.S. military assistance, however, was quite insignificant, and Eshkol now planned to change the situation. Encouraging Eshkol in his efforts were Golda Meir and Shimon Peres, then the deputy minister of defense. Although Peres was largely responsible for developing Israel's defense ties with France, he believed that the United States should be drawn in as an additional source of supply. In talks with Pentagon officials, Peres had explained that France felt uncomfortable in its role as the sole source of military equipment for Israel (Kennedy Library NSC Box 117–118).

Israeli officials believed that after it reached a settlement in Algeria, France would seek to improve its relations with the Arab countries, and this would affect the nature of its ties with Israel. Moreover, there were a number of sophisticated weapons that France simply did not manufacture. Adding to the importance of the United States as a source of superior weaponry was the fact that arms deals with the U.S. were generally concluded with generous terms of credit. For all these reasons— plus the fact that U.S.-Israeli relations were on the upswing, and Johnson was known to be sympathetic to Israel—the time appeared ripe for a new Israeli initiative.

In June 1964, Eshkol became the first Israeli prime minister to be officially invited to Washington. In a series of cordial talks with Johnson, Eshkol presented an Israeli request for M-48 Patton tanks with conversion kits and 105 mm guns. Although the United States possessed a newer tank, the M-60, there seemed little likelihood that Israel could receive these tanks. However, when converted and outfitted with the larger guns, the M-48 was virtually identical to the M-60. U.S. officials argued that they would prefer Israel to purchase the tank frames in West Germany while the conversion kits could be supplied by either the United States or Britain. Eshkol, for his part, argued that purchasing the entire tank from the United States would have great importance as a deterrent to Arab military buildups.

In a joint declaration published at the end of the visit, there was no reference to either a tank deal or the balance of arms principle. Johnson, however, had indicated that the request would be favorably reviewed, and had also reaffirmed Kennedy's earlier commitment that, "America would not be idle if Israel is attacked, and that this undertaking given by both his predecessors and himself, was a solemn and serious commitment" (Peres 1970, 103).

In fact there were several good reasons for approving the deal. Soviet deliveries to Egypt and Syria had given both these countries a qualitative and quantitative advantage in armor. In addition, the Johnson administration had given approval for the sale of 180 Patton tanks to Jordan. It was conceivable that the administration could have acted as the Eisenhower administration had done in 1957 and supplied tanks to Jordan while withholding them from Israel. But circumstances had changed: Washington had learned that the pro-Western Arab states feared Egyptian subversion (as evidenced in the war in Yemen) no less than they feared Israel. As a result, there was far less need to take Egypt's reaction into consideration. Even John Badeau, the U.S. ambassador in Cairo, did not object to the new U.S. policy of supporting pro-Western states such as Jordan, Saudi Arabia, and Israel. Badeau requested only that the government once again inform Nasser in advance of its moves, as it had done in the case of the Hawk missile deal. This was a notable change from the attitude that had prevailed during the 1950s, when great stress had been laid on the possible Egyptian reactions to any U.S. move.

The administration's decision was also influenced by its appreciation for the positive role that Israel had filled in the 1957 and 1958 crises in the region. The United States had come to realize that Israel was a country whose presence was useful to the West. In addition, the relations which had developed among Israel, Iran, Turkey, and Ethiopia after 1958 were highly appreciated in Washington, as were Israeli development and assistance programs in Africa.

Despite all this, it took the better part of a year before the tank deal was finally concluded. A decisive point in the negotiations was reached in March 1965, when veteran U.S. diplomat and statesman Averell Harriman arrived in Israel accompanied by Robert Komer, a senior staff member of the National Security Council. One of their goals was to convince Israel to refrain from publicly criticizing the U.S.-Jordanian arms deal that was already in the process of implementation. Admitting that the stationing of M-48s on the West Bank would constitute a serious threat to Israel, Harriman and Komer undertook to obtain a commitment from King Hussein of Jordan that the tanks would not cross the Jordan River to the west. The possible sale of planes to Israel was also discussed; it was agreed that an Israeli delegation would present its case at the Defense Department.

In November 1965, negotiations concerning the sale of Skyhawk planes commenced, with Ezer Weizman, the head of the Israeli air force, in charge of the Israeli delegation. The first deal, involving 48 Skyhawk planes, was signed in February 1966; soon thereafter, the administration approved the sale of an additional 52 planes. Negotiations for the planes proved far less complicated than those involving the tanks, perhaps because Johnson had already taken a stance in favor of the deal following the Harriman-Komer mission to Israel.

On February 6, 1966, after a series of leaks to the media, the State Department published a statement concerning the tank deals with Israel and Jordan. One passage of this statement is of particular interest:

> The established U.S. policy has been to refrain from becoming a major supplier of arms in this area while retaining the option of helping the countries of the area to meet their defense requirements through occasional selective sales. These exceptions to our general policy have been on careful case-by-case examinations and a determination that such a sale would not be a destabilizing factor. The United States has made over the years repeated quiet efforts to encourage limitations on arms build-ups in the area. Until these bear fruit, however, the U.S. cannot be indifferent to the potentially destabilizing effect of massive Soviet sales of arms to the area. Over the years, to meet modernization requirements, we have sold to the Government of Israel various items of military equipment to help it meet its own defense and internal security requirements. These have included Patton tanks (*Keesing's Contemporary Archives* 1966, 21321).

Of particular significance in this statement was the mention of "modernization requirements," which introduced a totally new element in U.S. Middle East policy. Rather than merely seek to maintain an arms balance, the United States was now introducing a new factor—modernization—that would help determine its arms supply policy. Further, the tank deal was evidence that the U.S. government was no longer limiting itself to the sale of purely defensive weapons.

In deciding whether to approve the Skyhawk deal, the administration, as in the past, was guided by a number of considerations. Two were especially important this time: the need to balance Soviet shipments to the Egyptian, Syrian, and Iraqi air forces; and the fact that the Johnson administration had decided to sell three squadrons of F-104 Starfighter planes to Jordan.

It is clear, in retrospect, that U.S. policy in the sphere of arms supplies had advanced substantially since the 1962 Hawk deal. However, not all the barriers had been removed. As one senior official in the State Department pointed out in June 1967, "the overriding consideration was for the U.S. not to be identified as a heavy or principle supplier to either of the antagonists in a potential conflict. Secondly, we wanted to maintain as much suasion as we could in the Arab countries. We felt that (influence in the Arab states) would have been decreased if we had become a large single source supplier to Israel." (*Middle East Record* 1967, 58).

Upon the outbreak of the Six Day War in June 1967, the Johnson administration announced its decision to stop all arms deliveries to the region. This decision had two principal motives: to signal to the Soviet Union to limit its own deliveries to Egypt, Syria, and Iraq; and to portray the United States as a country opposed to sending arms to states engaged in hostilities.

It soon became apparent, however, that the American gesture was ignored, since the Soviet Union continued supplying arms to Arab states in the region. In the June 23–25 summit conference in Glassboro, New Jersey, Johnson unsuccessfully attempted to extract guarantees from Soviet leader Alexei Kosygin that in the future, U.S. and Soviet arms deals would either be made public, or else details concerning such deals would be supplied by one government to the other. According to the proposal, the United States and the Soviet Union would first see to it that a balance of arms between the Arab countries and Israel would come into effect. Thereafter this balance would be meticulously preserved (*The New York Times* September 28, 1967).

In the meantime, the U.S. suspension of arms continued. According to Yitzhak Rabin, then Israeli ambassador to Washington, the consequences of the suspension were severe,

> not only in the refusal to approve new orders, but also in that the deliveries which had been approved and orders which had been contracted by the two states were held up and not sent to Israel. Thus the United States was in breach of signed agreements because of the illusion that this would convince the Soviet Union to slow down the pace of its own deliveries of arms to the Arab states . . . [in fact the] Soviet Union interpreted the suspension as American weakness and increased the arms deliveries to Egypt and Syria (Rabin 1978, I:221).

On July 14, Secretary of State Dean Rusk told the Senate Foreign Affairs Committee that the United States should consider renewing arms deliveries in order to prevent the Soviet Union from having a monopoly and gaining predominant influence in the area. Several weeks later, Rusk admitted that the administration was disappointed by the arms limitations efforts (*Department of State Bulletin* October 30, 1967). On October 24, 1967, the State Department announced that the United States would resume deliveries to Arab states (Jordan, Lebanon, Saudi Arabia, Morocco, Libya, and Tunisia) and to Israel. According to Nicholas Katzenbach, a Rusk deputy, one of the most important considerations behind this decision was the fact that the Soviet Union had not only replenished arms that had been lost but was also offering arms to Arab states such as Jordan that were considered traditional friends of the United States (Katzenbach 1971, 48).

For Israel, the first significance of the announcement was that deliveries of the Skyhawks would finally begin. Beyond this, however, Israeli officials hoped to be able to purchase additional aircraft. French president Charles de Gaulle had imposed an arms embargo following the outbreak of the Six Day War, and this embargo was still in force in so far as 50 Mirage V planes were concerned, even though Israel had already paid two thirds of their cost. It appeared that France had no intention of releasing these planes in the foreseeable future. As a result, Israel turned to the United States at the end of 1967 with a request for 50 Phantom planes.

The first U.S. reaction was reserved. In January 1968, Eshkol followed through with a visit to President Johnson's ranch. Although the talks were friendly, Johnson refrained from making a definite commitment to supply the planes. He said that the United States needed additional time before reaching a decision—possibly up to a year. However, he added, if the decision was to supply the planes, delivery would commence shortly thereafter.

The president's hesitation emanated from a wish to examine the Soviet Union's position concerning arms limitations. Johnson also relied on expert appraisals that Israel currently enjoyed a military superiority over its neighbors, and would thus not be placed in any jeopardy by having to wait several months for a reply. Eshkol, for his part, was satisfied with the meeting, having gained an impression that there was no opposition in principle to the sale of the Phantoms. The statement at the conclusion of the talks, although silent on the Phantoms, was also satisfactory to Israeli officials; among other things, it noted that the President had "agreed to keep Israel's military defense capabilities under active and sympathetic examination and review. . . ." (*Keesing Contemporary Archives* 1968, 22565).

The Soviet invasion of Czechoslovakia in August 1968 was a severe blow to the U.S. attempt to reach an arms limitations agreement with the Soviet Union. Although Rusk raised the issue once again with Foreign Minister Andrei Gromyko in October 1968, he did so merely in order to prevent the Soviets from arguing that the United States had not exhausted all possible diplomatic means before deciding on additional deliveries. Following that meeting, Johnson's decision to approve the sale of the Phantoms was published (October 9). The decision was undoubtedly facilitated in part by a congressional resolution passed three weeks before as part of the U.S. Foreign Assistance Act. The resolution called on the president, "to negotiate an agreement with the Government of Israel providing for the sale by the United States of such a number of supersonic planes as may be necessary to provide Israel with an adequate deterrent force capable of preventing future Arab aggression by offsetting sophisticated weapons received by the Arab states and to replace losses suffered by Israel in the 1967 conflict" (*Middle East Record* 1968, 82; see also Rabin, 1978, 225).

Several obstacles remained, however, even after the decision to sell the planes was announced. Foremost among these was a demand that Israeli military production and research institutions be placed under U.S. supervision (Rabin 1978, 236 and 243). Opposing this demand, Rabin argued that if the deal were delayed, President-elect Nixon would be able to gain the credit for supplying the planes. The difficulties were eventually ironed out to Israel's satisfaction and on December 27, the official agreement was published (*Middle East Record* 1968, 83).

The fact that 1968 was a presidential and congressional election year undoubtedly worked in Israel's favor. So did other, more objective factors. One was the continued Soviet military aid to Egypt and Syria. Coupled with the invasion of Czechoslovakia, this act strengthened the U.S. resolve to counter Soviet moves. The French refusal to release the Mirage V planes purchased by Israel was another factor in the decision to sell the Phantoms, as was the assessment that relations between the United States and moderate Arab states were not likely to be damaged, especially since American arms deliveries to Jordan had created a kind of symmetry in U.S. actions.

The Phantom deal constituted a watershed event in the history of U.S. military aid to Israel, one that paved the way for what was to take place thereafter. The most important aspect of the Phantom deal was that it provided Israel with a qualitative edge, since the Phantom was far superior in performance to any of the Soviet aircraft being supplied to the Middle East. The Arabs themselves were aware of the significance of the deal, as evidenced by Nasser and Sadat's frequent references to the planes in their speeches attacking the United States (see, for example, *The New York Times* February 15, 1970 and September 10, 1971). Despite this, the administration was wary about having its decisions regarded as binding precedents rather than ad hoc decisions. Two basic considerations that had guided the Johnson administration—the goal of attaining an arms limitation agreement with the Soviet Union, and a desire to avoid becoming the major Western supplier of arms to the Middle East—persisted in theory if not in practice even after the Phantom deal was concluded.

The Nixon Administration

Richard M. Nixon expressed his position on the issue of arms supplies to Israel on several occasions during the 1968 election campaign. On

April 22, 1968, for instance, he stated that, "the first urgency is for America not to allow the balance of power to shift in favor of the militant Arab states in a new war . . . the United States must see to it that Israel's military is never at a level vis-à-vis the Arab militants that will invite a war of revenge" (see *Near East Report* May 1968). Several months later he admitted that, "certainly a balance of power is a short-term solution, but when survival is at stake, short-term solutions are necessary." Israel's situation was such, he said, that, "the balance must be tipped in Israel's favor . . . [we] support a policy that would give Israel a technological military margin to more than offset her hostile neighbors' numerical superiority. If maintaining that margin should require that the United States supply Israel with supersonic Phantom F-4 jets—we should supply those Phantom jets" (Speech to B'nai B'rith quoted in *The New York Times* September 9, 1968).

It is interesting to compare Nixon's pre-election speeches and post-election policy. His statement on the need to provide Israel with a "technological military margin," for example, represents an advance on the previous terminology of "balance of forces" (though as noted, Johnson's Skyhawk and Phantom deals had already set the precedent for providing Israel with a qualitative edge). However, during the first three years of the Nixon administration, there was no real implementation of Nixon's stated policy. For the first year there was no need to provide additional arms, since the Phantom deal was just then being implemented. Gradually, however, it became apparent that the Nixon administration was looking to advance its interests among the Arab states as well as in Israel, and that restraint in its military supply relationship was one means towards this end.

Jerusalem was particularly concerned by the administration's willingness to open talks early in 1969 with the Soviet Union on the question of how to settle the Middle East conflict, and its agreement to hold talks on the matter throughout 1969 in a forum consisting of the permanent members of the Security Council (the United States, Britain, the Soviet Union, and France). At a press conference on January 27, 1969, Nixon noted that the Middle East was like a powder keg that could explode at any moment unless defused. Such a statement demonstrated Nixon's perception of the conflict as part of a global complex, and thus an urgent issue on his agenda (*Department of State Bulletin* February 17, 1969). The Israeli fear was that the United States might be willing to make concessions to the Soviet Union in an attempt to reach agreement. There were also indications that in order to further its interests in the Middle East the administration would attempt to improve its relations with several Arab states, notably Egypt. Nixon mentions in his memoir that in the beginning of April 1969, he told King Hussein that he regretted the fact that the United States had no diplomatic relations with a number of Arab states; the following day, he notes, these comments were passed on by Hussein to Egyptian foreign minister Mahmud Fawzi (Nixon 1978, 519).

Nixon's perception of the danger inherent in the Middle East situation was heightened by the renewal of the War of Attrition in March 1969. In the meantime, however, deliveries of the Phantoms continued. In September 1969, Prime Minister Golda Meir requested additional arms, including 25 Phantoms and 100 Skyhawks. Meir was not at first concerned when she was told that an answer would be several months in coming. At the beginning of 1970, however, Nixon decided to indefinitely shelve the Israeli arms request. He had two motives for doing so—first, a desire to send a positive signal to the Soviet Union; and second, to attempt to increase U.S. influence in the Middle East by seeking to renew diplomatic relations with Egypt and Syria.

Henry Kissinger, then Assistant to the President for National Security Affairs, offers in his memoirs a different explanation for the decision to put off consideration of a new aircraft deal, the decision itself being made public on March 23 by Secretary of State William Rogers. According to Kissinger, Nixon had originally been inclined to comply partially with the request. At about that time, however, an incident occurred in Chicago in which French president Georges Pompidou—who had recently approved a Mirage aircraft deal with Libya—was heckled by a pro-Israeli crowd. The incident so angered Nixon that he decided to indefinitely put off responding to the Israeli request. Beyond this, Kissinger continues, the assessment of all sectors of the administration was that Israel's military edge was likely to continue for another three to five years. Thus, there was no urgent need to approve an additional aircraft deal. In retrospect, Kissinger points out, both the assessment and general approach proved to be wrong: during the Yom Kippur War it became apparent that Israel's military advantage, despite additional U.S. military aid between 1970 and 1973, had not been so striking, given the fact that the Soviet Union had supplied Egypt with Sam-3 surface-to-air missiles operated by Soviet crews. The administration, he writes, should have shown much greater determination in countering the Soviet moves (Kissinger 1979, 561–572).

On March 18, 1970, Nixon met with Ambassador Yitzhak Rabin with a proposal regarding future arms agreements. Nixon's proposal, later relayed by him in a letter to Golda Meir, was that U.S. aircraft would be sold to Israel on the basis of actual losses sustained by the Israeli air force. There would be a flexible timetable in making new agreements, and the deals themselves would be negotiated without public disclosure (Rabin 1978, 283).

The proposal troubled Israeli officials for several reasons. If no specific timetables were set, the air force would be unable to plan and carry out on a long-term basis the development of its force, and would be forced to use its planes with extreme care and restraint if it was uncertain when new supplies would arrive (Rabin 1978, 308 and 359). Moreover, there were ominous political implications in the proposal. There seemed to be a hint that even this piecemeal approach to arms deliveries might be linked with political developments, i.e., Israeli concessions of some sort. Public announcement about completed arms deals had a deterrent effect on the Arab countries. Moreover, disclosure even prior to the consummation of a deal could work to Israel's advantage by galvanizing U.S. public opinion in support of Israel's request.

Despite Israeli objections, Nixon's guidelines went into effect. Although designed to keep the supply line open in practice, since Nixon had not prescribed any overall number of planes, delays in implementation were the rule (Kissinger 1979, 574). Thus in the interval between March 1970 and February 1972, when a new U.S.-Israeli aircraft deal was finally concluded, there were a number of fairly large arms deliveries approved by the Nixon administration. In each case, however, an atmosphere of uncertainty prevailed over the exact number of items approved and the exact timetable for deliveries.

Since the time of the Kennedy administration, the Israeli government had made great efforts to obtain a U.S. commitment that arms supplies would be provided on an ongoing basis. This meant that the administration would refrain from creating a linkage between Israeli policies and U.S. arms. The new Nixon guidelines, as implemented, made Israel wonder whether its efforts were not destined to fail. In December 1969, three months after Israel's request for additional aircraft, Secretary of State Rogers had unveiled a new U.S. plan for peace in the Middle East. The "Rogers Plan," as it became known, called for an almost total Israeli withdrawal from territories captured in the Six Day War in return for a "binding peace agreement." Although the plan was rejected by Israel and Egypt alike, the U.S. government did not shelve it. This caused Israel to suspect that the Nixon administration continued to expect Israel to make the concessions envisioned in the plan. Nixon's arms policy seemed to confirm Israel's fears.

One clear instance of linkage occurred in June 1970, when the administration proposed a 90-day cease-fire in the War of Attrition, during which time UN mediator Gunnar Jarring would conduct indirect talks between Israel and Egypt. According to the administration, the goal of such talks would be to "carry out Security Council Resolution 242 in all its parts." To encourage Israeli compliance, the administration simultaneously announced approval of a list of military supplies for

Israel that included 200 of the most up-to-date M-60 tanks, 175 mm long-range artillery, electronic systems, two dozen Phantoms and a similar number of Skyhawks (*Facts on File* 1970, 765). But there was also a qualification—progress in the political negotiations would determine whether shipments of these items would be continued or suspended. Protesting this, Golda Meir urgently appealed to Nixon to separate the issues of political negotiations and the military supplies that had been approved. The U.S. reply was somewhat ambiguous: there was no intention to create a linkage, yet delivery schedules would be reviewed if negotiations showed signs of success (Kissinger 1979, 576).

Such carrot and stick tactics were not discontinued even when, immediately after the U.S. engineered cease-fire along the Suez Canal went into effect, Egypt violated the agreement's standstill clause by moving its Sam-3 missiles eastward. In a meeting with Meir a month later Nixon responded, in Rabin's words, with "fine noncommital words about his concern that the balance not be disrupted to Israel's detriment." Concerning the planes, he merely promised that if the cease-fire was broken and the Egyptian missiles used, "the United States would discuss with sympathy an Israeli request for additional planes, in so far as Israel would need a larger number than that promised by the United States" (Rabin 1978, 308). Several weeks later, Prime Minister Meir sent a note requesting the supply of 54 Phantoms and 120 Skyhawks, and U.S. abandonment of the Rogers Plan (Quandt 1977, 102). This appeal was no more successful than previous ones. Although Kissinger informed Moshe Dayan in December 1970 that the administration would continue the supply of Phantoms and Skyhawks during the first six months of 1971, the quantity approved was much smaller than that requested by Israel.

A number of rather disturbing conversations also took place about this time between U.S. and Israeli officials. On one occasion, Kissinger asked Rabin whether Israel was confident it could withstand heavy American pressure that could take the form of a suspension of military supplies. On another occasion, in March 1971, Nixon warned Israeli president Zalman Shazar that U.S. military supplies to Israel should not be taken for granted. They could cease one day, Nixon said, and while this would not happen as long as he was President "I shall, after all, not serve forever" (Rabin 1978, 336).

Then, in December 1971, a long hoped for change occurred in U.S. policy. Golda Meir had once again come to Washington to plead Israel's case. Following a meeting with Nixon on December 2, a White House spokesman released a statement which noted that

President Nixon confirmed that the United States will continue to maintain its ongoing relationship of financial assistance and military supply to Israel. In this context it is recognized that the Israeli armed forces must maintain a long-term program of modernization and that the United States will continue to discuss how it can help in the process (*Facts on File* 1971, 944).

The use of the phrases "ongoing relationship" and "long-term program of modernization" symbolized a turning point; although the term "modernization" had first appreared six years earlier in the State Department bulletin, the reference this time was far more encompassing.

A second significant aspect of the Nixon-Meir meeting, according to Rabin, was that the president gave assurances that arms supply and the political problem were two separate subjects that would be treated separately (Rabin 1978, 366). According to Quandt, the Israeli prime minister

argued that Israel needed to be assured of continuing flow of aircraft and other equipment well into the 1970s. The Soviets had no hesitation in helping their friends. Why did the Americans insist on punishing Israel by withholding arms? That only increased Arab intransigence. A long-term agreement would convince the Soviets and the Arabs that they could not separate the United States from Israel and that a military solution was impossible, and such an agreement would allow Israel to negotiate from strength. . . . Nixon and Kissinger were basically in agreement with Mrs. Meir's points. In addition, a long-term agreement would help to avoid periodic squabbles over new arms agreements. Each time a new arms package was requested the United States and Israel argued over the terms and the timing. The Arabs saw the quarrels as encouraging signs, but then felt disillusioned when the United States eventually provided the arms (Quandt 1977, 146–147).

Another important shift in U.S. policy that occurred at this time was related to Henry Kissinger's growing ascendancy over Secretary of State Rogers. According to Kissinger, Nixon decided in December 1971 to begin handing over to him the operational control of U.S. policy in the Middle East. While avoiding handing full control over to Kissinger, Nixon charged him with the task of keeping an eye on U.S. policy in the region to ensure that the presidential election year of 1972 would pass as smoothly as possible (Kissinger 1979, 1285 and 1289).

On February 2, 1972, a memorandum of understanding was concluded between Israel and the United States concerning the supply of 40 Phantom and 82 Skyhawk planes. Delivery of the aircraft was to be in phases

lasting until June 1974. In light of past U.S. policy, Rabin was at first
skeptical about the delivery schedule. A number of years later, however,
he admitted that "the supply of American planes for the years 1972,
1973, and 1974 worked out to our satisfaction" (Rabin 1978, 376). A
second memorandum of understanding, signed at about the same time,
provided for the transfer of technical information from the United States
to Israel. Nixon also issued instructions to supply the Israeli aircraft
industry with Phantom engines needed for the manufacture of the Kfir
plane. These instructions were announced in March 1973 (*Facts on File*
1973, 204).

March 1, 1973 marked another meeting between Nixon and Meir.
Once again the outcome for Israel was positive: Nixon approved the
supply of an additional 48 planes, half of them Phantoms and half
Skyhawks. Delivery was to begin after the previous shipments had ended
and was to continue in phases until 1975 (*Facts on File* 1973, 204).

Israel had finally gotten what it had so long desired—a long-term
military supply relationship with the United States. According to Kissinger, the U.S. administration also benefitted from the new policy, since
it enabled the government "to avoid the periodic brawls that had resulted
from trying futilely to keep Israel on a short leash" (Kissinger 1979,
1289 and 1982, 22). What were the factors leading to the abandonment
of the "carrot and stick" approach that had prevailed during the first
three years of the Nixon administration? Apart from Kissinger's growing
influence, the following were also important considerations:

Soviet intransigence—Throughout the Nixon administration, the Soviet
Union had rejected American proposals concerning limitations of arms
deliveries to the Middle East and had escalated their military involvement
with Egypt and Syria. During negotiations conducted between the two
powers in 1969, the Soviet Union had shown no flexibility on the Middle
East issue. Thus, administration policy gradually began shifting towards
taking a harder line vis-à-vis the Soviet Union.

Israel's strategic importance—The events of September 1970 in Jordan
convinced Nixon that the radical Arab states, in this case Syria supported
by the Soviet Union, constituted a danger to American interests. As a
pro-Western state, Israel had demonstrated during this crisis its potential
as a strategic ally of the United States. This impressed Nixon deeply.

The United States as arms supplier—Successive U.S. administrations
had gradually accepted the fact that the United States had turned into
a major arms supplier to the Middle East, especially to Israel, Jordan,
and Saudi Arabia. Maintaining a balance of arms between Israel and the
Arab states was accepted as the best means of preserving the status quo.
The Nixon administration had come to rely on this policy to an even
greater extent than the Johnson administration. This development oc-

curred simultaneously with significant progress in the supply ties between the United States and Jordan. In 1970 American military aid to Jordan amounted to only $200,000; the amount escalated to $60 million in 1971 following the Jordanian crisis and the American decision to strengthen this state. Aid of a similar magnitude was granted Jordan in the last three years of the Nixon administration as well. As of 1973 this increased aid reflected the American commitment made to Jordan in February 1973 to aid it to modernize its army. Jordan had submitted a five-year plan for the development of its army and the administration changed nothing in this plan. Among other things, it was agreed that the United States would supply 600 modern M-60 tanks.

The single most crucial action taken by the United States in the Middle East during the Nixon administration was undoubtably the airlift of military supplies to Israel during the Yom Kippur War. Ordered by Nixon in response to a massive Soviet resupply of arms to the Arabs, the airlift delivered supplies that were valued at $825 million. On October 19, 1973, Nixon asked Congress to approve $2.2 billion to cover the costs of the airlift and subsequent military aid to Israel. This sum represented a four-fold increase in the amount of military aid provided in the previous peak year of 1971—and one and a half times the amount of military aid provided to Israel from 1948 onwards.

The relative size of the airlift was also significant. According to Kissinger, the administration decided to provide at least 25 percent more arms than the Soviet Union had sent to Egypt and Syria. The purpose of this was to demonstrate U.S. military and technological superiority, as well as its unqualified support for Israel (Kissinger 1982, 531). Also noteworthy was the fact that the airlift and subsequent U.S. actions did not seriously damage U.S. relations with other Arab states. In the aftermath of the war, the United States continued to provide both military and political support to Israel, despite the Arab oil embargo. The embargo was eventually lifted; in Nixon's view, "for the first time in the Arab-Israel conflict the U.S. [had] conducted itself in a manner that not only preserved but greatly enhanced our relations with the Arabs while we were massively resupplying the Israelis" (Nixon 1978, II:502).

Once the actual fighting was over, however, the administration moved in the direction of trying to influence a settlement. Nixon informed Golda Meir in November 1973 that a policy of constantly preparing for war was "no policy at all" (Nixon 1978, II:476). Preparations were made for the Geneva Conference to be attended by representatives of the United States, Israel, Egypt, Jordan, and the Soviet Union. Kissinger notes that when differences arose between Israel and the United States concerning preparations for the conference, "Nixon wanted to hold up one quarter of the 2.2 billion dollar postwar supplemental aid request for Israel as insurance of Israel's good behavior. I opposed it, convinced that desperation would make Israel more defiant . . . the idea was dropped" (Kissinger 1982, 792). This incident underscores the fact that the concept of linkage had not been totally adandoned.

Notwithstanding, it was the carrot more than the stick that was employed during the balance of Nixon's administration—the carrot being a U.S. commitment of long-term economic and military aid to Israel. A joint communique issued after Nixon's visit to Israel in June 1974 made this clear:

> President Nixon . . . reiterated the commitment of the United States to the long-term security of Israel . . . the President . . . affirmed the continuing and long-term nature of the military supply relationship between the two countries . . . future economic assistance by the United States to Israel would continue, and would be the subject of long-range planning between the two Governments. The United States in accordance with congressional authorization would continue to provide substantial economic assistance for Israel at levels needed to assist Israel to offset the heavy additional cost inherent in assuring Israel's military capability for the maintenance of peace (*Keesing's Contemporary Archives* 1974, 26598).

These commitments were taken very seriously by both the Meir government and the Rabin government that succeeded it. U.S. economic and military assistance was considered a crucial form of compensation for the territories Israel had given up in the framework of the disengagement agreements with Egypt and Syria. Moreover, the costs of the Yom Kippur War were extremely high; U.S. economic aid and supplies were vital in building up and strengthening the Israel Defense Forces. The United States, for its part, accepted the Israeli argument that giving up territories involved a tangible sacrifice as long as the prospect of peace remained as elusive and uncertain as ever.

The Ford Administration

In September 1974, shortly after Ford took office, Rabin visited Washington, D.C. to meet the new president. During their talks Ford assured Rabin that the United States would abide by the commitments made by Nixon. No question would be asked concerning the need to maintain Israeli military strength. In accordance with these sentiments, Ford issued instructions to carry out deliveries of vital military equipment valued at $750 million within the next seven months. This decision was fully implemented; all the equipment reached Israel before Rabin's next visit to Washington in June 1975.

In the interim, however, negotiations between Israel and Egypt concerning a further agreement in the Sinai reached a deadlock in March 1975. Kissinger's shuttle diplomacy was cut short, and the Ford administration announced on March 24 that it was starting a "reassessment" of its Middle East policy. In a speech given a week later, Secretary of Defense James Schlessinger noted that

> any future U.S. military assistance to Israel must be held in abeyance until Washington completed the review of its Middle East position . . . the U.S. had agreed to supply Israel with a substantial amount of arms by April and most of it had been received. Israel wanted a much longer term commitment with respect to security supplies but such a matter will have to wait (*Facts on File* 1975, 209).

The reassessment lasted close to six months (March-September); during this period, the United States refused to sign any new arms deals with Israel, although it continued to supply the items (including tanks, guns, and aircraft) concerning which agreements had already been signed (Rabin 1978, 465).

Israeli leaders understandably reacted to the "reassessment" with concern. The U.S. refusal to enter into negotiations on new arms deals contradicted its previous commitments concerning "ongoing and long-term" military aid: the policy of linkage had clearly returned. Also put on hold during the reassessment was an Israeli request for a multi-annual review of its defense needs (the "longer term commitment" referred to by Schlessinger). Matters remained frozen until after Rabin's June 1975 visit to Washington concerning the continuation of Kissinger's shuttle diplomacy. During the visit, Rabin once again raised the subject of U.S. aid:

> I said that we were requesting two and a half billion dollars per annum from the United States within the framework of our acceptance of the interim agreement, in order to compensate Israel for abandoning the oil fields and to strengthen it. I wanted to get the president, the Houses of Congress and public opinion in the U.S. to think in terms of large amounts of money for Israel . . . in this way we were actually saying that the linkage of arms and political issues was permissible—but only when it served the Israeli interest (Rabin 1978, 475–476).

Between June and August negotiations continued on the interim agreement with Egypt, while at the same time a set of U.S.-Israeli agreements was also being worked out. These latter agreements were summarized in a joint memorandum of agreement signed by Kissinger and Israeli foreign minister Yigal Allon in which U.S. commitments were spelled out even more clearly than had been the case in previous documents. Among the articles in the memorandum was a U.S. pledge to be "fully responsive . . . on an ongoing and long-term basis to Israel's military equipment and other defense requirements, to its energy requirements and to its economic needs." Another article specified that Israel's long-term military supply needs would be the subject of "periodic consultations between representatives of the U.S. and Israel defense establishments." In an addendum to the document, the U.S. commitment was spelled out even more specifically:

> The United States is resolved to continue to maintain Israel's defensive strength through the supply of advanced types of equipment, such as the F-16 aircraft. The United States Government agrees to an early meeting to undertake a joint study of *high-technology and sophisticated items, including the Pershing ground-to-ground missiles with conventional warheads*, with the view to giving a positive response. The U.S. Administration will submit annually for approval by the U.S. Congress a request for military and economic assistance in order to help meet Israel's economic and military needs (*Keesing's Contemporary Archives* 1975, 27431—emphasis added).

The main significance of these agreements was that they set the foundation for the wide-scale U.S. military aid in effect from 1975 onwards. In the introduction to the document, the United States recognized the principle that the Israeli "withdrawal from vital areas in Sinai constitutes an act of great significance on Israel's part in the pursuit of final peace." In 1979, when Israel agreed to withdraw from the rest of Sinai, the Carter administration entered into a similar agreement with Israel. In it the administration reaffirmed the Nixon-Ford commitments, mentioning specifically the September 1975 memorandum.

During a January 1976 visit to Washington, D.C., Rabin discovered that Ford had not only approved aid to Israel above a level recommended by the National Security Council but had given instructions to place Israel ahead of all foreign countries in the supply of U.S. arms. In 1975, the administration approved the sale of 100 F-16 and 50 F-15 planes to Israel. Because of financial limitations Israel ordered 25 F-15 planes of the second model only. On the other hand, no progress was made with regard to Israel's request to be granted a license to manufacture F-16s in Israel; the reason given for U.S. refusal was that existing agreements with a number of European countries precluded the granting of a license to manufacture the plane in any additional countries (Rabin 1978, 494 and 497). Another cause for Israeli concern was Ford's delay in approving the sale of a list of advanced technology items. Approval was finally granted less than a month before the November 1976 elections.

On the whole, however, the Rabin government was highly satisfied with U.S. policy during the Ford administration. Discussing the growth of the Israel Defense Forces during the three years he headed the government, Rabin noted that, "the tank force had grown by more than 50 percent, mobile artillery by more than 100 percent, APCs by 800 percent, planes by 30 percent. This growth was due, of course, to a large extent to American aid" (Rabin 1978, 505).

The Carter Administration

The major U.S. achievement in the Middle East during the Carter administration was the Egyptian-Israeli peace treaty of March 1979. Israel's withdrawal from the Sinai—including abandonment of three airbases there—for example, was compensated by U.S. help in financing and construction of two alternative bases in the Negev. Egypt, for its part, became the recipient of vastly increased U.S. military aid.

In contrast with the previous two administrations, no attempts were made to link U.S. military aid with Israeli concessions in the course of the arduous negotiations leading to the peace treaty. The "carrot" approach prevailed, Carter evidently believing that the best way to obtain Israeli concessions was to assure Israel's security. Tactics of suspensions, reassessments, or delays in supplies were a double-edged weapon, as the experiences of the Nixon and Ford administrations had shown.

Despite the lack of pressure, the Israeli government did not find the Carter administration totally satisfactory. At a meeting with Carter in March 1977, for instance, Rabin was disappointed to learn that the president had lowered Israel's priority in the list of nations receiving U.S. supplies. Previously, as noted before, Israel had been at the top of the list. On one occasion during the Ford administration, it had even received supplies at the expense of U.S. army bases (Rabin 1978, 519). Carter was also demonstratively cool on the subject of supplying U.S. military technological know-how to Israel, and made no changes in the policy of not granting Israel a license to manufacture F-16 planes in Israel.

U.S. military aid to Egypt and Saudi Arabia was perhaps the most sensitive issue affecting U.S.-Israeli arms relations during the Carter administration. In February 1978, the administration presented Congress with a $4.8 billion proposal to sell planes to Israel, Egypt, and Saudi Arabia. Carter emphasized that the package was to be approved or rejected in its entirety. The Israeli share of the package, valued at $1.9 billion, consisted of 15 F-15s and 75 F-16s. Saudi Arabia was to be sold 60 F-15s at a cost of $2.5 billion and Egypt a package consisting of 50 F-15s at a cost of $400 million. According to Secretary of State Cyrus Vance, the decision to sell planes to Egypt was based on the necessity to ensure Egypt's security to enable it to pursue peace negotiations, while Saudi Arabia was to be sold weapons by virtue of its apparent pro-Western, anti-Communist stance that seemed to make it a major force for moderation in the region.

After considerable debate, Congress approved the Carter package in May 1980. However, a number of concessions had been made in the course of the deliberations. To compensate Israel, the administration agreed to sell it an additional 20 F-15s. Congress was also given an assurance that Saudi Arabia would receive the planes without extra fueling tanks that could extend their range.

Although Carter was not the first to link aid to Israel with aid to the Arab states, he was the first to do so after the far-reaching presidential commitments of 1974 and 1975. None of these commitments had provided for such linkage.

Another issue of disagreement between the two countries arose during the Israeli invasion of Lebanon (Operation Litani) in 1978. It became known that Israel had used U.S. cluster bombs in the course of the operation. The administration demanded, and received, an Israeli commitment to limit the future use of these bombs to "hard" targets. The issue of the bombs had actually been raised during Carter's first days in office, when Vance informed Israel that the United States had decided to stop manufacture of these bombs altogether. (Four years later the subject came up again when the Reagan administration decided on July 29, 1982 to hold up an additional delivery of cluster bombs to Israel, in reaction against their having been used in the war in Lebanon.)

In addition to the package deal negotiated in Congress, the United States began supplying tanks, APCs and 40 F-4 Phantom planes to Egypt in September 1979. The purchase was financed by American military aid in the form of both loans and grants amounting to $1.5 billion in that financial year (*Facts on File* 1979, 762). Shortly afterwards, in February 1980, the Carter administration approved the sale of F-15s and F-16s to Egypt. Because of the high price of the F-15—$20 million each—Egypt preferred to purchase 40 F-16s at $12 million each (*Facts on File* 1980, 140). During the last months of the Carter administration, contacts were also begun with Saudi Arabia concerning the purchase of AWACS planes.

The First Two Years
of the Reagan Administration

The first two years of the Reagan administration were characterized both by continuity in the military sales policy to Israel and the use of punitive measures such as suspensions of deliveries on occasions when it disapproved of specific Israeli actions. In general, the administration adhered to the military aid commitments initiated by the three previous administrations. On several occasions these commitments were reaffirmed by Reagan; such was the case, for example, when Israel withdrew from the Sinai in April 1982 (*Facts of File* 1982, 280).

The first instance of Reagan administration sanctions occurred in June 1981, following the destruction of Iraq's experimental nuclear reactor near Baghdad by the Israeli air force. Secretary of State Alexander Haig informed Congress that the president had decided to suspend "for the time being" the "immediate shipment" of four F-16s provided for in the 1978 package deal. According to Haig, the suspension was intended to enable the administration to determine whether Israel was in breach of the 1952 Mutual Defense Assistance Agreement that permitted the supply of arms for defense purposes only. The Israeli government argued that the bombing was in fact an act of self-defense, since Iraqi nuclear weapons would pose a clear threat to Israel's existence. Following clarifications between the two states, Israel made a commitment that in the future it would "always take the interests of the United States, our friend and ally, into consideration" (*Facts on File* 1981, 948). This announcement enabled Reagan to give instructions for the renewal of deliveries at the beginning of July. Several days later, however, Reagan once again ordered a suspension in the wake of the Israeli air force bombing of PLO headquarters in the center of Beirut. On August 17, 1981, Reagan cancelled the suspension following a Lebanese cease-fire arrangement attained through American mediation. A total of 10 planes had been held up in delivery; the remainder of the F-16s and F-15s of the Carter deal were sent to Israel on schedule. U.S. sanctions were once again resorted to on December 14, 1981 after the Knesset passed a law effectively annexing the Golan Heights. Just two weeks before, on November 30, the United States and Israel had signed a memorandum of understanding on strategic cooperation. A series of meetings had been scheduled to arrange enactment of the memorandum. The State Department cancelled the meetings, explaining that Israel ignored an obligation implicit in the understanding that "each party [would] take into consideration in its decisions the implications for the broad policy concerns of the other" (*Facts on File* 1981, 948). Also placed on hold was consideration of an Israeli option to purchase an additional 75 F-

16 planes. The suspension was lifted on May 24, 1982, when the administration informally informed Congress of its intention to sell the planes. By law, Congress would be allowed 50 days to exercise a veto on arms deals; within 20 days, the administration was expected to present formal notification of its intentions. The outbreak of the war in Lebanon caused the administration to refrain from making this notification. It was only in May 1983, after the signing of an Israeli-Lebanese agreement providing for the withdrawal of all foreign forces from Lebanon, that the administration finally sent formal notification to Congress.

A third punitive act against Israel was the administration's refusal to purchase various items from the Israeli arms industry. The Carter administration had approved such purchases up to a sum of $100 million. Although the Reagan administration had initially shown willingness to increase this sum to $200 million, it postponed all action in this matter after the Golan law was passed. It was the U.S.-Saudi Arabian AWACS deal, however, that caused the most severe crisis in U.S.-Israeli relations during the first two years of the Reagan administration. Shortly after taking office, the administration informed Congress of its intention to sell Saudi Arabia $8.5 billion worth of military equipment, including ground radar stations and additional fueling tanks for the F-15 planes—an item that the Carter administration had assured Congress it would not sell to Saudi Arabia—along with five Airborne Warning and Control System Surveillance Aircraft (AWACS). The entire package encountered strong Congressional opposition. On October 28, 1981, however, the U.S. Senate narrowly voted (52–48) to reject a House of Representatives resolution of disapproval, thus making the deal possible.

Once again, it was the U.S. perception of Saudi Arabia as an anti-Communist, pro-Western linchpin in the Middle East that provided the main impetus for the sale. Backed by former presidents Nixon, Ford, and Carter, the administration strongly disputed the argument that the deal endangered Israeli security. In testimony to Congress, for instance, Secretary of Defense Caspar Weinberger stated, "I don't have the faintest idea why they [the Israelis] have raised opposition to it. . . . They could shoot down this plane in less than a minute and a half" (*Facts on File* 1981, 876).

At the same time, however, the administration took pains to reaffirm its commitment to Israel's security. It pledged an additional $600 million in military aid to Israel to be provided in two fiscal years. Regarding the actual AWACS deal, Reagan sent a note to Congress on October 28, 1981 in which he detailed the following safeguards:

(a) U.S. technological secrets would not be divulged to the Saudis;

(b) Saudi Arabia would be obliged to pass along any information received on its radar;

(c) AWACS were to be used only over Saudi territory, unless otherwise agreed between the two sides;

(d) The planes would be used "solely for defensive purposes as defined by the U.S."; and

(e) Until 1990, American crews would operate the planes; after this time, American technicians would share responsibility with the Saudi crews.

In summary, Reagan expressed his confidence that the deal did not pose a threat to Israel: "I remain fully committed to protecting Israel's security and to preserving Israel's ability to defend against any combination of potential hostile force in the region" (*Facts on File* 1981, 876).

Since President Reagan is still in office at the time of writing (1983), it is much too early to attempt to evaluate his administration's record on arms supply to Israel. It is clear, however, that in the first two years of his tenure he did not shy away from carrot and stick tactics. Early in 1983, it seemed that disagreement concerning the best means of settling the Arab-Israeli conflict was about to bring about a major confrontation between the United States and Israel. Rumors abounded that the administration was seriously considering cancelling all aid to Israel as a means of exerting pressure. Weighty considerations militated against the likelihood of this threat materializing, however. Even a temporary cutoff of aid would constitute a breach of existing U.S. commitments and the abandonment of its well-established policy of safeguarding Israel's security, while a long-term total denial of aid would disrupt the regional military balance to Israel's detriment. Paradoxically, the United States would then become the major factor responsible for tilting the arms equilibrium in favor of the Arabs, if U.S. military supplies to Egypt, Jordan, and Saudi Arabia were to continue.

In such a scenario, U.S.-Israeli relations would soon deteriorate to a level not seen since the mid-1950s. In the course of the last two decades, however, relations between the two countries have been quite cordial, occasional sharp disagreements notwithstanding. In its policy towards Israel the United States has shown a kind of consistency and adherence to commitments that is extremely rare in the realm of international relations. U.S. credibility as an ally and guarantor has been enhanced as a result; it is doubtful that the administration would choose to do anything to jeopardize this reputation.

Conclusion

Large-scale U.S. arms supply to Israel has its origin in the early 1960s and has been offered on a vastly increased level for the past 10 years. It must be assumed that significant American interest first led to the making of this policy and ensured its continuance by six presidents, three Democrats and three Republicans, over a 25-year period. At the same time, it appears undeniable that the question of Israel's strategic importance to the United States is still a matter of occasional controversy within the U.S. foreign policy establishment. Unless this were the case, the United States would not have signed the memorandum concerning strategic cooperation with Israel so reluctantly in 1981, and would not have suspended its implementation so lightly only several weeks later. The history of frequent, albeit brief, suspensions of U.S. arms deliveries to Israel may also point to differences of opinion in Washington concerning Israel's strategic value.

It is possible that supply disruptions are meant to demonstrate to the Arabs that Israel's needs and desires do not necessarily have first claim with Washington: that this may be so is indicated by Caspar Weinberger's reported declaration on February 1, 1983 that the security of the Arab states is no less important to the United States than that of Israel. If this statement accurately reflects U.S. thinking, it is presumably based on the assumption that Israel's strategic role is intrinsic to her existential dilemmas and can be taken for granted. As long as specific American policies towards the Arab states and the Soviet Union do not cause Israel any obvious damage, the administration feels there is no reason not to go ahead with them; while Israel is free to present its objections, the United States reserves the right to determine how valid these objections are and to ultimately act according to its own considerations.

Yet another facet of the U.S.-Israeli relationship is the clear linkage between U.S. military aid and the continuation of the peace process. This nexus—in existence particularly since the Yom Kippur War—has manifested itself in various agreements worked out between the two countries. Both the United States and Israel have acknowledged that U.S. military and economic aid constitute compensation for the territorial concessions Israel has been forced to make. This policy is based on the assumption that pacification of the Middle East serves both U.S. and Israeli interests. However, another U.S. interest, that of keeping Israel militarily strong if not superior, is seen as perfectly compatible with the pursuit of peace efforts.

Principal Dates in the Military Supply Relationship Between Israel and the United States

1958—*The Eisenhower administration* approves the sale of 100 recoilless guns, the first weapons deal between the two states since Israel's establishment.

1960—*The Eisenhower administration* approves the sale of a radar system.

1962—*The Kennedy administration* approves the sale of several batteries of surface-to-air Hawk missiles. Even though it involves a defensive weapon, this deal marks a change in U.S. policy because of the sophistication of the missile, and the actual magnitude of the deal (approximately $30 million). Equally important is the administration's statement that the sale is meant to prevent the creation of an arms imbalance as a result of the influx of Soviet arms into the region.

1965—*The Johnson administration* approves the M-48 Patton tank deal, which includes conversion kits and 105 mm guns. After conversion and up-gunning, the tanks are almost the equal of the most sophisticated of U.S. tanks, the M-60s.

1966—*The Johnson administration* approves the Skyhawk deal.

1968—*The Johnson administration* approves the Phantom deal.

1970—*The Nixon administration* approves the sale of additional planes on an ad hoc basis. It also approves an M-60 tank deal and the sale of modern electronic equipment for countering Soviet missiles. U.S. military aid reaches a sum of $545 million in 1971 compared to $30 million in 1970 and $85 million in the peak year of 1969. Nixon also undertakes to supply military equipment to Israel on an ongoing basis in order to modernize the Israel Defense Forces.

1973—*The Nixon administration* sends a massive airlift during the Yom Kippur War to resupply Israel with arms.

1974—*The Nixon administration* undertakes a commitment towards the government of Golda Meir to ensure military supplies on a long-term, ongoing basis. Military aid in this year reaches a sum of $2.483 billion.

1975—*The Ford administration* signs a memorandum of agreement with Israel that reaffirms the commitments made by Nixon; it also promises to supply F-16 planes.

1976—*The Ford administration* approves a deal that includes 100 F-16s and 50 F-15s. Military aid reaches a sum of $1.5 billion.

1978—*The Carter administration* links the approval of the sale of planes to Israel with sales to Saudi Arabia and Egypt. Military aid in the years 1977 and 1978 amounts to $1 billion per annum.

1979—*The Carter administration* signs a memorandum of agreement
with Israel following the peace treaty between Israel and Egypt, which
reaffirms the commitments of the previous administrations concerning
long-term supplies. Military aid reaches a sum of $4 billion—three
billion more than in previous years. This includes $2.2 billion in special
assistance to help finance Israel; and redeployment in the Negev, in
particular the construction of alternative air bases there.

Bibliography

Books

Bar-Zohar, Michael. *Ben-Gurion* (Hebrew). Tel Aviv: Am Oved, 1975.

Ben-Gurion, David. *Negotiations with Nasser*, Privately published, *circa* 1972.

Bowles, Chester. *Promises to Keep—My Years in Public Life, 1941–1969.* New
York: Harper and Row, 1971.

Campbell, John. *Defense of the Middle East.* New York: Frederick A. Praeger,
1960.

Eban, Abba. *An Autobiography.* Jerusalem: Steinmatsky Agency, 1977.

Forrestal, James. *The Forrestal Diaries.* New York: The Viking Press, 1951.

Gazit, Mordechai. *President Kennedy's Policy Towards the Arab States and Israel.*
Tel-Aviv: Shiloah Center Studies Series, 1983.

Katzenbach, Nicholas. *Middle East Record.* Jerusalem: Israel Universities Press,
1971.

Kissinger, Henry. *Years of Upheaval.* Boston: Little Brown, 1982.

———. *White House Years.* Boston: Little Brown, 1979.

Nixon, Richard. *Memoirs of Richard Nixon.* New York: Warner Books, 1978.

Peres, Shimon. *David's Sling.* New York: Random House, 1970.

Quandt, William. *Decade of Decisions, 1967–1976.* Berkeley: University of California Press, 1977.

Rabin, Yitzhak. *Pink as Sherut* (*Rabin Memoirs*, in Hebrew). Tel Aviv: Ma'ariv
Publishers, 1979.

Safran, Nadav. *Israel: The Embattled Ally.* Cambridge, Mass.: Harvard University
Press, 1981.

Sharett, Moshe. *Yoman Ishi* (*Personal Diary*, in Hebrew). Tel Aviv: Ma'ariv
Library, 1978.

Special Paper

Berglas, Eitan. "*Defense and the Economy: The Israeli Experience,*" *Maurice Falk
Institute for Economic Research in Israel*, January 1983, 28–30.

Newspapers and Periodicals

Congressional Quarterly
Facts on File

Keesing's Contemporary Archives
Middle East Record
Near East Report
The New York Times
Yediot Aharonot
Ma'ariv

Government Publications and Archives

U.S. Department of State
Department of State Bulletin
Foreign Relations of the United States (FRUS)
John F. Kennedy Presidential Library, Boston, Mass.
Public Papers of the Presidents of the United States
State of Israel
Israel State Archives
(*Documents on the Foreign Policy of Israel*)
World Zionist Organization, The Central Zionist Archives

FOUR

U.S. Aid to Israel: Problems and Perspectives

LEOPOLD YEHUDA LAUFER

Overview of U.S. Aid to Israel

Official assistance by the U.S. government to the government of Israel has been a permanent feature of the complex relationship between the two countries almost since the establishment of Israel in 1948. It supplemented and eventually surpassed by far the assistance provided from private sources, mostly Jewish, in the form of Israel Bonds, United Jewish Appeal contributions, etc.

Total official U.S. assistance to Israel from 1949 to 1983 totaled more than $25.5 billion—more than the total U.S. assistance to South Vietnam, and more than seven times as much as U.S. assistance to the Philippines, another country to which the United States has had firm political, strategic and moral commitments.[1]

During the last ten years (1974–1983), U.S. assistance to Israel averaged more than $2 billion annually, two thirds of it in the form of military assistance. This amount represented almost one third of all U.S. assistance during this period, and as such, marked both an extraordinary level of commitment for the United States and an unprecedented political achievement for Israel (see Table 4.1).

What have been the goals and patterns governing the U.S. aid program for Israel? What administrative and political processes influence the size and character of this program? What role has aid played in the political relations between the United States and Israel? What are the political and economic implications for Israel of the current aid relationship with the United States? What are the prospects for the current aid relationship

Table 4.1
U.S. Assistance to Israel, 1950–1983* (millions of dollars)

Year	Total U.S. Aid	Total U.S. Aid to Israel	Economic Loans to Israel	Economic Grants to Israel	Military Loans to Israel	Military Grants to Israel	Soviet Jew Resettlement Funds
1950	4.850	-	-	-	-	-	-
1951	4.380	0.1	-	0.1	-	-	-
1952	3.839	86.4	-	86.4	-	-	-
1953	6.496	73.6	-	73.6	-	-	-
1954	5.793	74.7	-	74.7	-	-	-
1955	4.864	52.7	30.8	21.9	-	-	-
1956	5.402	50.8	35.2	15.6	-	-	-
1957	4.976	40.9	21.8	19.1	-	-	-
1958	4.832	61.2	49.9	11.3	0.4	-	-
1959	4.954	50.3	39.0	10.9	0.5	-	-
1960	4.804	55.7	41.8	13.4	-	-	-
1961	4.737	48.1	29.8	18.3	-	-	-
1962	7.034	83.9	63.5	7.2	13.2	-	-
1963	7.314	76.7	57.4	6.0	13.3	-	-
1964	5.215	37.0	32.2	4.8	-	-	-
1965	5.310	61.7	43.9	4.9	12.9	-	-
1966	6.989	126.8	35.9	0.9	90.0	-	-
1967	6.440	13.1	5.5	0.6	7.0	-	-

Table 4.1 Cont.

1968	6.894	76.8	51.3	0.5	25.0	-	-
1969	6.791	121.7	36.1	0.6	85.0	-	-
1970	6.787	71.1	40.7	0.4	30.0	-	-
1971	8.078	600.8	55.5	0.3	545.0	-	-
1972	9.243	404.2	53.8	50.4	300.0	-	-
1973	9.875	467.3	59.1	50.4	307.5	-	50.0
1974	8.978	2.570.7	-	51.5	982.7	1.500.0	36.5
1975	7.239	693.1	8.6	344.5	200.0	100.0	40.0
1976	6.413	2.229.4	239.4	475.0	750.0	750.0	15.0
Transitional Quarter	2.603	278.6	28.6	50.0	100.0	100.0	0
1977	7.784	1.757.0	252.0	490.0	500.0	500.0	15.0
1978	9.014	1.811.8	266.8	525.0	500.0	500.0	20.0
1979	13.845	4.815.0	265.0	525.0	2.700.0	1.300.0	25.0
1980	9.694	1.811.0	261.0	525.0	500.0	500.0	25.0
1981	10.549	2.189.0	0	764.0	900.0	500.0	25.0
1982	12.324	2.219.0	0	806.0**	850.0	550.0	13.0
1983	14.202	2.498.0	0	785.0	850.0	550.0	13.0
Total	243.542.0	25.608.2	2.104.9	5.792.3	10.262.5	6.850.0	277.5

*Does not include Export-Import Bank Loans, American Schools and Hospitals Program, or amounts of less than $50,000.
**This figure includes $21 million in economic assistance reprogrammed from the Israeli account in FY 81.

Source: Agency for International Development: *U.S. Overseas Loans and Grants* (Annual Reports); Compilation prepared by the Congressional Research Service, Library of Congress, November 29, 1982.

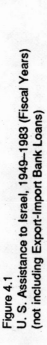

128

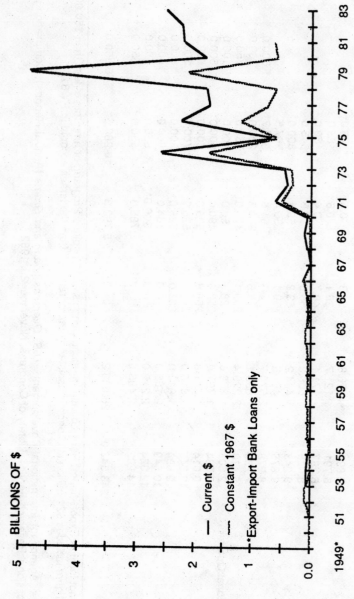

Figure 4.1
U. S. Assistance to Israel, 1949–1983 (Fiscal Years)
(not including Export-Import Bank Loans)

BILLIONS OF $

5

4

3

2

1

0.0

—— Current $

~~~ Constant 1967 $

*Export-Import Bank Loans only

1949* 51 53 55 57 59 61 63 65 67 69 71 73 75 77 79 81 83

Source: Based on Table 4.1.

to continue? And finally, what if any, conclusions can decisionmakers draw from an analysis of this element in the U.S.-Israeli relationship? These are the principal questions that will be addressed in this study, in the hope that they will help identify significant issues and problems that affect U.S.-Israeli relations.

The extensive use of government-to-government assistance is one of the new phenomena which characterizes international relations in the post-World War II era. Initiated by the United States with the inauguration of the Marshall Plan, it quickly became a major element of U.S. foreign relations. This fact reflected not only the wealth and the humanitarian concerns of the United States in relation to the rest of the world, but also the realization that aid could serve a useful purpose in carrying out U.S. foreign policy. The countries of post-World War II non-Communist Europe, together with Latin America and most non-Communist newly developing countries, came to regard such aid as part of their relationship with the United States.

It is not surprising therefore that, once the United States had decided to recognize the new state of Israel and support it politically, aid became an important element in the new relationship.

With the benefit of hindsight, we may distinguish two distinct periods of U.S. aid to Israel, the first from 1949 to 1970, and the second from 1971 to 1983, the time of writing. Major substantive differences between the two periods relate not only to magnitudes and types of aid, but also to the political environment and the implications to be drawn therefrom.

First Period

The beginning of this period may be dated from the visit by Israel's first president, Chaim Weizmann, to President Harry Truman on May 25, 1948, just ten days after the proclamation of the state. Weizmann recalls the visit in his memoirs:

> We . . . discussed the economic and political aid which the State of Israel would need in the critical months that lay ahead. The President showed special interest in the question of a loan for development projects and in using the influence of the United States to insure the defense of Israel—if possible, by preventing Arab aggression . . . or . . . by insuring that we had the necessary arms (Weizmann 1949, 481).

In fact, U.S. military aid played almost no role during the first 14 years of Israel's existence, as the United States sought to stay out of the arms race between Israel and the Arab countries. Even later it did not reach a significant level until 1966, when Israel's deteriorating relations with France, combined with President Nasser's growing aggressiveness, threatened to leave Israel dangerously exposed to a massive new Soviet weapons buildup in the area.

On the economic side, however, the United States proceeded quickly in carrying out President Truman's promise. The aid program began in 1949 with a $100 million loan from the Export-Import Bank, supplemented in 1951 by another $35 million Export-Import Bank loan. Half of these funds went for agricultural development, and the rest for the development of industry and essential infrastructures. In 1952, the United States inaugurated a program of economic grants designed both to help Israel absorb the thousands of destitute refugees streaming into the country and to finance commodity imports, thus alleviating Israel's balance of payments deficits. At the same time the Food-for-Peace program (PL 480) was initiated, under which $635 million worth of U.S. wheat, feed grains, dairy products, fats and oils were transferred to Israel between 1952–1973. About 10 percent of these imports were grants to finance free school lunches and programs for the needy, while the rest were long-term loans, most of which until 1968 were repayable in Israeli currency and were plowed back into the Israeli economy. The first major achievements of the Food-for-Peace program were to relieve the food shortages of the early 1950s that had led to food rationing, and to provide further stimulus to economic growth through the use of local currencies (counterpart funds) generated by the sale of the agricultural commodities. In 1955, a program of development loans linked to specific projects was initiated and maintained until the onset of the second period of U.S. aid in the early 1970s.

The important characteristics of U.S. assistance during the first period can be summarized as follows:

(a) While the decision to grant aid was political, based on a basic commitment to Israel by President Truman that all subsequent presidents have reaffirmed, the goals and framework of the program were primarily oriented towards relief and economic development.

(b) Except for 1966 and 1969, military assistance played only a minor role during this period. Israel received virtually no military assistance from the United States prior to 1962, and even when significant military assistance was extended during the period immediately prior and subsequent to the Six Day War (1966–1969), it did not exceed the amount transferred for economic assistance.

(c) As Israel became economically stronger during the late 1950s and 1960s, economic aid became relatively less important to the development of the economy. A study of Israel's import surpluses, compared to the growth in Israel's national product, shows a declining ratio. In the 1950s, the ratio of the import surplus was about 45 percent while in 1967 the ratio was only about 10 percent (Michaely 1977). Coincidentally, but not entirely unrelated, this was also the year when U.S. assistance to Israel reached an all-time low of $13.1 million.

(d) Despite the growing strength of the Israeli economy, Israel continued to depend on U.S. aid to finance better than 20 percent of its import surplus. But the composition and terms of the assistance underwent significant changes. Technical assistance was terminated by mutual agreement in 1962, grant programs were gradually phased down, and development loans were progressively reduced and finally eliminated in 1968. Food assistance was prominent throughout the first period, and towards its end accounted for virtually all of the economic aid Israel was receiving from the United States.

(e) Except for Food Assistance (PL 480), most of the aid was appropriated from the category of "development assistance," which under U.S. legislation requires economic justification and detailed monitoring, and which is usually related to specific projects. Total U.S. aid to Israel (excluding Export-Import Bank loans) for the entire first period (1951–1970) amounted to slightly more than $1.26 billion, about 1.1 percent of all U.S. assistance to developing countries.

Considering Israel's small size and comparatively advanced stage of development, this was not an insignificant share of the total aid pie, but it clearly did not mark Israel as a major client of the United States (e.g., India received more than 12 percent of total U.S. aid during the same period). Furthermore, the policy goals behind the type of assistance program described above reflected, first, a desire—though not fully realized—to avoid military aid; and second, a plan to strengthen the economy to the point where assistance could be terminated. These trends can be seen in Table 4.1 and Figure 4.2.

Second Period

The change which occurred in the second period of U.S. aid to Israel is so drastic and all-encompassing, that it makes the earlier program almost unrecognizable in today's setting.

First of all, the magnitudes: The quantum jump occurred in 1971, when the program increased almost nine-fold, from $71.1 million in 1970 to $600.8 million in 1971. From that point the level never declined below $400 million per annum, and in 1979 reached an all-time high of $4.81 billion. After that, the annual level hovered around $2.2 billion, until 1983 when it reached almost $2.5 billion. Israel is the largest

Figure 4.2
U.S. Assistance to Israel, 1949–1970 (Fiscal Years)
(not including Export-Import Bank Loans)

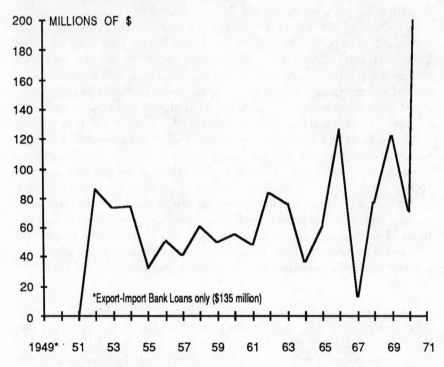

Source: Based on Table 4.1.

recipient of U.S. assistance, and in 1983 is receiving nearly one fifth of all U.S. assistance.

The bulk of U.S. aid is in the form of military assistance, which has accounted for about two thirds of the total during this period. Initially, this assistance was in the form of long-term credits, but beginning with 1974 a substantial portion of these credit obligations has each year been forgiven, thus in effect converting them into grants. About 38 percent of all military assistance during the second period has been in the form of grants, but during the last few years the proportion of grants has been rising.

On the economic side, not only the magnitudes but the character of the program has been totally transformed. Beginning in 1974, food assistance that had totalled between $50–60 million annually was drastically reduced; it was discontinued altogether in 1980. On the other hand, most economic assistance to Israel, starting in 1972, was appropriated under the so-called "Security Supporting Assistance" category, which is designed to support friendly countries in cases where

> economic and political stability is threatened and U.S. security interests are involved. This assistance, although economic in form, is usually granted primarily for political or security reasons rather than solely for economic development (Comptroller General of the United States August 18, 1978, 1).

In line with this definition, Security Supporting Assistance (SSA) funding requires virtually no economic development justification and little monitoring or cumbersome project-related transfer procedures. Its purpose is clearly political: it is legislatively linked with military assistance in a separate authorization (the International Security Assistance Act of 1977), and it passes through the same political review channels of the State Department as does military assistance.

During the last 10 years of the existence of the Supporting Assistance Program for Israel, the terms and conditions of the program have undergone several significant changes. The Israel program began in 1972 with a so-called "cash grant" of $50 million, which was not "tied" to purchases from the United States. In 1975, when the program level rose to $324.4 million, a new concept—the Commodity Import Program (CIP)—was introduced, limiting that portion of the funds to purchase of an approved list of commodities from the United States, and providing some of the funds (usually about one third) in the form of concessional loans rather than grants. The Commodity Import Program assured that the funds would be used on the basis of an approved list of commodities. However, as assistance levels to Israel increased, the list had to be progressively broadened, and the device had no significant effect on increasing total U.S. civilian exports to Israel. Moreover, the documentation of authorized purchases proved cumbersome and resulted in the delayed transfers of assistance funds.

In 1981, the CIP method of transfer was abandoned, as was the formula of providing one third of the SSA funds in the form of loans. For the last two years, economic assistance to Israel has been entirely in the form of so-called "cash transfers," i.e., grants transferred to the Israeli government in four annual installments. The only limitations on the use of these grants are: (a) total civilian imports from the U.S. must at least equal the amount of economic assistance; (b) U.S. funds must not be used in the "Occupied Territories, or for military purposes"; and (c) 50 percent of grain shipments from the United States must be carried in U.S. ships. Except for the last condition, which increases the cost of imported U.S. grain because of above-market U.S. shipping costs, these limitations impose no significant restrictions on the Israeli government.[2]

In reviewing the evolution of the assistance program during the second period, it is clear that beyond the dramatic increase in size and the preponderance of military aid, the terms and conditions of U.S. aid have also greatly changed in Israel's favor. Considering the general U.S. approach to foreign aid—with its strong emphasis on accountability and supervision—the aid program for Israel has been stretched almost to the limits of flexibility.

One technical problem still at issue is Israel's desire to have the total U.S. cash commitment transferred at the beginning of each fiscal year instead of four yearly installments, thus saving the Israeli treasury another $20 plus million dollars.

The remaining issues are only partly technical: Should Israel's share of the aid pie be further increased in order to take account of inflation, which reportedly has been particularly severe for military hardware? Can this be done in the face of total aid program levels that since 1971 have virtually stagnated at the $8–9 billion a year figure? Should the proportion of grant-to-loan in the military program be further increased in Israel's favor in order to lessen the long-term debt burden? Israel claims that for every $100 million of grant rather than loan, it saves $22 million in debt service obligations. U.S. officials, on the other hand, explain that every grant obligation is a full charge to the national budget, whereas Military Sales Credits do not constitute a budget obligation unless there is a default in repayments. And finally, should Israel be automatically entitled to some kind of compensation (probably additional military hardware) for every major new arms deal between the United States and Arab countries—a reverse version of the "evenhandedness doctrine?" Clearly these issues bear thorough and dispassionate technical examination, but their resolution will be politically determined. The generally rising volume of U.S. aid can be seen in Figure 4.3.

The Aid Process

The record of U.S. financial and military support for Israel just described is unique in history. It could not have taken place without a continuous dialogue between the two governments, the deep involvement of the U.S. Congress, and the support of the U.S. public. In order to understand this larger picture, it is necessary to comprehend the U.S. administrative and political process leading to the point where decisions are made on the aid program in general, and on assistance to Israel in particular.

Figure 4.3
U.S. Assistance to Israel, 1971–1983 (Fiscal Years)
(not including Export-Import Bank Loans)

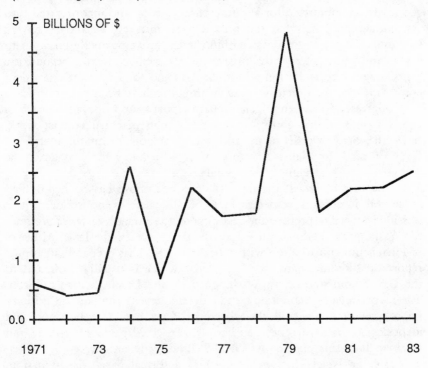

Source: Based on Table 4.1.

The Role of the Executive Branch

The preparation of country assistance programs is the reponsibility of the executive branch of the U.S. government. In the case of most countries that receive aid from the United States, the country mission of the U.S. Agency for International Development (AID) consults with the host government in preparing annual proposals in line with general policy guidelines sent from Washington. These proposals are evaluated at AID headquarters and discussed with other interested U.S. government agencies, including in particular the Office of Management and Budget (OMB), which imposes a budget ceiling on the AID program as a whole. In the case of military programs, U.S. military attaches in host countries play an important role in developing the proposals, while the Bureau for International Security Affairs of the Department of Defense, the Defense Security Assistance Agency, and the Arms Export Control Board, an interagency body chaired by the State Department, have major responsibility for the Washington review process.

At the end of this elaborate review exercise, the final country program proposals are submitted for White House decision and incorporated into the budget proposal that the president submits every January to the Congress. The review process within the executive normally takes up to a year and does not usually involve the recipient countries beyond the initial stage of consultation with their AID and/or Defense Department contacts. Once the executive branch proposals have been transmitted to the Congress, government officials must support their proposals at hearings before Congressional committees and through personal contact work. AID, the State Department, and the Pentagon maintain a staff of Congressional "specialists," whose job it is to lobby for passage of the administration's foreign aid proposals.

In the case of Israel, the process described above has been modified in several important respects. First of all, there is no resident AID mission in Israel to prepare and recommend the annual assistance program for Washington review. Instead, for the last 13 years, the Israel Ministry of Finance, in consultation with other ministries, has prepared an annual report on "Requirements for U.S. Aid," which is usually presented to the U.S. administration in Washington by the Israeli finance minister. The report reviews economic trends, details Israel's civilian and military import requirements and their balance of payments implications, and identifies the hard-currency gap between expected payments abroad and receipts. It is this gap for which U.S. funding is sought.

While the Israeli document serves as a formal basis for discussion, both within the U.S. administration and between the United States and Israel, the president's ultimate proposal to the Congress on aid to Israel must clearly take account of other factors as well.

There follows a series of consultations both within the U.S. administration and with Israeli officials on the details of the aid package, including additional visits of senior Israeli officials to Washington. Informal briefings and discussions are held with key members of Congress even before the executive decides on its request to Congress. At the same time (since 1979), AID is also required to prepare a special report to the Congress on "The Israeli Economy and Debt Repayment Prospects." The purpose of the report seems to be to supply additional background on the Israeli economy, and to justify the terms and conditions of the aid with regard to Israel's debt-carrying capacity. During the last few years, these reports have tended to support the administration's contention that a substantial portion of the aid can continue to be extended in the form of loans rather than grants without overtaxing Israel's debt-carrying capacity. This is one of the perennial issues which comes up in U.S.-

Israeli discussions on the aid package. The principal issue, of course, is the magnitude of the package itself, i.e., whether the United States should be prepared to finance all or only a certain part of the gap in Israel's balance of payments. Traditionally, the "gap" identified in the Israeli report has been higher than the amount of aid proposed by the U.S. administration to the Congress. In 1983, for example, the "gap" identified by Israel stood at $3.2 billion, whereas the U.S. administration's request amounted to $2.5 billion. The policy message seems to be that the administration is prepared to finance a large part of Israel's expected balance of payments deficit (nearly 80 percent in 1983, for example) but not all of it.

The process leading up to the presentation of Israel's aid request to the Congress, described above, illustrates the unique character of Israel's case. Unlike other aid recipient countries, Israel is closely involved both in the presentation of its needs to the executive branch, and in the internal review and consultative process which follow. The device of using its own report as the basis for discussion is an added tactical advantage for Israel, but it should not obscure the basic fact that the magnitude of the package is primarily a political judgment in which economic factors do not necessarily play a decisive role. Thus it was personal intervention by former Defense Minister Ezer Weizmann with President Carter in 1979 that reputedly yielded an extra $200 million in aid for Israel; while the understanding that Israel would receive an extra $600 million in military aid was meant to sweeten the pill of the 1981 AWACS sale to Saudi Arabia.

However, the importance of the close and sustained relationship between Israel and the U.S. executive branch in the preparation of the aid request should not be underrated. In the next stage of the aid process—consideration by the Congress—the presentation of Israel's case by its representatives and friends is perhaps even more important.

The Role of Congress

Under the U.S. constitutional system, the president has the responsibility and authority to conduct the country's foreign policy. Accordingly, as we have seen, it is the executive branch which determines the general magnitudes and conditions of the foreign aid program, selecting as well the countries that are to benefit from it. However, since foreign aid involves significant sums of money and the Congress has decision-making authority over all expenditures of government funds, the influence of the Congress on foreign aid is greater than on other foreign policy issues. The Congress exercises this influence through extensive committee hearings at which administration spokesmen, as well as proponents and

opponents from the public, present their views on the proposed aid legislation. The Congressional committees are central to the processing of the legislation through the Congress, for in an age of growing complexity and specialization, the legislative bodies have come to rely increasingly on the recommendations of their specialized committees. Even within the committees and subcommittees, there are particular members or staff advisors who, by virtue of position, personality, knowledge, dedication, or seniority, can exercise exceptional influence on foreign aid legislation.

The process itself is lengthy and complicated. As is the case with all legislation requiring the expenditure of funds, the foreign aid proposal requires two consecutive (or sometimes parallel) legislative decisions—an "authorization," which establishes policy guidelines and an overall monetary ceiling, and an "appropriation," which provides the actual funds within the limits established under the authorization.

The authorization process for aid to Israel, for example, begins in both the Subcommittee on Europe and the Middle East of the Foreign Affairs Committee of the House of Representatives, and in the Subcommittee on Near East and South Asian Affairs of the Senate Foreign Relations Committee. These subcommittees hold public and private hearings as well as "mark-up" sessions at which the proposed legislation is examined in detail and often modified. The recommended bills are then considered by the full committee, and are ultimately "reported out" to the House and the Senate respectively. More often than not, the aid authorization approved by the two chambers is not identical, and thus goes to a conference committee of both chambers that seeks to arrive at a compromise version likely to be acceptable to the House and the Senate. This compromise version is submitted to the two chambers for final approval, after which it goes to the president for his signature. A similar procedure takes place for the appropriations process. There the legislative process begins in the Appropriations Subcommittee on Foreign Operations of the House Appropriations Committee, moves on to the Appropriations Subcommittee on Foreign Operations of the Senate, and so on. The legislative process is complete only after identical authorization and appropriation bills have been approved by the House and Senate and signed by the president. At numerous points along the way legislation can be changed, sidetracked, or stopped altogether. This holds true particularly for controversial legislation such as foreign aid.

Historically, foreign aid has had a difficult time in the Congress, and even in the executive branch it is at times regarded with considerable ambivalence. Symptomatic of this fact is that although the United States has had an offical foreign aid program since the end of World War II, the agency administering the program has never been established as a permanent entity of the U.S. government. Foreign aid is generally not popular with the American public or Congress, and it lacks a strong domestic constituency ready to lobby on its behalf. Because of these reasons, the annual battle for foreign aid is usually drawn-out and painful. The administration struggles hard to explain and justify its program to the public and the Congress; yet almost every year, its funding proposals are cut and provisions are added to restrict its flexibility in administering the program.

The outstanding exception to this norm has been the aid request for Israel, which has consistently had strong support in the Congress. A recent study analyzed the period of 1970 to 1977 from the point of view of Congressional action with respect to Israel, including decisions on foreign aid. It found that during this period the Congress with two minor exceptions consistently and significantly increased appropriations for Israel beyond the administration's request. With regard to economic aid, Congressional appropriations for Israel exceeded administration requests by 30 percent; military assistance was increased by about three percent above the request. Total assistance in both categories was increased by $703.4 million, or 8.7 percent above the requested amount. This record of action is particularly impressive in the face of parallel annual actions by the Congress to slash the overall aim program requests of the administration. During the same period, 1970 to 1977, for example, the Congress reduced total foreign aid requests of the administration by 23.5 percent (Feuerwerger 1979, 29–30).

In appropriating more funds for Israel than requested, the Congress has at times risked a direct clash with the administration. Thus, in 1972, the Congress appropriated $50 million unrequested economic aid for Israel under the International Security Assistance Act, despite the threat of the head of the agency, John Hannah, to impound the funds; and in 1976, Congress voted an unrequested $200 million in military assistance and $75 million in economic support for the "transition quarter" between two fiscal years, in face of a presidential veto threat for the bill as a whole (Feuerwerger 1979, 31). (Neither threat was carried out in the end.) Moreover, the action of the Congress in appropriating economic support funds along with military aid set an important precedent that was subsequently accepted by the administration, and which has resulted in channelling $6.7 billion in economic aid to Israel during the period between 1972–1983.

Other Congressional initiatives on aid to Israel included support for the absorption of Soviet Jewish refugees in Israel and the construction of a nuclear power and desalting plant (Feuerwerger 1979, 32, 40, 49). In addition, the Congress since 1971 has earmarked most of the funds going to Israel to prevent any possible diversion, and has repeatedly

eased the terms and conditions of aid. The 1976 Security Assistance
Act, for example, provides that of a total of $2.37 billion in aid, $1.5
billion "shall be available only for Israel"; the same act goes on to
stipulate that, "Israel shall be released from one half of its contractual
liability to repay the United States Government" (Feuerwerger 1979,
33). In the most recent instance of action to ease conditions of aid to
Israel, the Congress, (over administration objections) transferred more
than half a billion dollars in the 1983 appropriation bill from the
proposed loan category to the grant category.

The aid process described above has shown the operational stages of
decision-making with respect to the U.S. aid program, along with the
special features which distinguish the aid program for Israel from the
other 90 plus countries which receive U.S. assistance. What has not been
shown are the policy considerations, institutional elements, and moti-
vational sources which impinge upon the operational process just described.

Shaping Aid Policy Toward Israel

In 1983 (the time of writing), more than 17 percent of total worldwide
U.S. assistance is going to Israel. Moreover, there have been years in the
recent past (e.g., 1976) when Israel's share represented more than one
third of total U.S. assistance. As we have also seen, much of this assistance
is given as a grant that comes at the end of a decision-making process
in which Israel itself participates as a partner. These exceptional circumstances raise several questions regarding the shaping of U.S. aid policy.

First, why has the United States been prepared to sustain its aid
program to Israel over such a long period of time—and for the last
10–12 years at such unprecedentedly high levels?

Second, why is the U.S. Congress prepared, even in times of economic
crisis and in the face of serious cuts in domestic programs, to continue
supporting the present high aid levels to Israel? In this connection, why
has the Congress consistently been more generous to Israel than the
executive branch?

The answers to these questions go to the heart of the overall relationship
between the two countries. Briefly stated, they include the following
precepts and perceptions:

(a) The United States recognizes a moral commitment to the continued
existence and welfare of the state of Israel;
(b) The United States has a political interest in supporting and
sustaining one of the few outposts of democracy outside Western Europe
and North America;

(c) The United States has a strategic interest in strengthening Israel as part of a deterrent bulwark to potential Soviet expansionism towards the Indian Ocean, the Persian Gulf, and key communication links in the eastern Mediterranean; and

(d) The United States believes that its aid can encourage the Arab-Israeli peace process by making Israel feel more secure, and by signalling to the Arab states that Israel is here to stay.

How firmly are these precepts and perceptions rooted in the American political consciousness, and how are they articulated through the policy mechanism?

Moral Commitment. This first and probably the most permanent precept of the U.S.-Israeli relationship dates back to the creation of the state of Israel. It was implicit in President Truman's decision that the United States would be the first country to recognize Israel and was followed by the previously mentioned commitment to Chaim Weizmann on Israel's security and economic well-being. Since then, this moral commitment has been affirmed by both political parties. Its roots probably go back deep into the American psyche—the redemption of the Biblical promise combined with a mixture of guilt and outrage over the Holocaust—both of which were clearly part of President Truman's inspiration.

Israel as Outpost of Democracy. The perception of Israel as an outpost of democracy is firmly anchored in U.S. political thinking about the world outside of Europe, and about the Middle East in particular. It adds a strong ideological tie to the moral commitment, placing Israel in the position of an ally of the United States whose continued existence and welfare supports U.S. foreign policy objectives. The strength of this perception has been manifest almost since the beginning of the relationship, despite the absence of any formal contractual agreement or alliance.

Strategic Consensus. This doctrine began to gain plausibility with the emergence of Israel as a regional military power after the Six Day War, and it increased in popularity with Israel's greatly increased military strength after the Yom Kippur War. According to this doctrine, Israel's military capability, beyond its defensive dimension, can serve U.S. strategic interests by deterring potential Soviet expansionism or other forms of extremism in the region.

As one long-time U.S. advocate of this thesis has put it: "The Israel Defense Forces have as their principal task the deterrence of Soviet military adventurism in the region. To achieve such deterrence, Israel's military technology must remain at the sharp edge of conventional power . . . The U.S. assistance package is the hard steel necessary for Israel's edge."[3] Some administration and Congressional pronouncements have lent credence to this doctrine, even in the absence of a formal alliance between the two countries. The high point of acceptance of the thesis was probably the signature of the (now suspended) U.S.-Israel Strategic Cooperation Agreement of 1982.

Israel's Security. The basic premise of this doctrine is that Israel will be ready to engage in a negotiating process involving compromise and risk-taking only if it feels economically and militarily secure. This was the general approach taken by former Secretary of State Henry Kissinger to smooth the way in the various stages of the lengthy and often painful negotiating process that was initiated during the Nixon and Ford administrations, and which continues to this day. The sharp escalation of aid beginning with the Nixon administration can be seen as a corollary to this doctrine, as can U.S. acceptance of the notion that Israel must maintain a qualitative and technological edge over its regional adversaries. U.S. support for a "secure" Israel also carries its own indirect message to the Arab states—namely that the United States is prepared to back up its moral commitment to Israel with concrete steps designed to ensure its security.

The above precepts and perceptions form the basis for the U.S. interest in Israel and for an assessment that must be renewed annually—namely, that this interest is served through the assistance program. However, neither the assessment nor the doctrines supporting it are static. They stand or fall with the political environment between the two countries; specifically, with their acceptance by the administration, the Congress, and by U.S. public opinion. When seen in this context, the cluster of U.S. interests which support aid to Israel is being continuously tested against other clusters of U.S. interests as well as against changes in the intensity and validity of these doctrines and perceptions.

Thus, the "moral commitment" of 1983, though sanctified by time, cannot have the intensity of the early period with its vivid memories of the Holocaust, homeless refugees, and the perception of a "little" Israel threatened by overwhelming Arab power. Some observers claim in fact that the "moral commitment" doctrine is virtually defunct, except for Christian fundmentalist support for "the return to Zion"—a not insignificant but basically secondary element of the doctrine. And indeed, it would be unrealistic to pretend that this set of beliefs and perceptions remains unaffected by the passage of time and the enormous increase in Israel's power in relation to the Arab countries, especially with regard to the Palestinians. As a result of this change in the power relationship, one can discern an emerging countertendency, i.e., sympathy for the Palestinians as the underdog, and more outspoken advocacy of America's "moral commitment" to the "rights of the Palestinians." However, as long as one U.S. administration after another takes pains to affirm its moral commitment to Israel, it would be premature to write off the political significance of this precept.

U.S. Assistant Secretary of State Nicholas Veliotes, testifying before a Congressional committee on the administration's 1984 aid request for Israel, stated:

> "Support for Israel's security and economic well-being is a basic firm principle of American foreign policy. Our support for Israel grows out of a longstanding commitment to a free nation which has been a haven for immigrants from all over the world, and which shares many of our own social and democratic traditions" (*Jerusalem Post* March 4, 1983).

Similarly, the perception of Israel as an outpost of democracy continues to draw U.S. support, although here too, treatment of the Palestinian issue has somewhat tarnished Israel's democratic credentials, and annexation or near annexation of territories beyond the 1967 boundaries have raised questions regarding Israel's dedication to the peace process. For example, after the Knesset adopted a law in 1981 subjecting the Golan area to Israeli civil jurisdiction, a public opinion poll in the state of New York reportedly showed a drastic decline in support for aid to Israel. According to the same source, this loss has never been fully made up.[4] Thus, it may represent a permanent erosion of support for Israel, caused by a weakening of Israel's democratic image.

The strategic consensus doctrine has also been buffeted by the strong winds of dissension between Israel and the United States during the last few years. Its unspoken but implied condition is that it be part of a wider regional strategic consensus emerging from an attenuation of the Arab-Israeli conflict. The absence of further movement in this direction since the signing of the peace treaty with Egypt, together with continuous U.S.-Israeli disagreement about the goals of the Camp David peace process, have raised doubts about the realism of the doctrine. Thus it should not have been too surprising that the United States, while recognizing the existence of common strategic interests, has at times downplayed their significance and failed to give the doctrine an operational dimension. In fact, the almost casual ease with which the U.S. government suspended the Strategic Cooperation Agreement with Israel in reaction to Israel's "Peace for Galilee" operation—almost before the ink had dried on the document—seems to downgrade the importance of the doctrine in the eyes of the United States.

The "secure Israel" thesis, on the other hand, has not been questioned—in fact, Assistant Secretary of State Veliotes, in opening Congressional testimony in March 1983, emphasized that the administration was not attaching political conditions to its large aid package for Israel, but simply wanted Israel to feel "supersecure" (*Jerusalem Post* March 4, 1983). At other times U.S. administrations have emphasized that whatever the cost of making Israel "secure," it is far cheaper than financing the costs of war, as the United States did in the aftermath of the Yom Kippur War.[5] What may be at issue, however, is not the principle, but the quantities of hardware and dollars required to ensure Israel's "supersecurity." In light of Israel's repeatedly demonstrated military and technological superiority over her adversaries, U.S. estimates tend to lag behind those of Israel.

In sum, the foundations upon which Israel builds its expectations of U.S. aid are subject to changes in their appeal and intensity, depending partly on Israeli policy and partly on other or shifting U.S. interests over which Israel has little control. Successive U.S. administrations, responding to some of these conflicting or at least competitive interests in the Middle East, have for many years espoused the so-called "evenhandedness doctrine," the notion that whatever Israel gets should in some way also be given to the Arab states.

I.L. Kenen, the former director of the American-Israel Public Affairs Committee (AIPAC), whose Washington career spans almost the entire period of U.S. aid to Israel, has pointed out that when he began his pro-Israel lobbying activities in Washington in 1951, the new Eisenhower administration planned to allot $23.5 million in economic assistance to Israel and an identical amount to the Arab states. In the end the amounts changed, but $50 million of the first economic aid package for Israel was labeled "refugee aid" in order to parallel another $50 million being requested for Arab refugees (Kenen 1981, 72 ff). Another attempt at "evenhandedness" was applied to Israel and Jordan in the two decades prior to 1970, when except for food assistance, both countries ran neck and neck in the receipt of U.S. economic development aid.

This concept lost much of its relevance in the 1970s as oil politics, deteriorating relations with the Arab states, and the new U.S. commitment to Israel's military security outweighed "evenhandedness" considerations. Lately, however, the doctrine has seen a strong revival in relation to Egypt, which has openly demanded "equal treatment" with Israel in terms of military and economic aid. In the afterglow of the Camp David accords, these demands fell on fertile ground with both the Carter and the Reagan administrations, gaining as well a favorable response in the Congress. The result is a certain symmetry in both military and economic assistance between Israel and Egypt since 1979. In that year the United States assumed the role of principal military supplier to Egypt at an initial military assistance program level of $1.5 billion; in addition, the United States continued to provide Egypt with economic assistance which in 1979 amounted to about $1 billion. The symmetry is particularly apparent in the allocation of economic assistance (not including food aid), which was roughly equal for both Egypt and Israel over the 1977–1982 period, amounting to $4.75 billion and $4.66 billion respectively.[6]

The "evenhandedness" doctrine has also reemerged in the military area in relation to arms supplies for Saudi Arabia and Jordan. Without going into details on these issues, it is clear that as long as U.S. policy in the Middle East rests on maintaining or strengthening its influence with the "moderate" Arab regimes, "evenhandedness" considerations will affect the U.S.-Israeli aid relationship. In other words, the volume of aid flowing to Israel may also be affected to a significant extent by the state of relations between the United States and Israel's Arab neighbors. "Evenhandedness" may mean more competition for aid funds, but it may also mean a greater disposition to provide aid as a means of safeguarding peace and moderation. In any case, that seems to have been the experience with regard to the aid programs for Israel and Egypt during recent years.

Another potentially competing U.S. interest to aid for Israel (and incidentally also for Egypt) are the claims of almost 100 developing countries and half a dozen international agencies that also receive U.S. assistance. The fact that Israel, year by year, corners about 25 percent of total U.S. security assistance is not welcomed by parts of the U.S. foreign policy establishment responsible for safeguarding U.S. interests elsewhere, and of course by the other claimants themselves. In the Congress as well, some members have questioned the wisdom of the present policy, notably the chairman of the Foreign Affairs Subcommittee on Europe and the Middle East, Representative Lee H. Hamilton. In an article published in the *New York Times* on March 28, 1982, he wrote that this imbalance caused difficulties for the United States:

> First, our commitment to economic development in poor countries and to alleviation of suffering around the world are called into question. . . . Second, serious problems arise in our relations with other countries. . . . The imbalance breeds envy and suspicion . . . many countries believe we can control those who receive so much of our aid, (and) find it hard to believe that they as old friends, should receive so much less than Egypt, a new friend. . . . Third, there are risks for Egypt and Israel . . . because both are so dependent on our assistance, their economies are distorted, their debts burgeon, and their need for more aid grows. . . . Fourth, because of this concentration of assistance, we have not begun to address adequately the world's social and economic problems . . . we may soon face grave threats to security and stability caused, in part, by our neglect.
> A review of our foreign aid programs is warranted. Without turning our back on Egypt and Israel, we need to rethink the purposes of foreign

aid, what it can and must achieve, and whether the present distribution
of aid is the best we can do.

Partly no doubt in response to these competing thoughts and pressures,
the Reagan administration in February 1983 appointed a high-level
commission headed by former Ambassador Frank Carlucci to review
U.S. foreign aid policy. While the commission is not likely to recommend
a cutoff of aid to Israel, its work is bound to draw renewed attention
to the material and political cost of this program.

In the face of countervailing political and economic pressures, ag-
gravated during the past few years by economic crisis and persistent
policy disagreements between the United States and Israel, it is all the
more remarkable that the aid program for Israel has fared so well,
comparatively speaking. For while it is true that the total real purchasing
power of U.S. aid has declined as a result of inflation, this has affected
not only Israel but all U.S. aid recipients. Israel, in fact, has done better
than most other countries in this regard, since it has received some
compensation in the form of increased dollar allocations and better terms
(e.g., military assistance has risen from $1 billion in 1980 to $1.7 billion
in 1983), and has also been able to supplement concessional aid with
major medium-term loans from the U.S. Export-Import Bank.[7] The
secret of Israel's success remains the continued support for Israel in
American public opinion, and the effective articulation of this support
by the organized Jewish community in relation to the administration
and particularly the Congress.

The Pro-Israel Lobby

The American-Israel Public Affairs Committee (AIPAC), the major pro-
Israel lobby in Washington, began operations in 1951 with a tiny staff,
few resources, and its focus on key Congressmen who would be sympathetic to American aid for Israel.

One of the initial principles to be sorted out was AIPAC's relationship
to the Israeli government. After some discussion, it was decided that
AIPAC would represent the Jewish community in the United States and
would have no official relationship to the Israeli government. This decision,
which may appear at first glance to be more formal than substantive, is
actually of considerable importance. It means not only that there is no
legal requirement to register as an agent of a foreign government, but
also that AIPAC's policy line, energy, and effectiveness depend in the
final analysis on the support and enthusiasm of its U.S. supporters and
not on orders issued in Jerusalem. This greatly increases the credibility
of the organization as serving American and not "foreign" interests, but

it also makes it incumbent upon Israel's leadership to fashion its policies with a view towards maintaining the unstinting support of the organized Jewish community, the ultimate sponsor of AIPAC.

In the many years since the founding of AIPAC, this unwritten (but nevertheless real) proviso has not been of great importance, given the large measure of agreement between official Israeli government views and those of most of its U.S. supporters. However, during the past few years, differences have emerged between some important segments of the organized American Jewish community and the Israeli government over policies concerning the Palestinian issue, and AIPAC's automatic support of Israeli policy can no longer be taken for granted. Evidence of this became public when in September 1982, the Israeli government abruptly rejected the Reagan peace plan, while Tom Dine, Director of AIPAC, saw in it "great worth" despite some negative elements (*Ma'ariv* November 12, 1982).

Even though efforts were immediately made to patch up the differences, there is no denying that there are significant disagreements within the U.S. Jewish leadership, as well as among the grass roots supporters of Israel, which reflect more or less the policy split existing within Israeli society itself. Only the overriding loyalty to Jewish survival, which still animates the large majority of organized American Jewry, has thus far prevented these disagreements from affecting the operations of AIPAC and of its grass roots activists with respect to the annual aid program. Yet this precious moral capital, like the other previously described assets favoring U.S. aid to Israel, is neither inexhaustible nor immune to potential erosion. To ignore this fact is risky, to say the least.

Thus far, however, AIPAC has been a very effective instrument in mobilizing and articulating public support for aid to Israel. A recent study of the Congressional Research Service for the House Foreign Affairs Committee on information sources in foreign policy states that AIPAC is "widely regarded today as the most effective ethnic/foreign policy lobby on Capitol Hill." AIPAC and the Conference of Presidents of Major American Jewish Organizations, the report goes on to say, "have been most effective in insuring (sic) a relatively uninterrupted flow of military and economic aid to Israel, especially since 1967" (Congressional Research Service February 1982, 46–47).

AIPAC's strength is built on three foundations: know-how, information, and organization.

Know-How. AIPAC today is a highly sophisticated organization. It has a 40-person staff, including professionals, who represent a broad range of expertise on the U.S. political process—particularly the workings of Congress—foreign affairs, communications, and the operations of the U.S. Jewish community. I.L. Kenen, its first director, a journalist by profession, was a life-long Zionist activist and organizer who had deep roots in the American Jewish community and close ties to the founders of the state of Israel. Kenen was succeeded by Morris Amitay, who trained as a lawyer and served previously as a U.S. Foreign Service officer and Congressional aide.

The present director, Tom Dine, formerly worked for Senators Church, Muskie, and Edward Kennedy; he has an academic background in South Asian history and served as a U.S. Peace Corps volunteer in the Philippines. The AIPAC staff constantly keeps its ear to the ground to assess the problems and opportunities for advancing Israel's aid request. It begins its lobbying activities after Israel's annual request reaches Washington, first with the administration, and at a later stage with key elements in the Congress. Because of its broad range of knowledge and contacts, AIPAC is in a position to identify key elements, issues, and personalities before formulating its strategy. Although AIPAC's main focus is on Congress, the executive branch has also learned to respect and appreciate AIPAC's strength, particularly its ability to mobilize support for foreign aid. Its know-how has made AIPAC both an ally and a contender of the administration in the formulation and presentation of the annual aid bill—a contender in usually pressing for more or better conditions of aid to Israel than the administration wishes to provide, and a valuable ally in lobbying for passage of the generally unpopular foreign aid legislation as a whole. A State Department official is quoted as saying:

> There aren't hostile relations between AIPAC and the Administration. . . . Anyone sharing in the process knows that we are speaking of a complicated political activity in which many are involved, and the final product is a result of compromises by all the elements (*Ma'ariv* November 12, 1982).

The battle for approval of the 1983 aid package for Israel illustrates the use of this know-how. In 1982, the Israeli aid request (i.e., the balance-of-payments gap for which U.S. financing was sought) amounted to $3.22 billion. After internal consultations, the administration presented its own request to Congress, which amounted to $2.485 billion (of which $1.025 billion was a grant). AIPAC, working with the key Senate Foreign Relations and House Foreign Affairs Committees, persuaded them in April and May 1982 to approve authorization on more favorable terms, i.e., a higher proportion of grants and, in the case of the Senate Committee, the addition of $125 million to the economic aid allotment requested by the administration. In June came the "Peace for Galilee" operation with subsequent increased tensions and conflicts between the U.S. and the Israeli governments. AIPAC and its friends in the Congress counselled against convening the Senate and House Appropriations

Committees that had to approve the funding requests. The strategy paid off, for by December 1982, hostilities had ceased and there seemed to be prospects for a political solution. The Congressional climate and public opinion vis-à-vis Israel had improved, although tensions between the Reagan administration and the Israeli government persisted. In the improved atmosphere, the committees and the full House and Senate met and approved the original administration request—but with the much improved terms authorized earlier in the year, translating into an additional half a billion dollars in grants rather than loans. The Congress took this decision despite last-minute high-powered administration pressures against it. "I feel very good about the whole thing," said AIPAC director Tom Dine, whose machinery had been very much involved throughout the lengthy process of approval (*Jerusalem Post* December 24, 1982).

Information. Much of AIPAC's strength and credibility derives from its ability to produce timely and accurate information of direct relevance to Congress and AIPAC supporters among the public at large. AIPAC's principal regular information outlet is *The Near East Report*, a weekly newsletter produced under AIPAC's sponsorship that both summarizes and analyzes Mideast developments, and monitors the progress of legislation of interest to AIPAC supporters. The newsletter is sent to every member of Congress in addition to some 60,000 subscribers. AIPAC's research and legislative departments also produce many special studies and papers as needed.

The previously cited study on information sources for Congress notes:

> AIPAC and the other groups comprising the Israeli lobby are as effective as they are in part because of the services they supply to members of Congress and their staffs. These principally involve the production of carefully crafted and packaged information, designed to be of maximum value to a busy legislator (Congressional Research Service February 1982, 48).

The study goes on to stress the importance of information as a means of gaining access to legislators and building personal and institutional relations. It cites the findings of another researcher to the effect that "in a moment of perceived crisis (AIPAC) can put a carefully researched, well-documented statement of its views on the desk of every Senator and Congressman and appropriate committee staff within 4 hours of a decision to do so" (Congressional Research Service February 1982, 48).

Similarly, AIPAC has an effective communications network to other Jewish organizations and its grass roots supporters all over the United States. Through letters, telegrams, and telephone calls, AIPAC can rapidly transmit important information or requests for organizational action.

Organization. Within the characteristic framework of American politics, all of AIPAC's political know-how and information-gathering abilities would be of limited value without the back-up of articulate and preferably (but not necessarily) influential political activists. AIPAC has succeeded in tapping into this grass roots strength by way of a computerized "key contact" list that can be activated at a moment's notice. In the previously described battle for improvements in the 1983 aid program for Israel, this network was mobilized to produce personal communications from consitituents, including from important campaign contributors and others known personally to the legislators. "Without Jewish political action we wouldn't have won," one pro-Israel lobbyist said after the campaign (*Jerusalem Post* December 24, 1982).

This political action is nurtured by a stream of information and specially prepared material that explain to AIPAC's 34,000 dues-paying members (as well as other supporters) how to use effectively the American political process of which they are a part. For example, a pamphlet entitled "The U.S. Congress: A Guide to Citizen Action" begins by explaining in some detail the Congressional legislative process—before going on to suggest how citizens can influence this process. Another pamphlet, the "AIPAC Congressional Handbook," lists the names and party affiliations of all Representatives, Senators, and Congressional leaders, as well as members and staff directors of key committees. To supplement this broad-gauged educational effort, AIPAC is in the process of organizing "Political Action Workshops" designed particularly for states with relatively small Jewish communities. AIPAC officials also meet regularly in Washington with representatives of other major Jewish organizations in order to coordinate positions, so that when AIPAC representatives testify, they usually speak for the majority of the organized Jewish community.

Observers of the American political scene have pointed out that, perhaps because of the Jewish historical experience, American Jews are more politically involved than other ethnic groups. Voter participation among Jews has been estimated at 80 percent—higher than that of any other ethnic group. Contributions to election campaigns are also thought to be out of proportion to population size (*Ma'ariv* November 12, 1982). AIPAC and the American Jewish community have learned to utilize these general qualities of good citizenship in order to influence American policy towards Israel, and more specifically to benefit the U.S. aid program for Israel.

In the final analysis, however, U.S. aid policy towards Israel is shaped by the precepts and perceptions of U.S. interests as seen by the U.S. government and supported by both public opinion at large and, to a growing extent, the media. An ethnic lobby, no matter how effective and sophisticated, cannot in the long run prevail against such a power combination, as was shown in the AWACS controversy. But Israel's problem is even somewhat more complex, for it must in the first instance retain the loyalty and support of its Jewish supporters before working with them to secure the support of governmental decision-makers and the U.S. public as a whole. Israel's spectacular success in obtaining U.S. aid has been possible because all along this complex line of political perception and action, the vision affecting the ultimate decisions has been more or less identical among the various actors. Whether this will continue into the future depends principally on the resolution of basic conflicts between the two governments concerning the Palestinian issue.

Aid Leverage in Crisis or Near-Crisis Situations

The question of the existence and use of leverage with regard to U.S. assistance for Israel is one of the most controversial and complex issues in U.S.-Israeli relations. First of all, what consititutes aid leverage? Is it just the application of political pressure against the background of aid, i.e., the threat that non-compliance would have negative effects upon the aid program? It is certainly that, but there are at least two other types of leverage which must also be considered. One type of leverage is formally incorporated into all military aid agreements concluded by the United States in the form of a pledge by the recipient country not to utilize arms aid except for defensive purposes and not to transfer the arms received to third parties without U.S. consent. Similarly, since the mid-1970s, U.S. policy is to withhold aid from countries engaged in consistent gross violations of human rights. Theoretically, any violation or suspected violation of these provisions could result in a partial or complete aid cutoff or suspension. A third, more subtle form of leverage, can be invoked merely by nurturing public discussion of possible aid cutoffs, reductions, or suspensions.

In reviewing the extent to which aid leverage has been applied in U.S.-Israeli relations, it is useful to clear away some of the psychological cobwebs surrounding the issue. As we have seen, part of the leverage conferred upon the United States originates from legal provisions which form part of the U.S. Foreign Aid legislation. While the definitions are left deliberately vague and flexible, both donor and recipients are clearly aware that they could at some point form the basis of leverage.

The nonformal types of leverage, through direct political persuasion or more subtle psychological pressure, are also no secret to international relations. The current U.S. Ambassador to the United Nations, Jean

Kirkpatrick, wrote in a recent report regarding the motives for U.S. assistance: "Obviously, when the administration proposes assistance to another country, and when the Congress votes it, both have in mind specific and important reasons for doing so. These can range from key geostrategic location, to economic or political (factors). . . . " (*Jerusalem Post* March 1, 1983).

According to this description, foreign aid is clearly part and parcel of U.S. foreign policy, to be used in the furtherance of U.S. foreign policy objectives. It follows therefore that aid is either extended to support those objectives, or can be withheld or otherwise manipulated whenever those objectives seem threatened. The effectiveness of such leverage depends of course on a number of factors, most notably the importance of the aid to the recipient country. Applying this analysis to the U.S.-Israeli relationship, we may draw the following conclusions:

(a) When U.S.-Israeli relations are calm and foreign policy objectives or tactics are identical or at least similar, aid leverage is a hypothetical matter which barely penetrates into public or official consciousness;

(b) The potential for the application of aid leverage to Israel is real and powerful, particularly in light of periodic divergences in objectives or perceptions between the United States and Israel and the enormously important place U.S. aid has assumed in the Israeli economy; and,

(c) U.S. aid leverage is part of the price Israel pays for the security and relative comfort which aid buys.

But its potential for the United States is not unlimited—despite Israel's enormous aid dependency—as long as Israel enjoys substantial support in the U.S. Congress and among the U.S. public. America's ability to apply aid leverage is also limited by the knowledge that an Israel free of aid strings might be more problematic for U.S. foreign policy than in the present conditions of dependency. Thus, in Israel's case, any invocation of aid leverage is conditioned both by Israel's unique place in the consciousness and political framework of the United States and by countervailing consideration within the framework of U.S. foreign policy itself. It is perhaps this set of often complex and even contradictory considerations which explains the relatively judicious use of aid leverage in relation to Israel. But to deny that aid leverage does play a role in U.S.-Israeli relations would be to deny reality.

Direct Sanctions

B'not Yaacov Hydroelectric Project. Early in the Eisenhower administration, in 1953, Israel's hydroelectric power construction project in the demilitarized zone of the Jordan Valley north of the Sea of Galilee was challenged by Syria, which took the issue to the United Nations Security Council. Major General Vagh Benikke, the chief of staff of the UN Truce Supervisory Organization (UNTSO), ruled that Israel would have to obtain Syrian consent to the digging of a water diversionary channel, thus giving Syria veto power over the development project. Israel considered the ruling unjustified and continued its construction activities. At this point, in September 1953, the U.S. government suspended all aid to Israel, pending resolution of the conflict. The pro-Israel lobby in Washington intervened with Secretary of State John Foster Dulles, but to no avail, as U.S. policy was to support the UN as arbiter of the armistice agreements, regardless of the merits of the case. After more than a month of pressure, Israel notified the Security Council that work on the project was being suspended, and the next day, U.S. aid was resumed (Neff 1981, 44).

Sinai Campaign, 1956. Israel's preventive blow in Sinai, coordinated with simultaneous action at the Suez Canal by Britain and France, was perceived by the Eisenhower administration as an unmitigated disaster. It not only smacked of a return to colonial intervention but also seemed to doom Washington's favorite strategy of drawing the Arab and other Near Eastern countries (except for Israel) into the Western alliance system. All U.S. efforts in the aftermath of the invasion were therefore aimed at "limiting the damage" by getting the three invading countries to accept a UN cease-fire and to withdraw as quickly as possible from occupied territories along the Suez Canal, in Sinai, and in the Gaza Strip. The invader's grievances, which included Israeli security concerns over Egyptian-directed terrorist attacks, the blockage of Israel's Red Sea maritime approaches, and the denial of access to the Suez Canal, were considered of secondary importance.

As the documents of the period show, threats to cut U.S. aid to Israel—then amounting to approximately $50 million in economic assistance—were used repeatedly in an effort to persuade Israel to conform to U.S. wishes. Soon after the operation began, Secretary Dulles was quoted as saying to an assistant: "It looks so bad we may have to stop our aid. They (the Israelis) don't think we would do that" (Neff 1981, 365). During the following weeks and months of negotiations, the aid theme remained a major one in discussions between the Israeli and U.S. governments, although aid was never apparently suspended. However, when Israel sought to delay its final withdrawal in the hope of extracting better terms, the United States threatened to turn another screw. Undersecretary of State Herbert J. Hoover Jr., amplifying a sharp letter from President Eisenhower to Ben-Gurion, told the Israeli minister in Washington that, "Israel's attitude will inevitably lead to most serious measures, such as the termination of all U.S. *governmental and private* [emphasis added] aid, UN sanctions and eventually expulsion from the United Nations" (Neff 1981, 365). The same idea was repeated in another personal letter from President Eisenhower to Prime Minister Ben-Gurion in February 1957, despite a groundswell of pro-Israeli sentiments in Congress and the press.

Finally, on March 1, 1957, Israel announced its willingness to withdraw in exchange for a UN Emergency Force (UNEF) presence in Gaza and Sharm el Sheikh. In the aid sphere, Israel's "reward" was U.S. support for a substantial World Bank loan to Israel, as well as continuation of direct U.S. economic assistance ($40.9 million in 1957). But the confrontation had left deep imprints of resentment and even hostility on the consciousness of the U.S. foreign policy establishment, as reflected in the following private remarks by Secretary Dulles:

> I am aware how almost impossible it is in this country to carry out a foreign policy not approved by the Jews. . . . The Jewish influence here is completely dominating the scene and making it almost impossible to do anything they don't approve of. The Israeli Embassy is practically dictating to the Congress through influential Jewish people in this country (Neff 1981, 433).

These remarks illustrate, perhaps more clearly than any other, the hidden emotions and calculations which at times affect not only the use or non-use of aid leverage but the entire fabric of U.S.-Israeli relations. However, it was the clash of strategic interests and perceptions which no doubt largely determined the thrust of U.S. policy and tactics in the first Sinai crisis.

Indirect Sanctions

With the coming of the Nixon administration, the application of aid leverage with regard to Israel took a somewhat different course, although once again it was a crisis and a divergence of strategic interests flowing from it which triggered the process.

As Israel struggled to recover and snatch victory from the great psychological and military trauma of the Yom Kippur War, there emerged three vital strategic Israeli objectives: (a) demonstrating to the Arab world the futility of military solutions; (b) ensuring itself against any such eventuality; and (c) assuring continued political, economic, and military support from the United States. The U.S. connection in particular became a matter of life and death in light of the military losses Israel sustained on the battlefield and the wave of hostility towards it which swept the world.

U.S. strategic perspectives and objectives looked quite different. They were primarily the following: (a) bringing an end to the oil embargo and ensuring against its repetition; (b) limiting Soviet involvement in the Middle East; and (c) demonstrating the essential role of the United States to both parties in the Arab-Israeli conflict. These goals required a central U.S. mediating role, a conciliatory posture towards the Arab states, and protection for Syria and Egypt from the consequences of Israel's military victory.

Whether by design (as asserted by some) or by happenstance (as maintained by others), aid became a prime instrument signalling the course preferred by the United States.

The delay in the immediate U.S. resupply of arms, planes, and ammunition—whether superbly orchestrated from above or the result of resistance from lower levels of the Pentagon and State Department bureaucracy—carried the message that Israel's military victory would have to be limited. President Nixon's message to Congress on October 19, 1973, asking for $2.2 billion in military aid for Israel "to maintain a *balance* [emphasis added] of forces and thus achieve stability" carried a similar message (Sachar 1976, 784).

Nixon's tactics (as opposed to those of Kissinger) tended later towards the invocation of direct sanctions. In his book, *Years of Upheaval*, Kissinger cites at least four such instances—first, a threat to hold up one quarter of the $2.2 billion arms package "as insurance of Israel's good behavior" at the upcoming Geneva peace conference; second, a directive to cut off aid unless Israel changed its position in the Syrian disengagement negotiations; third, an order to suspend current arms deliveries and receipt of new arms requests until Israel agreed to a comprehensive peace agreement (this order was never carried out since Nixon resigned three days later, before he had signed the necessary papers); and fourth, a muted warning during Nixon's visit to Israel in June 1974 that in return for continued massive aid, the United States expected Israeli "flexibility" in negotiations (Kissinger 1982, 792).

Kissinger's more subtle tactics may also have included use of the leverage conferred by Israel's dependency on U.S. aid, particularly in the military sphere. According to several sources, both the initial resupply operation in 1973 and later arms deliveries were manipulated by Kissinger in order to extract Israeli concessions in conformity with U.S. strategic objectives in the post-Yom Kippur War era (Luttwak and Laqueur 1974, Golan 1976).

According to Israeli journalist Matti Golan, who based himself on Israeli sources, U.S. arms and deliveries unaccountably slowed down again in July 1974, as U.S. pressure mounted to bring Israel and Jordan into peace negotiations. The slowdown was reputedly due to a new

Kissinger directive to the Pentagon to stall on deliveries—"not enough to hurt, but enough to be felt" (Golan 1976, 220). Finally, at the end of the period of Kissinger's "shuttle diplomacy" between Israel and Egypt in March 1975, a frustrated Secretary of State announced a "reassessment" of U.S. policy towards Israel which, again according to Golan, was accompanied by a drying up of the delivery pipeline and cancellation of planned talks on new deliveries. Israeli officials also feared possible suspension of economic aid (Golan 1976, 243–246). After holding out for three months, Israel yielded and agreed to U.S.-supported Egyptian demands to evacuate the Sinai passes and return the Abu Rodeis and Ras Sudr oil fields.

Although the details of Kissinger's operations may be contested, the use of indirect sanctions and the carrot and stick approach would appear to fit well into the Kissinger style of diplomacy. And as the "reassessment" crisis has shown, the hint of economic sanctions, combined with the military supply pressures, may have been enough to bend Israel to the will of the United States.

Indirect leverage—in this case through a steady stream of rumors and speculative press leaks about U.S. intentions with respect to Israel's aid program—also appears to have been used by the Reagan administration in the aftermath of Israel's invasion of Lebanon in 1982. While it is impossible at this writing to gauge the ultimate effectiveness of this effort, it is likely that these indirect sanctions do have some restraining effect upon Israeli government actions. The same can also be said for the more formal sanctions invoked in accordance with the aid legislation.

Formal Sanctions

As indicated earlier, leverage resulting from formal sanctions can only be applied if there is an actual or suspected violation of the provisions under which the aid has been granted. While there has never been a determination that such violations have occurred in relation to Israel, questions have been raised regarding possible violations in a number of instances where Israel has resorted to military action. These have included the bombing of the Iraqi nuclear reactor, numerous air strikes against Lebanese targets, the ground action of March 1978 known as the "Litani Operation," and most prominently, the June 1982 "Peace for Galilee" war in Lebanon. The latter action triggered the suspension of the delivery of so-called "cluster bombs" and an embargo on the sale of previously promised F-16 fighter planes. The Reagan administration, moreover, has evidently decided to extract maximum leverage from finding that a violation "may have occured," without going so far as to charge Israel with an actual violation. A State Department spokesman explained, echoing earlier (but less precise) remarks by President Reagan:

As the President pointed out, under law, any weapons supplied must be for purposes of legitimate self-defense. . . . While Israeli forces remain in Lebanon, concerns arise as to whether it would be consistent with the spirit of the law to go ahead with the Congressional notification regarding (the sales of) these aircraft, which has been held up since Israel went into Lebanon. . . . However, the President was not stating that he was making a determination of ineligibility under U.S. law (*Jerusalem Post* April 3, 1983).

By taking this line, the U.S. government seeks to derive the benefits of leverage under the mantle of law—thus avoiding the odium of a political act which could be interpreted as hostile to Israel, and protecting itself against attack from pro-Israel elements in the Congress and the public.

No matter which type of sanction or the manner in which it is applied, it is clear that aid leverage has played and continues to play a significant role in U.S.-Israeli relations. And it could not be otherwise, given the circumstances of the relationship. However, it is also worth pointing out that, by and large, the United States has used its aid leverage on Israel with restraint and that rarely, if ever, has the aid pipeline actually been cut. Most recent American policymakers have tended towards the Kissinger thesis that a "satisfied" Israel, i.e., militarily and economically secure, is more likely to show flexibility than one which is pushed against the wall by threats of abandonment and punishment. Nevertheless, the fact that the United States may at any time decide to curtail or suspend aid is one that is poised, like the sword of Damocles, over the heads of Israeli policymakers.

Dependency and Its Alternatives

As has been pointed out before, during the early period of U.S. governmental assistance to Israel, the aid provided an important stimulus to Israel's economic development; while in the food sector, it enabled Israel to cover a significant portion of its food emports. Although this aid played a significant role in Israel's economic life, it was overshadowed by transfers from other major sources such as Jewish communities, Israel Bonds, German reparations and restitution payments—a large proportion of which were non-repayable contributions. From 1948 to 1970, transfers from these four sources amounted to $6.535 billion, whereas U.S. government aid came to $1.523 billion, or less than one quarter of this amount (Congressional Research Service September 1976, Table 2). In terms of Israel's chronic balance of payments deficit, U.S. government aid financed about one fifth of the import surplus.

The year 1971—with its quantum jump in U.S. military assistance to Israel—changed the picture radically. German reparations ended in 1970, and while contributions from Jewish communities, Israel Bonds, and German restitution payments held their own, they lost in importance relative to the increasing aid allotments from the U.S. government. This was also reflected in the increasing importance of U.S. aid in the financing of Israel's import surplus. Since 1974, U.S. aid has covered between 65–75 percent of Israel's annual trade deficit and, in absolute terms, far overshadows the remittances from Israel's other sources of assistance.

At the same time, although the terms of U.S. government assistance to Israel are very favorable and almost two thirds of the aid is in the form of grants, Israel's indebtedness to the United States has been growing steadily. In 1977, Israel's debt service payments to the United States amounted to $375 million, about half of total U.S. economic assistance for the year (Controller General of the United States August 18, 1975, Appendix II and AID 1978). By 1981 the annual payments had risen to about $700 million; in its January 1981 "Report on the Israeli Economy and Debt Repayment Prospects" (p. 13), the U.S. Agency for International Development noted that this amount almost equaled U.S. economic assistance to Israel for the year. And in 1983, payments (according to Israel Finance Ministry estimates) are expected to exceed $900 million, substantially more than the $785 million in U.S. economic aid. According to its report, "Israel's Requirements for U.S. Aid for Fiscal Year 1981" (September 1979, Appendices 7 and 8), Israel's debt to the United States in 1973 accounted for 26 percent of its total foreign debt, whereas by 1983 it is expected to reach 51 percent.

The inescapable conclusion that flows from the above figures is one of Israel's enormous and constantly growing economic dependency on the United States. This economic dependency forms the background for Israel's additional dependency in the military and political sectors, where the United States has emerged as Israel's sole supplier of major weaponry and often its sole defender in the international-political arena.

Aside from financing a large portion of Israel's trade deficit the United States also assures Israel's access to the international financial market through its economic and political support. Such access is vital in financing that portion of the foreign currency gap not covered by the United States. In the absence of any material change in the basic situation, any threat to the U.S. aid flow could quickly produce a major economic emergency by simultaneously drying up short-term commercial borrowing. Although the bulk of Israel's foreign debt is long or medium term and at concessional rates of interest, the financial journal *Euromoney* recently classified Israel as one of the riskiest countries for short-term lending—just ahead of Turkey, Jordan, Cyprus, and Italy (Razin 1983,

Table 4.2
Forecast of Israel's Foreign Debt Service,
1978–1983 (millions of U.S. dollars)

	1978	1979	1980	1981	1982	1983
Outstanding						
Foreign Debts	12,184	14,300	16,920	19,185	21,400	23,195
thereof: U.S.						
Government	4,626	5,557	7,029	8,549	10,333	11,485
Total Interest						
Payments	938	1,005	1,210	1,395	1,640	1,875
Total Debt						
Service	1,925	2,205	2,310	2,595	2,940	3,275
thereof: U.S.						
Government	561	534	635	750	851	939

Source: Israel Ministry of Finance, Jerusalem 1979.

39). Recent economic developments are adding to Israel's exposed economic situation. The year 1982 saw a mostly stagnating economy, with increased imports, declining exports, and no growth in the Gross National Product. The estimated import surplus in 1982 reached $4.9 billion, some $500 million more than in 1981 (*Jerusalem Post* December 31, 1982).

Under such circumstances, Israeli and U.S. policymakers face only a limited number of options in any attempt to reduce Israel's economic, military, and political dependence on the United States.

Israel's Options

The only effective way to reduce Israel's dependency on U.S. aid is to strive to close the gap between its exports and imports, i.e., to do away with or at least reduce, Israel's chronic deficit in its balance of payments. However, this would require a stringent economic policy aimed at drastically reducing imports—including defense imports which account for a large portion of the import surplus—while making supreme efforts to increase exports. In the absence of peace, such restraints may be judged incompatible with the country's security. On the civilian side, restrictions on foreign travel (another nonproductive source of consumption of foreign currency) and consumer goods imports, together with relocations of manpower to import substitution and productive export sectors, were suggested in 1975 by a group of academicians to the executive committee of the Likud government coalition. The proposal, entitled "Guidelines for Preparation of an Emergency Economy" was submitted but never again heard from.[8] Perhaps the reason was that the proposal's total effect, according to the authors of the report, would have been to roll Israel's living standard back by four years to 1971 levels. Recent calls by Likud Knesset members Yigal Cohen-Orgad and Yigal Hurvitz for a policy of "more production, more export, and less consumption" went similarly unanswered by the government leadership (*Jerusalem Post* January 1, 1983).

By their inaction, Israel's leaders have tacitly decided to continue the policy of relying on massive U.S. aid to sustain Israel's prevailing standard of living and defensive capacity. The price for continuing this policy is the risk that U.S. government aid leverage may be invoked directly or indirectly at any time, and that the total dependency on the U.S. may have negative effects on Israel's international credit worthiness and economic and political health, as well as on the internal fabric of Israeli society.

Is there a relationship between today's manifestations of cynicism and erosion of moral fiber within Israeli society and the many years of a "shnorrer" (beggar) policy? Are the outbursts of hostility and frustration which have increasingly crept into U.S.-Israeli relations another part of the price for chronic dependency to which there seems to be no end? There is no evidence that Israel's leadership has sought to address these difficult questions to any extent in shaping its policy decisions.

U.S. Options

U.S. policymakers, like their Israeli counterparts, face complex questions in deciding on their aid policy for Israel. To what extent can or should they invoke their awesome power over Israel's future to make Israel conform to U.S. policy objectives in the Middle East? Some of the complexities of the relationship have been stated eloquently by Secretary Kissinger in his memoirs:

> Israel is dependent on the United States as no other country is on a friendly power. . . . The Arab nations blame us for Israel's dogged persistence. Israel sees in intransigence the sole hope for preserving its dignity in a one-sided relationship. . . . It takes a special brand of heroism to turn total dependence into defiance; to insist on support as a matter of right rather than favor; to turn every American deviation from an Israeli cabinet consensus into a betrayal to be punished rather than a disagreement to be negotiated. And yet Israel's obstinacy, maddening as it can be, serves the purpose of both countries best. A subservient client would soon face

an accumulation of ever-growing pressures. It would tempt Israel's neighbors to escalate their demands.

It would saddle us with the approbium for eventual deadlock. That at any rate has been our relationship with Israel—it is exhilarating and frustrating, ennobled by the devotion and faith that contains a lesson for an age of cynicism; exasperating because the interests of a superpower and of a regional ministate are not always easy to reconcile and are on occasion unbridgeable. Israel affects our decisions through inspired persistence and a judicious, not always subtle or discreet, influence on our domestic policies (Kissinger 1982, 484).

In light of these considerations, U.S. policymakers also appear to have opted for the status quo in their aid policy towards Israel. They realize that the turmoil a total aid cutoff would create is not in the U.S. interest, and might not be sustained by Congress or U.S. public opinion. However, they also seem to realize that something much less drastic—while perhaps symbolically important—is not likely to affect seriously Israeli political decisions. They appear to believe that aid leverage can continue to be invoked partially, i.e., indirectly through hints, or formally by reference to the aid legislation. Such restrained use of aid leverage may not bring any breakthroughs from the American point of view, but it serves at least to restrain Israeli policy, and to strengthen the hand of the more moderate elements in the Israeli government.

What could produce a fundamental change in U.S. aid policy towards Israel? The following contingencies, while speculative, do not appear to be beyond reason: First, if Israel chose to take major action totally contrary to U.S. policy objectives, such as the formal and total annexation of the West Bank, permanent Israeli occupation of large parts of Lebanon, or large-scale expulsion of Palestinians from the West Bank and Gaza. Second, if growing perceptions of Israeli "aggressiveness" and of Palestinian "rights" were to result in a gradual but persistent erosion of support for Israel among the U.S. public and Congress.

The fact that neither of these contingencies have yet been triggered affords Israeli and American leadership an opportunity to review fundamentally the current aid relationship. The question for the policymakers in such a review would be whether the long-range interests of U.S.-Israeli friendship are best served by the status quo aid relationship, fraught as it is with many elements of mutual frustration, hostility and potential instability; or by a gradual, mutually agreed upon reduction of U.S. aid, coupled with other appropriate economic measures to ensure the viability of the Israeli economy.

Notes

1. Statistics based on U.S. Agency for International Development, "U.S. Overseas Loans and Grants, 1945–1980," and U.S. Library of Congress Congressional Research Service statistical compilation, "U.S. Assistance to Israel, 1948–1983," November 29, 1982. Figures do not include U.S. Export-Import Bank Loans and the American Schools and Hospitals Program unless specifically mentioned, and refer to U.S. fiscal years.

2. Civilian imports from the United States came to about $16 billion in 1981—thus economic assistance only accounts for a fraction of imports from the United States; as to the second restriction, the Israeli government has no difficulty applying U.S. economic assistance funds outside of the "Occupied Territories" and the military sector, and of using other funds for these areas.

3. *Jerusalem Post*, October 19, 1982, Letter to the Editor by Joseph Churba, Director, Center for International Security, Washington, D.C.

4. Statement by Dr. David Luchins, Special Assistant to Senator Daniel Moynihan, Jerusalem, January 25, 1983.

5. Secretary of State Cyrus Vance, letter to Senator Frank Church, April 23, 1979, quoted in *Hearings Before Senate Foreign Relations Committee on Middle East Peace Package*, GPO 79, p. 130.

6. U.S. Agency for International Development, "U.S. Overseas Grants and Loans, 1945–1980," pp. 13, 18; FY 1983 Security Assistance Submission to Congress, p. 17.

7. Loans to Israel from the Export-Import Bank amounted to $301.4 million in 1980, and $265.7 million in 1981.

8. The report also included a chapter co-authored by the present (as of writing) Defense Minister, Professor Moshe Arens, which called for greatly strengthened domestic military production.

Bibliography

Books

Feuerwerger, Marvin C. *Congress and Israel—Foreign Aid Decision-Making in the House of Representatives 1969–1976*. Westport, Conn.: Greenwood Press, 1979.

Golan, Matti. *Secret Conversations of Henry Kissinger*. New York: Quadrangle/ N.Y. Times Book Co., 1976.

Kenen, I.L. *Israel's Defense Line*. Buffalo: Prometheus Books, 1981.

Kissinger, Henry. *Years of Upheaval*. Boston: Little Brown & Co., 1982.

Neff, Donald. *Warriors at Suez*. New York: Linden Press/Simon & Schuster, 1981.

Sachar, Howard M. *A History of Israel*. New York: Alfred A. Knopf, 1976.

Weizmann, Chaim. *Trial and Error*. New York: Harper & Brothers, 1949.

Articles

Edward Luttwak and Walter Laqueur. "Kissinger and the Yom Kippur War." *Commentary*, September 1974.
Michaely, Michael. "Israel's Dependence on Capital Imports." *The Jerusalem Quarterly*, No. 3 (Spring 1977).
Razin, Assaf. "Foreign Aid of the United States to Israel." *Skirah Chodsheet*, No. 1 (January 1983).

Newspapers

Jerusalem Post
Ma'ariv
The New York Times

Government Publications

Comptroller General of the United States.
Reports to the Congress of the United States.
U.S. Agency for International Development (AID).
Annual reports: "U.S. Overseas Loans and Grants."
U.S. Library of Congress—Congressional Research Service.
"Foreign Assistance to the State of Israel: A Compilation of Basic Data." September 1976.
"U.S. Assistance to Israel, 1948–1983." November 29, 1982.
"Executive-Legislative Consultation on Foreign Policy." February 1982.

FIVE

U.S. Aid to the West Bank and Gaza: Policy Dilemmas

LEOPOLD YEHUDA LAUFER

Evolution of U.S. Assistance Policy
Toward the West Bank and Gaza[1]

Except for the limited conflict in Lebanon, the Arab-Israel confrontation has for better than a decade been contained and prevented from spilling over into another general Middle East war. More than that, the Israel-Egypt peace treaty, despite some shortcomings, has laid the basis for further dialogue and the opening up of the peace process with Jordan and other Arab states. U.S. diplomacy has played an important role in these developments, its effectiveness boosted by the infusion of unprecedentedly large amounts of military and economic assistance. The scale and character of this assistance are well-known and have been analyzed elsewhere (see, for example, Laufer in this volume and Weinbaum 1983).

Less well-known is the U.S. attempt, beginning in 1975 (coinciding approximately with the launching of the large-scale assistance program for Egypt and Israel), to smooth the way for American contacts with the Palestinian population of the administered territories of the West Bank and Gaza (held by Israel since the Six-Day War of June 1967)[2] through a small-scale economic assistance program.

When the West Bank and Gaza came under Israeli occupation as a result of the Six Day War of June 1967, the official U.S. economic presence was small and in large part indistinguishable from private charitable activites. Jordan on the West Bank and Egypt in Gaza gave low priority to the development of these territories, and the U.S. aid programs with these countries reflected this policy. A survey undertaken by the Israel Economic Planning Authority in December 1967, for example, estimates (p. 23) that only about 10 percent of Jordan's $46 million development budget for 1966—largely funded by U.S. assistance funds—had been expended on the West Bank.

Except for a strategically important Jerusalem–Dead Sea highway that had been completed earlier, U.S. assistance projects on the West Bank prior to 1967 were confined to small tourism and water projects and food assistance. The latter, made available under the Food-for-Peace grant program (P.L. 480, Title II), benefited several hundred thousand persons in Gaza and on the West Bank on the basis of government-approved lists. The distribution of food assistance and management of related small-scale economic projects (Food-for-Work) were in the hands of American private voluntary organizations (PVOs), notably the Catholic Relief Services (CRS), the Lutheran World Federation (LWF), the Mennonite Central Committee (MCC), the Near East Council of Churches (NECC), and the Cooperative for American Relief Everywhere (CARE). Under an agreement between these agencies and the Israeli government concluded in September 1967, the former agreed to continue their operations while the latter accepted the provisions of contracts that had been worked out with the Jordanian government, including tax and customs privileges and financial participation in certain program and administrative expenses. Similarly, in accordance with Jordanian practice, the Israel Ministry of Labor and Social Welfare was designated as the supervisory authority over the operations of the PVOs (Elazar 1982, 163).

It is doubtful that the U.S. government decision to continue operations under Israeli occupation in accordance with previous Jordanian guidelines represented more than an administrative judgment, or at best a tacit desire not to "rock the boat." Under this arrangement, the PVOs continuted their food distribution and small project programs in cooperation with Israeli authorities. The Jordanian pattern of social welfare-oriented programs was retained, and while contacts between the PVOs and Israeli authorities were few, they were apparently without friction. Similarly, U.S. government involvement through either the State Department or the Agency for International Development (AID) was minimal, so that the PVOs were largely left to their own devices. This pattern of operations continued until the Yom Kippur War.

The post-Yom Kippur War period of 1974–1975 represented a watershed for U.S. policy development in the Middle East. Israel had snatched military victory from temporary defeat on both the Egyptian and Syrian fronts, but only at the price of increased dependence on the

United States. Shortly after the war, an activist U.S. policy thrust was launched, stage-managed by Secretary of State Henry Kissinger through his shuttle diplomacy, which sought to wrest an opening towards a political solution of the Arab-Israel conflict. As a sweetener, Israel, Egypt and perhaps also Syria were to be rewarded with greatly increased U.S. assistance. One result of this policy thrust—in addition to a quantum jump in aid to Egypt and the continuation of already high levels of assistance to Israel—was the creation of a $100 million Middle East Special Requirements Fund (MESRF) in the foreign aid package for fiscal year 1975. The purpose of the fund as defined by Congress was "to meet contingency needs important to efforts by the United States in helping to achieve peace in the Middle East" (House Report No. 93–1471 1974, 25). Kissinger's testimony before the House Foreign Affairs Committee indicates that the administration intended to use a major portion of this fund for Syria. In addition, Congress earmarked $6 million to be used to cover part of a deficit incurred by the UN Relief and Works Agency (UNRWA), along with an unspecified amount to be allotted to socioeconomic projects on the West Bank and Gaza. In describing the purposes of this particular program, the committee report stated that

> some of the funds authorized for the Special Requirements Fund should be made available to support projects and expand institutions in the occupied territories of the West Bank and Gaza. It is believed that such assistance can help build the socioeconomic underpinnings necessary to preserve peace both for the immediate and long-term futures. In particular, the committee believes that such funds should be used to expand the activities of educational and vocational training institutions in the occupied territories. In the view of the committee, these are the kinds of worthwhile projects the United States can usefully be associated with in the coming years as we hopefully move towards a lasting peace in the Middle East (House Report No. 93–1471 1974, 26).

Several U.S. policy elements in this statement are worth noting. First, the program was conceived as part of the peace-making process in the region. Second, it was to be a discreet new program for the West Bank and Gaza, unrelated to assistance for Israel or the surrounding Arab countries, and not merely an add-on to ongoing food assistance activities. Finally, its emphasis was to be on support of "educational and vocational training institutions in the occupied territories." This was a rather modest formulation of the parameters of the program; in administration testimony before the House Appropriations Committee, a potentially broader scope was indicated:

Some (funds) may be utilized . . . for development projects—for example, in areas presently under occupation which could be involved under the terms of a settlement. The latter projects are likely to be of special urgency as large numbers of Palestinians look to the established regimes—rather than the revolutionary organization—to help them fulfill their aspirations. What is important . . . is that the U.S. Government be in a position to sustain its lead in moving all parties to this dispute towards a negotiated settlement. . . . (House Report 94–53 1975, 32).

In retrospect, this more ambitious goal has not been realized. Nonetheless, it has remained in the consciousness of U.S. officials involved in the program, and seems to have led over time to certain subtle changes in the content and public image of the program. The first indication of such change appeared in a Congressional committee statement in connection with fiscal year 1977 aid legislation that perhaps for the first time placed special emphasis on the direct U.S.-Palestinian character of the assistance:

> The Committee believes that the activities and programs of American private voluntary agencies . . . should continue to be supported and that the *bilateral American-Arab character of the program* (emphasis added) be maintained. These modest assistance programs . . . serve long-term American interests and provide a logical and appropriate channel for providing assistance to the Arabs living in the West Bank and Gaza (House Report 95–274 1977, 21).

The following year the program in the West Bank and Gaza was formally removed from the Middle East Special Requirements Fund (an ad hoc arrangement) and placed in the regular security assistance portion of the foreign aid legislation. In the words of the House subcommittee, the program "is now considered to be a continuing requirement for which economic assistance can be planned." The subcommittee went on to express the hope that PVO activities would be increased and that "new development projects [would] be focused specifically on development needs in the West Bank and Gaza during a transition phase in the peace process" (Hearings February/March 1978, XIII).

Noteworthy, in addition to the inclusion of the program in the regular annual aid legislation, is the emphasis on the "development needs" of the territories, which has since become a major theme in the U.S. approach. Secretary of State George P. Shultz and former Undersecretary of State Lawrence S. Eagleburger in more recent days added to this formulation a concern with the "quality of life" in the territories. Eagleburger, in an address in January 1984, expressed U.S. policy in these terms:

If the acceptance by the Palestinians of the West Bank and Gaza of a peaceful future is to be nurtured, they must be given a stake in the future by greater opportunities for economic development, fairer administrative practices, and greater concern for the quality of their life (quoted in Benvenisti 1984, 1).

Thus, current U.S. assistance policy in the territories may be seen as favoring (a) direct U.S. contacts with the Palestinians through the PVOs; (b) economic development; and (c) improved quality of life. A comparison of these elements with those first enunciated when the program was born reveals similarities as well as significant differences. The direct U.S.-Palestinian link remains a constant theme, albeit with increased emphasis on economic development and the addition of the catch-all "quality of life" element. The latter in particular adds a new dimension that seems to transcend the socioeconomic sphere.

In summarizing, it is important to note that the development program whose evolution and political linkages has been described above is only one of three U.S. bilateral assistance efforts on the West Bank and Gaza. The others, of lesser political significance, are the Food-for-Peace program (PL 480, Title II) which, as mentioned previously, pre-dates the Israeli occupation; and the American Schools and Hospitals Abroad program. Together these three U.S.-funded programs have constituted an American presence that, though relatively small in monetary terms, has nevertheless been felt and noted.

Politics and Cooperation in U.S. Assistance

Total U.S. contributions to the three above-mentioned programs over the past ten years have amounted to about $75 million. On a scale of the degree of politicization, it may be said that the socioeconomic development program has been the most politicized and the food distribution program the least politicized, with the schools and hospitals program somewhere in the middle. This appears logical at first glance, considering that socioeconomic development and school assistance touch on clearly recognizable political issues in the territories, whereas food distribution evokes more of a humanitarian image. However, as will be seen shortly, the food distribution program has consistently contained a significant economic development element as well. The fact that this element has been accepted without causing political controversy suggests that the attitude of the particular PVO involved may have some bearing on the matter.

The dimensions and distribution of funds among the three programs can be seen in Table 5.1.

Table 5.1
U.S. Government Assistance to the West Bank and Gaza (in $ millions)

Program	1975	1976	1977	1978	1979	1980	1981	1982	1983	1984	Total
Socioeconomic Development (MESRF-ESF)	1.0	1.6	3.4	2.8	6.8	3.0	2.5	6.0	6.5	8.5	42.1
Food-for-Peace PL 480 Title II ($ equivalent of food)	8.7*	1.8	1.7	1.2	1.8	3.5	3.7	2.7	1.9	2.3	29.3
American Schools and Hospitals Abroad					1.5		0.8			1.0	3.3
Total	9.7	3.4	5.1	4.0	10.1	6.5	7.0	8.7	8.4	11.8	74.7

*This figure suggests a considerably larger than average food distribution program for the year 1975. No satisfactory explanation for this possibility has been advanced; it may be that the figure given is incorrect.

Source: U.S. Agency for International Development, Washington, D.C., 1984 (compiled from various sources)

Table 5.2
Food Relief Programs, Fiscal Year 1983

Activity	No. of Recipients
Maternal and Child Health	35,000
Regular School Feeding	4,600
Preschool Feeding	7,300
Other Child Feeding (Institutions)	10,100
Food for Work (Vocational Training and Demonstration Farms)	16,100
General Relief	33,200
Total Recipients	106,300

Source: "AID-Supported Programs in West Bank and Gaza," AID/Washington, Attachment 3, PIO/T No. 298-0150-3-624701, Sept. 1983, p. 4.

Food-for-Peace Grants

This is by far the oldest continuing U.S. program on the West Bank and in Gaza. In the past, as mentioned previously, it was administered by several private voluntary organizations, notably the Catholic Relief Services (CRS); the Mennonite Central Committee (MCC); the Lutheran World Federation (LWF); and the Cooperative for American Relief Everywhere (CARE). All of these agencies, except for CRS, have been gradually phased out of the program. Nonetheless, its size appears to have been fairly stable over the past ten years, numbering between 130,000–160,000 recipients per year until 1983, when the Sinai component of the Gaza program (24,100 recipients in 1983) was transferred to CARE/Egypt. The commodities currently included in the food grant program are flour, rice, oil, wheat soya blend, corn soya milk, bulgur, and non-fat dry milk. In fiscal year 1983 these commodities were distributed as follows:

Table 5.2 shows, inter alia, that in fiscal year 1983, nearly a third of the food recipients were welfare cases, while only about 15 percent were participants in development-oriented Food-for-Work programs. These figures, however, must be seen in the context of earlier years, when the social welfare character of the program was much more pronounced. In the period immediately after the Six Day War, for example, almost all of the 120,000 recipients in the Gaza Strip alone were defined as "needy" or "emergency feeding" cases (AID report on CARE 1967–1968, 3–4). The Israeli government subsequently conducted a census of aid recipients in the occupied territories that eliminated much abuse and duplication. At the same time CARE and CRS, the principal PVOs involved, were encouraged by AID/Washington as well as the Israeli government to place greater emphasis on economic rather than welfare programs. As a result of these dual initiatives, the character of the program changed, and became oriented more towards economic development and vocational training.

CARE put into operation an extensive Food-for-Work program that at one point accounted for a major share of the total CARE effort. This program enabled men and women to participate in vocational training courses, and also provided compensation for agricultural workers taking part in demonstration projects designed to introduce new crops or agricultural techniques. The balance of the food went to improving the nutritional status of women and children attending mother and child health clinics; the provision of hot meals at child care institutions, day care centers and elementary schools; and relief of needy persons.

The food program of the Catholic Relief Services has in the past been considerably smaller than the CARE effort, for it did not include the Gaza Strip or any Food-for-Work projects. In fiscal year 1982, for example, CRS provided food to 51,600 recipients on the West Bank, while CARE had 80,300 recipients (U.S. Embassy Paper 1983–1984). As of June 30, 1984, CARE terminated its program, leaving CRS as the only agency responsible for the official U.S. food distribution program. Although CRS has taken over part of the CARE program, the fiscal year 1985 program estimate made available to this researcher called for a 14 percent reduction in the total number of recipients in the West Bank and Gaza.

Most of CRS food distribution in the past was in support of a continuing nutrition and health education project funded by AID from its socioeconomic development program. This project is directed at training mothers and the staffs of private village health centers in nutrition, home first aid, and child development. The promise of supplementary food rations (supplied from the Food-for-Peace program) for pregnant or lactating mothers and their youngest child has served as an incentive and has thus far reportedly drawn more than 20,000 mothers from 111 West Bank villages to attend the six-month training courses. While this project has been carried on outside the Food-for-Work framework, it has clearly furthered socioeconomic development goals as well.

CRS also intends to take over a part of CARE's Food-for-Work program, under which some 4,000 workers are being trained in carpentry, mechanics, lathe operation, sewing, and knitting. Thus, while the number of beneficiaries seems to be declining somewhat with the departure of CARE, the program as such continues to reach some 100,000 persons on the West Bank and in Gaza, and provides an incentive for important health and development activities. Accordingly, the program is a significant component of U.S. assistance to the territories, and is likely to remain so.

Another aspect relevant to this inquiry is the role played by the Israeli government with regard to the food distribution program. There is every indication that Israel has favored this program in the past, and continues to do so. According to the terms of U.S. legislation, governments of recipient countries incur obligations for inland transportation, customs clearance, and warehousing of the commodities. In this case, the Israel Ministry of Labor and Social Welfare has assumed the obligation, as well as funding other local costs. The ministry has also made its own contributions to parts of the food program. In 1982, for example, it contributed 480 metric tons of flour, milk, and rice valued at $200,000 to the CRS food program, with the U.S. government contribution totaling 1,986.8 metric tons valued at $1,073,480 (CRS Jerusalem/West Bank Annual Public Summary of Activities 1982, 2).

The Israeli government apparently plays a role as well both in Food-for-Work projects and in determining the eligibility of welfare recipients. The latter is based on lists made available by the Israel Ministry of Labor and Social Welfare, which also supervises distribution of the food; Food-for-Work projects are as a rule coordinated with the Ministry of Labor and Social Welfare in the case of vocational training projects, or with local agricultural officers in the case of rural development projects. In 1984, for example, 25 percent of the food recipients in CARE's West Bank program were farmers who had agreed to participate in demonstration projects supervised by officers of Israel's agricultural extension service. The projects included the use of spray insecticides, grafting, improved livestock, herd inoculation, terracing, and land reclamation. This program, for reasons not immediately apparent, is not being continued with CARE's departure from the scene. However, CRS is initiating a Food-for-Work program of its own in coordination with the Ministry of Labor and Social Welfare and private charitable organizations on the West Bank. Under the program, some 11,000 workers and dependents will receive food rations while the workers attend various vocational training courses lasting up to ten months.

What is interesting in all the Food-for-Peace activites in the territories is the apparently successful application of a trilateral pattern of participation involving the Israeli government, American PVOs, and local Palestinian organizations.

American Schools and Hospitals Abroad

This grant program has thus far benefited two West Bank projects located in Bethlehem: the Mount of David Crippled Children's Hospital, and the planned construction of a new building for Bethlehem University.

The new children's orthopedic hospital opened its doors in 1983, and treats an estimated 1,300–1,500 patients a month on an in-patient and out-patient basis. AID made two grants totalling $2.25 million (44 percent of costs) towards the hospital's construction and purchasing of equipment during fiscal years 1979 through 1981, inclusive. According to knowledgeable officials, the hospital enjoys good relations with the Israel Ministry of Labor and Social Affairs, government-supported hospitals in the occupied territories, and Jewish hospitals in Israel. The sponsor of the hospital is the Holy Land Christian Mission International (HLCM), a Kansas City-based organization founded in 1936 that also conducts other charitable and educational activities in the occupied territories and in nine other countries (Holy Land Christian Mission International publication 1984).

Bethlehem University is an institution established in 1973 that enjoys financial and political support from the Vatican and Christian groups in the United States and western Europe, as well as from Arab sources. The $1 million grant made available by AID in fiscal year 1984 through the U.S.-based Brothers of the Christian Schools will finance one third of the cost of construction for a multipurpose academic building. The university has 1,200 full-time and 250 part-time students, and has been operating in crowded, partly makeshift quarters. Israeli authorities apparently delayed issuance of a building permit for some time, but were finally persuaded to do so because the broad-based sponsorship of the project included a number of countries friendly to Israel.

Socioeconomic Development Grants

This program is central to any assessment of U.S. policy towards the West Bank and Gaza, for as shown previously, its origins, rationale, and legislative history are closely linked to U.S. policy goals in the area. Because of this fact, the program assumes an importance quite out of proportion to the actual amounts of aid provided. (During several fiscal years, the food distribution program actually distributed more in dollar terms.) Nonetheless, the political significance of the socioeconomic program has been perceived by all three of the most directly interested parties—the Palestinians, the Israeli government and the U.S. government.

Knowledgeable Palestinians have come to regard the program as a bellwether of U.S. interest and involvement in the administered territories. Thus the East Jerusalem weekly *Al Fajr* featured a recent article (March 14, 1984) on the subject under the headline: "U.S. Aid in the West Bank: A Trickle for Development—American Money: Short Carrots Leading to the Promotion of U.S. Policy, or Humanitarian Aid for the Long-Term Improvement of the 'Quality of Life'. . . ." The late former mayor of Hebron, Fahd Qawasmeh, was even more outspoken when he commented on a visit to Washington, D.C. in 1979: "What we get from America is like giving a dying person aspirin. The West Bank gets only $3 million from the United States. The Israelis get $3 billion" (MERIP Reports, No. 83, 7). Elias Freij, the mayor of Bethlehem who is known as a moderate, put it perhaps more elegantly during his visit to Washington in March 1984, when he reportedly urged the administration to provide increased and direct assistance to the West Bank and Gaza without the intermediation of U.S. voluntary agencies (*Jerusalem Post*, March 30, 1984). The Palestinian position on the program can thus be paraphrased as follows: we need more, and we need it without strings attached.

The Israeli position, not surprisingly, is quite different. While the government early on endorsed the idea of U.S. economic assistance to the West Bank and Gaza, it also indicated, according to a U.S. General Accounting Office report, that Israel preferred to run the program itself (GAO Report July 7, 1978, 17). While this probably remains Israel's preference, Israel has accepted a much more loosely structured arrangement of participation and supervision. Nevertheless, the question of control remains a permanent Israeli concern, from time to time flaring up as a source of friction between the U.S. and Israeli governments and between Israeli officials and the voluntary agencies implementing the program—as well as with the program's purported beneficiaries, the Palestinians. Symptomatic of this concern for control is an article appearing in *Ha'aretz* on December 1, 1979 that reported on a growing disquietude among a number of high-level government officials at the "escalating" scale of U.S. activities in the territories. According to the article, U.S. activities were sometimes accompanied by anti-Israeli propaganda; they also encompassed

> various programs (in) the province of planning, which is supposed to be in the hands of the sovereign power and not in those of private voluntary organizations or foreign consulates . . . educational and propaganda activities have been on the upswing. The number of scholarships has increased, the number of American delegates of unknown identity has increased as well. . . . Tenders have been opened by American organizations for the establishment of a large-scale factory, supported by the springs of Ein Farah, for four villages in the Jerusalem vicinity and for the establishment of a trade center at Halhul. . . . We are talking here of welfare and relief activities which are in fact delineating a separate master plan in place of a joint plan with Israel. . . .

Benyamin Ben Eliezer, a former head of the Israeli Administration in the territories, put Israel's position more bluntly a few years later when he told *The New York Times*, "No voluntary organization has the autonomy to do whatever it pleases in this part of the world. Here on the West Bank there is law, order and administration. We know exactly who is who, who needs what, and to whom to render assistance" (quoted in *Ha'aretz*, April 13, 1984).

This rather hardline Israeli assertion of control can be traced to a combination of circumstances and motives, which might be summarized as (a) security; (b) politics; and (c) economics.

Security. As the occupying power, Israel has a clear and legitimate concern for security. Projects that could either directly undermine security in the territories or pose an indirect threat by inciting hostility against Israel or creating an anti-Israel power base are thus clearly suspect. The question, of course, is where legitimate considerations of security end, and oppression begins. The Israeli administration has taken the view that it does not need to justify its actions, and that a decision to reject a project on security grounds requires no further explanation.

Politics. More complicated is the political concern, which holds that U.S. assistance should not be used to prepare, create, or strengthen existing or potential centers of Palestinian political power likely to be hostile to Israel. This concern must be seen against the background of Israel's unwillingness—or inability so far—to create a pro-Israeli political force in the territories. Hopes for the emergence of such a force from the municipal elections of 1976 or later on from the framework of village leagues set up with Israeli support were both dashed, leaving the Israeli policymakers without an indigenous framework on which to base their occupation policy. The result, insofar as it related to the U.S. assistance program, has been for Israeli administrators to suspect hostile political motives behind many proposed projects that in other countries would go unquestioned. Israeli administrators seem to be particularly sensitive when it comes to the establishment or strengthening of cooperatives; according to one PVO source, only two cooperative projects out of more than a dozen submitted over a two-year period (1982–1984) were approved for implementation. Israeli officials deny any political bias against cooperatives, but are clearly opposed to projects they believe would strengthen their political enemies in the territories. In this regard it is important to note that a number of Palestinians who have been barred from engaging in political activities have reportedly come to look upon the cooperative movement as a potential alternative power base and a way of expressing their Palestinian identity.

In the absence of more clearly defined policy guidelines, the normal tendency of the Israeli bureaucracy has been to err on the side of caution and restrictiveness. Moreover, approval and disapproval of projects has also become a tool in the incessant political maneuvering taking place in the territories. The PVOs, well aware of the political ramifications of their work, have learned to operate and survive within this seemingly byzantine environment.

Economics. The economic concern arises from the fact that the Israeli administration views itself as both the political authority in the territories and as the entity responsible for all aspects of economic policy, planning, and development activity. The thrust of the Israeli approach is reflected in a recent pamphlet issued by the Israeli administration:

> The Israeli administration . . . has aimed . . . at encouraging solutions to practical problems and making further advances possible . . . . The complete opening of the borders between the areas and Israel removed an artificial barrier that had needlessly stymied economic growth and social progress for 19 years. Since then, Israeli policies—including the "Open Bridges" with Jordan—financial aid and expertise have helped stimulate unprecedented economic and social progress in the areas . . . (Israel Ministry of Defense November 1983, 1–2).

Following this somewhat paternalistic approach, the Israeli administration asserts its responsiblity to assess each proposed activity from the standpoint of economic viability. U.S. officials and thoughtful Palestinians have urged that Palestinians be permitted to make their own mistakes if need be, but with little success.

Another criterion for economic decision-making by the Israeli administration is compatibility with the notion of the territories and Israel as a single economic unit. Thus, project proposals have sometimes apparently been turned down for two totally contrary reasons: either because they could *not* compete with more efficient Israeli production; or because they *were potentially competitive* with Israeli production. In both instances, it was thought, the proposals violated the notion of a single economic unit.

Other Israeli economic decisions have been connected to the continuing political struggle. The rejection of a number of project proposals concerned with land reclamation, water development, electrification, manpower training, and industrial development, for example, have been rightly or wrongly attributed to the Israeli desire to keep the territories both in economic subjection and open to Israeli colonization.

The combination of security, political, and economic concerns that operate in the approval process presents formidable obstacles to the execution of a rational and well-integrated program of assistance. Distortions that have taken place in a large part of the program as planned by the PVOs were recently highlighted in a study of three of the five major voluntary organizations responsible for carrying out U.S. government-financed activities in the territories. The study showed, for example, that between 1977–1983, only 35 percent of project proposals in the field of agriculture were approved, (88 percent of approvals involving proposals to upgrade drinking water and sewage treatment). In the area of social and community services, 57 percent of the proposals were approved. The lowest percentage of approvals (23 percent) was in industry, while the highest (100 percent) was in food distribution (Benvenisti 1984, Table 8). Before attempting to interpret this data, however, it is necessary to examine in somewhat greater depth both the role and functions of the American PVOs responsible for the administration of the socioeconomic development program, and the Israeli officialdom involved.

The Role of U.S. Private Voluntary Organizations

As noted earlier, a number of American-sponsored PVOs were active on the West Bank and in Gaza prior to the Six Day War, largely in welfare activities involving the distribution of U.S. food commodities. When Israel took charge of the administration of the territories, it requested these agencies to continue their work under the same conditions as had prevailed under Jordanian and Egyptian administration (see the chapter by Levine in Elazar 1982). Since 1967, additional voluntary agencies from the United States and other countries have launched programs in the territories. Their focus was initially welfare-oriented, linked many times to local charitable or welfare organizations or agencies. In accordance with the spirit of Jordanian law that still governs much administrative practice on the West Bank, the Israel Ministry of Labor and Social Welfare was granted supervisory responsibility. It appears that as long as the agencies' activities were small-scale and welfare-oriented, supervision and interference by the Israeli authorities was minimal.

Even the new U.S. government initiative by way of the Middle East Special Requirements Fund (MESRF) began in 1975 with a mere $1 million and, as a consequence, seems at first to have caused barely a ripple. The change occurred only a year or two later with the increased size of the funds available, the entry of additional PVOs upon the scene, and a simultaneous reorientation of program goals on the part of some of the voluntary organizations. It seems apparent that the U.S. initiative was seen by the PVOs as a sign of increased American interest that could lead to increased funding. Since 1977, six U.S. voluntary organizations have been involved in carrying out U.S. government-financed assistance programs: CARE, the Catholic Relief Services (CRS), the Holy Land Christian Mission (HLCM), Save the Children/Community Development Foundation (CDF), the America-Mideast Education & Training Services (AMIDEAST), and the American Near East Refugee Aid (ANERA). The distribution and disbursement of AID funds among these PVOs can be seen from the table below.

Among other things, the tables show that CRS and ANERA were the first PVOs to take advantage of the newly available funds in 1975. In monetary terms, however, it is AMIDEAST—the last of the PVOs to join the program—which has for some time been receiving the largest allocation of AID funds. AMIDEAST also appears to have the largest pipeline of unexpended funds—2.8 million (28 percent) as of the end of 1983; the pipeline of most of the other agencies being well under 20 percent. The following brief summary and analysis of the operations of the PVOs elucidates some of the differences between them, and the implications thereof.

CARE

Known for its worldwide feeding and relief activities, CARE operated on the West Bank and in Gaza even before the Six Day War, continuing its activities after the war in cooperation with the Israeli authorities. The CARE program involved only Food-for-Peace commodities, which were used in part for outright relief to indigent persons and in part as incentive for economic and social development programs. As noted earlier, the latter activities principally involved vocational training, maternal and child health instruction, and agricultural development. In all cases the programs were designed and carried out in close collaboration with local government authorites, with the Ministry of Labor and Social Welfare providing central liaison when necessary. The agricultural development activities already described were as a rule also planned in consultation with the local farmers who were the direct beneficiaries. Perhaps because of this "bottom-up" approach, CARE programs were not subject to the Israeli central approval process, and thus experienced none of the difficulties encountered by other PVOs. During fiscal year 1984 alone, more than 8,000 farmers on the West Bank were scheduled to receive CARE food rations in return for participating in demonstration projects supervised by local agricultural extension officers.

Catholic Relief Services (CRS)

Of the six PVOs operating with U.S. government funds, CRS is the only one that uses both PL 480 food commodities and economic support funds. Since CRS has absorbed much of the CARE feeding program, its current fiscal year 1985 feeding program provides for approximately 100,000 recipients at an equivalent cost of about $2.5 million. Of the

Table 5.3
AID Funded Programs of U.S. Private Voluntary Organizations*
in the West Bank/Gaza: Obligations and Expenditures (in $ Thousands)
as of December 31, 1983

PVO/Project Title	FY	Obligated	Expended	Unexpended
AMIDEAST—Human Resource Development	1978	1.084	1.084	-
	1979	.998		
	1980	1.091	3.604 (for years 1979–1981)	-
	1981	1.515		
	1982	2.203	2.203	-
	1983	2.990	.163	2.827
AMIDEAST Subtotal		9.881	7.054	2.827
ANERA—Development Assistance	1975	.576	.576	-
	1976	.571	.571	-
	1977	.902	.902	-
	1978	1.259	1.259	-
	1979	2.100	2.100	
	1980	1.509		
	1981	.140	1.225 (for years 1980, 1982)	.597
	1982	.173		-
	1983	.544	-	.544
ANERA Subtotal		7.774	6.633	1.141
CRS—Rural Development I	1975	.142	.142	-
	1976	.501	.501	-
Socioeconomic Development	1976	.500	.500	-
Bethlehem University Science Wing	1977	1.100	1.100	-
Nutrition Education	1975	.282	.282	-
	1978	.094	.094	-

Table 5.3 Cont.

PVO/Project Title	FY	Obligated	Expended	Unexpended
Nutrition Education	1975	.282	.282	-
	1978	.094	.094	-
Rural Development II	1979	1.581	1.581	-
	1982	.573	.006	.567
Health Education	1979	.742	.742	-
	1982	.552	.552	-
	1983	.530	.015	.515
CRS Subtotal**		6.597	5.515	1.082
CDF—Community Development	1977	.712	.712	-
	1979	1.200	1.200	-
	1980	.400	.400	-
	1981	.801	.801	-
	1982	2.284	2.284	-
	1983	2.170	.346	1.824
CDF Subtotal		7.567	5.743	1.824
HLCM—Crippled Children's Hospital	1977	.702	.702	-
	1978	.250	.250	-
Preschool Education	1979	.180		
	1981	.044	.224 (for years 1979–1981)	
	1982	.215	.188	.027
	1983	.266	-	.266
HLCM Subtotal***		1.657	1.364	.293
Grand Total		33.476	26.309	7.167

*Not including Food-for-Peace distributions (PL 480) or funds obligated under the American Schools and Hospitals Abroad (ASHA) program.
**Also distributed in addition about $4.8 million worth of Food-for-Peace commodities.
***Also received $2.25 million American Schools and Hospitals Abroad grant.

Source: U.S. Agency for International Development, Washington, D.C., 1984.

recipients, some 75 percent are on the West Bank and 25 percent in the Gaza Strip. CRS uses some of the food commodities in conjunction with village training courses financed from economic support fund appropriations. These courses are designed for teachers and mothers and include nutrition, first aid, child development, and hygiene. Between 1979–1984, some 20,000 women completed these courses, which have been organized in cooperation with the local Union of Charitable Societies, an umbrella organization of 94 local Palestinian groups. The project reportedly covers 111 out of 430 West Bank villages, with 200 additional villages on the waiting list. Unlike the CARE program, the CRS village health education project operates without reference to the government health services. This situation does not seem to have provided an obstacle to its execution—though one might question the efficiency of the approach.

Since 1975, CRS has also been carrying out a rural development project that is designed to introduce such essential improvements into village infrastructures as improved access roads, electrification, water systems, community centers, clinics, and schools. The projects, usually small, stress the self-help principle and normally require at least a 30 percent participation in the cost by the villagers themselves. They are developed jointly by CRS staff and local communities, after which they are submitted to the Ministry of Labor and Social Welfare for approval. Implementation is monitored by a village committee that also includes representation from CRS, the ministry, and the local government administration. As of the end of fiscal year 1983, 67 projects had been completed and 27 were being implemented at a total cost of 3.3 million. No difficulties (except occasional delays) were reported in obtaining approval for subprojects by the Israeli authorities, although according to Table 5.3, disbursements slowed considerably in 1982 when the project was extended for two additional years. The previously cited Benvenisti report lists a 3.5 percent disapproval rate for CRS (Benvenisti 1984, Table 2), but CRS officials questioned "didn't know" of any projects that had been disapproved. Questions or problems are handled through a dialogue between CRS staff and the Ministry of Labor and Social Welfare, or during implementation through the implementation committee.

Although CRS prefers to concentrate on small, community-oriented projects, it has also served as a channel for AID support for the construction and furnishing of a new science wing at Bethlehem University. This project was implemented in 1977 with a contribution of $1.1 million from AID.

Holy Land Christian Mission (HLCM)

The smallest of the PVO programs, HLCM has received some $3.2 million from AID towards the construction and equipping of the Mount David Crippled Children's Hospital in Bethlehem, the equipping of satellite clinics in Nablus and Hebron, the training of medical personnel, and the upgrading of hospital services. The 73-bed modern specialized hospital facility primarily serves the population of the occupied territories.

Since 1977, HLCM has also received approximately $700,000 from AID to provide preschool education and mother and teacher training in six Palestinian refugee camps. This project covers an area of concern that is reportedly not served by the UN Relief and Work Agency (UNRWA) or other public agencies; it also includes the preparation and publication of a curriculum for preschool education, developed with assistance from U.S. volunteer experts. Some 800 children, mothers, and teachers appear to be benefitting from the project at any one time. Although the Israeli authorities are aware of the project, there appears to have been little supervision and no interference on the part of the authorities.

America-Mideast Educational & Training Services (AMIDEAST)

Although the last of the PVOs to join the U.S. government-funded program on the West Bank and in Gaza, AMIDEAST's association with the area goes back to 1951, when as the American Friends of the Middle East (AFME), it became active as a pro-Arab lobbying organization. More recently, AMIDEAST has concentrated on human resource development, principally on academic exchange programs under which students and faculty from Arab countries come to the United States for study. AMIDEAST's participation in the AID-funded program for the occupied territories began in 1978 with a $1 million grant, which by the end of 1983 had tripled in size (see Table 5.3). The initiative for AMIDEAST's participation reportedly came from AID.

The core of AMIDEAST's program is the support of the three major Arab universities in the territories—Bir Zeit University near Ramallah, An Najah University in Nablus, and Bethlehem University. The project finances the upgrading of faculty levels by offering scholarships for higher degree study in the United States, as well as providing scholarship assistance to undergraduates at these universities.

As of the end of 1983, a total of 63 faculty members had completed advanced degrees in the United States under this program and had returned to their teaching positions; 125 others were still studying in the United States (AMIDEAST Annual Report 1983, 14). The dropout rate has been estimated at 5–10 percent. The importance of this activity can be gauged from the fact that it appears to cover more than one third of all faculty members at the three universities.

AMIDEAST's undergraduate scholarship program amounted to $270,000 in 1983 and during that year provided full or partial scholarships to 194 students at the three universities. The institutions have had considerable flexibility both in selecting the scholarship students and determining whether to provide full or partial scholarships. Thus, while this project cannot be expected to have a major impact on a combined student body of some 6,000, it does strengthen the university authorities, by offering them the possibility of channeling scholarship assistance into priority areas. Whether this is in fact being done is not clear. It is also uncertain what proportion of graduates are able to find employment in the territories, though a recent article by Hillel Frisch (*Jerusalem Post* May 23, 1984) reported on growing numbers of graduates without a corresponding growth in job opportunities.

The last sub-project funded under the MIDEAST program provides between 15–20 short-term vocational or professional training visits annually, primarily to the United States. The recipients are nominated by the Palestinian universities, municipalities, U.S. government sources, or voluntary organizations. After a protest by the Israeli authorities several employees of government agencies in the territories have also been included. The professions of the trainees cover a wide range, from mental retardation and library science to mathematics, engineering, and food processing.

Shortly after the AMIDEAST project began, it was agreed with AID that an education sector assessment study should be undertaken. Soundings that were taken with Israeli authorities and local educators and institutions encouraged AMIDEAST to proceed with the project. However, when the study was actually undertaken in 1979, a number of difficulties developed that affected both its quality and usefulness. These problems were summarized in an AID evaluation report as follows:

1. In the Territories, there is no "host country" in the common usage of the term.
2. Although AMIDEAST had been assured by the Israeli authorities of their willingness to allow survey research to be carried out, in fact the Ministry of Labor and Social Affairs (sic) not only did nothing to assist the survey, but on several occasions impeded the researchers' efforts.
3. The three West Bank universities were unable to participate actively in the sector assessment because they could not spare existing trained faculty members or take time to train undergraduates to work in data collection. Moreover, they were reluctant to involve themselves in a

process that would require their asking approval of the Military Government.

4. Most disappointingly, the hoped-for cooperation with the Council for Higher Education never materialized. Not only was the Council lacking in effective organization and the ability to address itself to the questions raised in an educational sector assessment . . . but it functioned as much as a political forum as an educational planning body.

5. Finally, AMIDEAST tried to carry out the sector assessment before having established its acceptability among the individuals and institutions with which it was trying to work . . . (AID report on AMIDEAST 1981, 11–12).

The assessment study itself notes, inter alia, that AMIDEAST was informed by a Ministry of Labor and Social Welfare official that "AMIDEAST and its researchers were not to solicit information from any source in the Territories: government, private or international." It also concludes that, "the most immediate and important observation arising out of the sector assessment is that, indeed, education and most other basic human activities in the West Bank and Gaza are highly politicized" (AMIDEAST Assessment of Education in the West Bank and Gaza Strip July 1979, V and VII).

The tensions and conflicts noted here afflicted not only this particular project, but can be discerned as well in other AMIDEAST activities—whether in the agency's reluctance to include local government employees in the short-term training program lest this stain the program with a "collaborationist" label; in occasional delays by Israeli authorities in granting exit permits for study in the United States (sometimes reportedly for six to eight months); and in persistent Israeli demands to submit all elements of the program to their scrutiny.

Perhaps more important than the political problems in the long run is the question of whether the AMIDEAST project as now conceived is responsive to the present educational reality in the territories. There seems to be no indication thus far that AMIDEAST is preparing to deal with the problem of overproduction of graduates (particularly in the arts) from West Bank universities.

Community Development Foundation (CDF)

CDF is the only PVO that simultaneously maintains a program in the territories and in Israel. (The program in Israel is known as "Save the Children.") Its representatives point to the existence of these two programs as proof of CDF's "impartiality," but they are also quick to stress that there is no connection whatsoever between them in terms of funding, personnel, or policy. The purpose of their program in the territories, they emphasize, is to "assist and encourage local community groups in the selection, planning, implementation and evaluation of projects which improve the social and economic conditions of *their* (emphasis added) communities" (CDF Background Sheet October 20, 1983). Hence it is CDF's relation to the local community and the community's priorities that are the primary determinants for programming decisions of the agency.

Within this general framework, CDF has between 1977 and 1983 carried out a program totaling about $7.5 million in AID funds, matched in many cases by up to 50 percent of funds from "other sources." These could be locally raised resources, or contributions from Arab sources outside the territories. CDF does not inquire into the origins of the matching funds, but Israeli authorities reportedly sometimes disapprove or delay project proposals because of the origins of the funds. Nevertheless, the recent Benvenisti study reports a disapproval rate of only 18.4 percent for CDF, most of it in agriculture or water projects (Benvenisti 1984, Table 10). The reasons for disapprovals or delays of particular projects are often difficult to discover, since Israeli authorities, as previously noted, are under no obligation to provide the reasons or background for their decisions. A case in point is a CDF proposal for the improvement of preschool education submitted to the Israeli authorities in August 1983. Although experts on various sides of the political spectrum seemed agreed on the need for the activity, it took eight months until approval was finally granted.

The CDF program concentrates about half of its resources on community water, health, and sanitation projects, and the bulk of the remainder on rural community development, preferably cooperative and self-help projects, including farm-to-market roads, land reclamation, olive seedling distribution, maintenance of terraces, small agricultural or agro-industry enterprises, rural electrification, etc. A small part of the program is also devoted to the advancement of preschool and special education—areas of development which are greatly underserved at the present time.

Although, as indicated above, most of the CDF project proposals are eventually approved by the Israeli authorities, the organization appears to have opted for a somewhat confrontational style. In its concern for the confidence of the Palestinian population and the integrity of its program, CDF seems to believe that it must limit both its contact with the Israeli authorites and the information it provides them to the barest minimum. In this connection it was pointed out to the writer that CDF had not complied with routine reporting requirements of the Israeli authorities. It also appears that in making project or design choices, CDF seems to prefer a refusal or a delay by the authorities to any stance that could be interpreted as "collaboration" or "pacification." This political orientation has undoubtedly had a negative effect on the shape of the CDF program and Israeli attitudes towards it. The question remains an open one whether by virtue of its style CDF has been able to deliver a more effective program than those of its sister agencies whose style of operations is less confrontational.

In spite of CDF's policy orientation, the Benvenisti report (p. 15) holds that Israeli manipulation of project approvals has forced an emphasis on "consumption-oriented public works projects . . . (that) reduce the budgetary burden on the Israeli government." While this may be partly true, it is equally possible that without CDF support, the many small rural infrastructure projects partly financed by it would not have come into being, thus reducing further the development potential of the territories.

American Near East Refugee Aid (ANERA)

The most controversial of the U.S. agencies operating with AID support in the territories is ANERA, which was founded in 1968 to provide assistance to "Palestinian refugees and other needy individuals in the Arab world; to contribute to the more rapid achievement of self-sufficiency by supporting economic and social development . . . , and to inform the American people about the plight of the Palestinians" (Wynta 1978, 45).

The use of code phrases such as "self-sufficiency" and "plight of the Palestinians" betrays the basically pro-Palestinian political orientation of the organization, but this was apparently no barrier to its early involvement in the AID-funded program on the part of either AID or the Israeli authorities. The first two years of ANERA's activities (1975–1976), involving grants of about $1 million to some 20 charitable Palestinian organizations and training institutions, appear to have been largely noncontroversial. The activities funded included for the most part the purchase of equipment, vocational training, and institutional improvements, and were apparently administered from ANERA's Washington, D.C. headquarters. The turning point seems to have been fiscal year 1977 (beginning on October 1, 1976), which saw the establishment— at Israeli insistence—of a Jerusalem office of ANERA, together with a near doubling of its AID funding. With encouragement from AID, the thrust of ANERA's program was redirected towards economic development activities that would more directly boost the productive capacity of the territories. At the same time, ANERA also began to give preference to cooperatives as the most suitable pattern for such development activities. In this respect both CDF and ANERA follow similar lines, but it is worth noting that ANERA seems to have made especially great efforts in support of cooperative development.

The report of a study tour of officials from the U.S. cooperative movement that visited the territories in 1984 concluded that there is a great potential for cooperative development in the territories. This report cited data showing that as of 1983, there were 227 active cooperatives on the West Bank and another 175 awaiting registration by Israeli authorities; during 1982–1983 only 27 applications for registration had been approved ("Palestinian Cooperatives . . . " 1984, 29–35). There is no doubt that both CDF and ANERA have experienced special difficulties in obtaining Israeli approval for their cooperative project proposals. Israeli officials have denied that they are especially opposed to cooperatives. However, it does not appear farfetched that—remembering their own history—they regard cooperatives not only as instruments of development but also as potential instruments of political action and mobilization. The previously cited study tour report of U.S. cooperative officials lends some unwitting support to this notion in its strongly pro-Palestinian report when it notes that

> cooperatives are clearly seen as economic instruments for the strengthening of the Palestinian Community . . . (they) are viewed as an expression of Palestinian economic self-determination. . . . Only recently have they become an expression of Palestinian identity ("Palestinian Cooperatives . . ." 1984, 2).

In examining the project proposals submitted by ANERA for approval by the Israeli authorities in fiscal year 1984, it is striking that seven out of ten proposals are for cooperatives. Given the known Israeli reluctance concerning cooperatives, it suggests that ANERA may be more interested in building up a record of refusals than in embarking on productive development initiatives.

ANERA has also not hesitiated to align itself publicly with the Palestinian community in controversies with the Israeli authorities. Thus when Mayor Rashad al Shawa of Gaza resigned in a dispute with Israeli authorities in 1980, ANERA withdrew its support of a $1.5 million municipal sewage water recycling project until compelled by Israeli counterpressure to continue. Even now ANERA has not yet implemented a companion project for rainwater conservation in Gaza that was approved by Israeli authorities in February 1982. Similarly, ANERA put in abeyance an approved project for a municipal slaughterhouse in the town of Al-Bireh after the Arab mayor had been replaced by an Israeli military officer.

As to the quality of ANERA's operations, an AID evaluation of ANERA's program for 1975–1979 noted that project purposes and analysis were too general to permit an assessment of achievement. It went on to say: "AID/Washington remains critical of the quality of economic analysis in ANERA proposals. At times, more advocacy than analysis creeps into the proposal." At the same time the report also details indications of success in various ANERA projects, praising the fact that "eighty-eight percent of assisted institutions are continuing activity without further contribution from ANERA." On the broader political goals of the program, the report concludes:

> The purpose of the AID West Bank Voluntary Agency program was to communicate to Palestinians in concrete ways that it is possible for the U.S. Government and people to remain sturdy, reliable allies of Israel and still be genuinely concerned about the welfare of the Palestinian people. On ability to communicate U.S. concern about their welfare to West Bank and Gazan people, ANERA has fulfilled the Congressional purpose . . . (AID report on ANERA 1981, 12, 18 and 19).

Retrospect and Prospect

The most striking aspect about the U.S. government-funded aid program on the West Bank and Gaza is the large number of interested parties involved, all of whom can influence both the character of the program and the implementation process. Unlike "normal" AID-PVO programs, this is the only one operating in an area under military occupation. As if that were not enough of a complication, it is also a program that spans the crosscurrents of U.S. policy in the Middle East and thus engages the often conflicting goals and interests of various protagonists in the Arab-Israeli conflict.

Happily, the controversies have by and large not touched the Food-for-Peace (PL 480) program, which has accounted for more than a third of total U.S. government assistance to the territories (see Table 5.1). It seems that in this sphere the goals of the U.S. government, the PVOs, the Israeli authorities, and the local Palestinian institutions or organizations have coincided sufficiently to allow coordinated planning and programming. The direct benefits for nutritional and health levels of children and other vulnerable groups have been significant, as has been the economic development stimulated over a number years by CARE's many Food-for-Work projects. However, precisely because of its non-controversial character, this part of the program goes largely unrecognized. The Benvenisti report does not even mention CARE as one of the PVOs that has operated in the territories. It also makes no effort to distinguish between welfare and production-oriented uses of food assistance, relegating all food assistance to welfare activities.

It is true of course that only in the economic assistance program are the differing objectives and agendas of the various parties more clearly discernible. We must therefore look to this program and its management in order to gauge the expectations and outcomes of the total U.S. government aid effort.

The U.S. Dilemma

The hope of "opening a door" to the Palestinians and thus enhancing the peace process under U.S. leadership—a hope lying at the core of Congressional and State Department thinking when the assistance program was initiated in 1975—has been frustrated by conflicting U.S. interests and concerns of the executing agencies. The initial grant of $1 million out of a total package of $100 million for Middle East "special requirements" already indicated the relatively low priority of the program in American thinking. When Israeli authorities began to raise questions about the operation two years after its outset, U.S. policymakers realized that they would have to weigh the goals of the West Bank and Gaza program against the larger complex of factors in the overall U.S.-Israeli relationship. The first result of this new perception was an agreement that all the PVOs involved in the AID program would have to have a resident representative, and that all projects required the approval of Israeli authorities.

Without particularly wishing or planning for it, the U.S. embassy in Tel Aviv and the consulate general in Jerusalem were cast in the role of protector of the program and of the PVOs executing it. A division of responsibility also emerged, with the former assuming jurisdiction over the Gaza program (previously administered from the U.S. Embassy in Cairo), and the latter over the program on the West Bank. While described by U.S. officials as merely a matter of convenience, this jurisdictional division serves to emphasize and promote the role of the Jerusalem consulate as the U.S. government's representation to the West Bank. However, since the consulate is not accredited to the Israeli government and maintains no official relations with it—an anomaly of another kind in this tangled web of fact and fiction—it cannot deal with Israeli occupation authorities on matters pertaining to the aid program. Thus the PVOs must rely on the embassy for intervention or liaison with the Israeli authorities while on other matters reporting to the consulate. Inevitably, there are differences of perspective, as one U.S. entity is oriented towards the Palestinian Arabs on the West Bank, and the other one towards the state and government of Israel. This difference is reinforced by the special status the State Department has granted to the consulate, which makes it independent of the Tel Aviv embassy.

At the core of the complex situation described above lies the basic dilemma of U.S. policy towards the Arab-Israel conflict—on the one hand seeking to strengthen U.S. influence with the Palestinians by supporting their aspirations for self-determination, and on the other hand not wishing to go too far in opposition to Israeli positions and beliefs. As a result, U.S. policy management for the AID program has pleased none of the parties concerned.

Palestinian Expectations and Realities

When the aid program was initiated, it may have appeared to Palestinian leaders on the West Bank and Gaza as an important new card in the evolving U.S. thrust to draw Egypt, Jordan, and the Palestinians into a U.S.-managed peace process with Israel. They could find support for this belief in the administration's previously cited testimony to Congress in support of the $100 million "special requirements" fund, which seemed to imply a fairly large-scale effort. Palestinian disappointment with the relatively small amounts actually made available—especially when viewed against the background of multibillion dollar assistance to Israel—is not hard to understand. "U.S. Aid in the West Bank: A Trickle for Development," is the way a nationalist Palestinian weekly appearing in Jerusalem (*Al Fajr* March 14, 1983) characterized it, while a similar reaction by West Bank Palestinian leader Fahd Qawasmeh has been cited earlier in this study.

In the atmosphere of mistrust and suspicion characterizing the situation in the territories, it is not surprising that the U.S. motives in launching the program have been questioned. An official U.S. evaluation of the program in 1978 reports that

when U.S. assistance began in 1975, several (Palestinian) institutions approached by the voluntary agencies were hesitant about participating. This reluctance has reportedly diminished and the voluntary agencies report that Palestinians are becoming more and more receptive to U.S. Government efforts on their behalf. Increases in aid through the Middle East Special Requirements Fund, along with actions on the political front, have caused Palestinians to think of the United States in more favorable terms (GAO Report July 7, 1978, 17).

Whatever reservations may still be present—and it would be naive to presume their total disappearance—the Palestinian partners of the PVOs seem to have reacted with characteristic pragmatism to the opportunities presented by the U.S. aid program. On the critical question of how to relate to the Israeli authorities, they appear to take their cue from whatever PVO controls the funds. More recently there has also been pressure from at least one local Palestinian organization to administer an AID-funded activity without the intermediation of an American PVO. If this were to become a more general pattern, it would undoubtedly represent a significant change in the policy, character, and leadership of the program.

Even now, however, the program has a significance for the Palestinians that goes beyond the relatively small amounts of funds made available, being seen by them as a symbol—albeit a small one—of U.S. political interest and economic commitment. Moreover, in the general setting of stagnation that has characterized the economic situation in the territories during the past few years, the availability of even $6–9 million a year for development purposes assumes some importance. This is all the more true since all the PVO programs except for the scholarships awarded by AMIDEAST require local contributions ranging from 30–50 percent. Thus the total economic activity generated by the program may be almost double the AID input.

The source of these local counterpart funds has sometimes added another element of complexity to an already complicated situation. It is well known that despite Israeli occupation of the West Bank, Jordan continues to exert influence in the area through innumerable links of family, institutions, politics, trade, and finance (see, for example, Frisch and Sandler 1984, 66–67). The joint PLO-Jordan Fund set up by the Baghdad Arab summit meeting of 1978 and financed by the oil-producing Arab states has reportedly had as much as $150 million a year at its disposal to support West Bank economic and social development (*Yediot Acharonot Weekly* April 30, 1982, 7). Little is known about the criteria, mode of operation, or size of the fund, and estimates of hundreds of millions of dollars are no doubt greatly exaggerated. It is known, however, that in the absence of organizational infrastructure and appraisal capability on the West Bank, the fund has at times furnished the Palestinian counterpart share for AID-financed projects, relying in its decisions on the AID feasibility criteria and the PVOs, reputed managerial capacity for assurance of prospects for success. The intervention and availability of the Jordan-PLO Fund has at times apparently eased the problem of finding counterpart funds for the AID program, but its uncertain operations and Israel's power of veto have diminished its utility. It has also been noted that the local community commitment so important for the success of small community-based development projects is not achieved when the local contribution is in effect another donation from an outside source.

In sum, the Palestinian attitude and relationship to the AID program reflect all the complexities inherent in this highly sensitive situation. It seems doubtful, however, that many Palestinians would share the Benvenisti report characterization of the program (p. 14) as a "pacifier" that serves to actually strengthen Israeli occupation, given the pragmatic orientation of many of those involved in the program and their recognition of the real needs being served by it.

PVOs—Program Executors or Policymakers?

The basic theory governing the operation of the PVOs within the framework of the U.S. foreign assistance program is that the U.S. government sets the policy and the PVOs carry it out. While this may work well in many countries, it is fraught with difficulties in the Palestinian context, where virtually every technical move also becomes a political decision, and where symbols often count for more than realities and needs.

In assessing the work of the six PVOs involved in the AID program, it is helpful to once again briefly sketch their background and general program goals. Two of them—ANERA and AMIDEAST—are solely oriented towards the Middle East and have a long record of support for the Palestinian cause. Two others—CRS and the Holy Land Christian Mission—are Catholic organizations with both a broad program base and a special relationship to the "Holy Land" that may reflect Vatican interests in the area. CARE and Save the Children/Community Development Foundation both have a broad program base with worldwide interests and no known special interest in the area.

Perhaps because of the unique political/administrative situation prevailing in territories in which there is no "host country," as well as the great political sensitivity of the program, the official U.S. policy and administrative apparatus has been only minimally involved. The PVOs have thus dealt not only with program execution, but also with what might be called "policy development." Certainly the thrust of the program appears to be as much the creation of the PVOs as of AID and the State Department.

To the outside observer looking at the composite of the program, the diversity of policy approaches used is surprising. As described earlier, two of the agencies (CARE and CRS) have chosen the path of cooperation with Israeli authorities and have apparently had no difficulties in getting their project proposals approved. Two others (ANERA and, to a smaller extent, CDF) seem to have chosen the path of confrontation and have experienced frequent long delays, as well as refusals of project proposals. Some of these proposals, however, may have been initially put forward in the knowledge that they would be rejected and thus fuel the struggle against the occupation or bolster the standing of the particular PVO with its Palestinian clients. The remaining two agencies (AMIDEAST and HLCM) appear to wish to avoid confrontation, but resent Israeli "interference" and have sometimes taken approaches that have led to friction with the Israeli authorities.

Thus it can hardly be said that there is a uniform and consistent U.S. policy implemented by the PVOs. Instead there appear to be several different policies, and it is not at all clear whether these are the policies of the U.S. government or of the particular PVOs. For instance, is it consonant with U.S. policy interests to continue support for expansion of higher education on the West Bank—especially in the arts which account for more than half the AMIDEAST scholarships—in the face of growing academic unemployment? Is the continuing strong preference of ANERA and CDF for cooperative production justifiable in light of the prevailing individualistic economic and cultural patterns of the region, the reportedly unimpressive record of accomplishment of cooperatives in the territories, their reputed politicization going back to the days of Jordanian rule, and Israel's persistent opposition? Is the ambivalent attitude of some of the PVOs towards the local professional government apparatus in the territories (e.g., in agricultural extension) consistent with the economic development goals of the program? It seems that these and other important questions of policy are ripe for a thorough review—not by the PVOs, but by the U.S. government.

As the program grows in size, the techniques for project development and implementation may also require a review. Specifically, it may be questioned whether preparation of feasibility studies should be an in-house responsibility of the PVO concerned or of a disinterested third party, as required in most AID programs. Similarly, it would seem that, given the sensitivity and complexity of this program, evaluations might be conducted more than once in three years as seems to be the present pattern, and might be carried out by investigators who have no connection with the program itself. Finally, Food-for-Work projects, or a combination involving both economic and food assistance, might be strengthened beyond their present limited scope.

The Israeli Quandary—Another Conflict of Interests

As has been pointed out earlier, Israeli policies towards the AID program have been governed by a variety of economic, security, and political considerations. If these have sometimes been ambiguous or contradictory, they reflect the absence of clear policy towards the Palestinian problem as a whole, and in particular towards the occupied territories. In such circumstances, bureaucracies—as, for instance, the Israeli bureaucracy responsible for the West Bank and Gaza—seek shelter in protecting the status quo, i.e., allowing as little change as possible while at the same time invoking the classic tactic of punishing enemies and rewarding friends. Except for the relatively brief period of 1967–1973 when economic and educational growth was encouraged, this has been the thrust of Israeli occupation policy. However, various extraneous elements have intervened to disturb this policy thrust, among them the U.S. government and its assistance program.

Israeli officials apparently did not anticipate the course the program would take when it was introduced in 1975, regarding the U.S. initiative as simply another version of the largely noncontroversial Food-for-Peace program. Thus, although they would have preferred to run the program themselves, they welcomed the additional U.S. assistance and during the first few years apparently paid little attention to it. Once they realized the anti-status quo orientation of the program and the pro-Palestinian sympathies of most of the PVOs involved, they set out to try to control it and limit its impact. But this held the potential of conflict with the United States—Israel's best friend and protector. Was it worth damaging this relationship for the sake of a few million dollars' worth of U.S. funds going to the territories?

The existing non-system and cat-and-mouse game that has characterized the relationship of the Israeli authorities to the program and its PVO implementers can be ascribed in large measure to these conflicting interests. As indicated earlier, the Israeli authorities introduced a complicated and cumbersome system for project submission and approval, invoking political and security, as well as economic, criteria. Both because of the diverse and sometimes conflicting goals and perceptions of the PVOs and the Israeli authorities and in the absence of basic trust between them, the information provided by the two sides and communication between them have often been inadequate. Israelis complain that proposed project submissions are too sketchy because of PVO attempts to hide their real purposes, while the PVOs point out that aside from unreasonable delays, refusals have frequently been given without explanation and without attempts to obtain clarification of dubious points.[3] When Israeli authorities in January 1984 introduced a new system of implementation reports, most of the PVOs balked, and the U.S. embassy intervened. Israeli authorities were unhappy about the matter, but in view of U.S. patronage of the agencies, were reluctant to take strong action against non-compliance.[4] From time to time Israeli frustration with the program has spilled over into the daily press, as in a recent *Ha'aretz* article by Tsvi Barel (April 13, 1984) that charged PVO-American consulate collaboration in an attempt to "lay the economic and administrative groundwork for the Palestinians, thus sowing the seeds for a Palestinian state."⁵ True or not, Israeli and U.S. agendas and approaches in the territories have been far from identical, and the U.S. assistance program has come to symbolize in some measure a continuing divergence between the two countries.

The economic stagnation in the territories during the past few years has also served to increase the relative significance of the program. It is one of the few sources of development capital in the territories, equaling, according to the *Ha'aretz* article cited above, one quarter of the government's development budget.

However, far greater than the economic weight has been the political significance of the program. Israeli authorities have contributed to it through erratic and sometimes overly restrictive policies that have both contributed to the deteriorating image of the Israeli occupation and have sometimes produced minor U.S.-Israeli confrontations. While the significance of these confrontations within the larger framework of U.S.-Israeli relations should not be exaggerated, they do represent an irritant that, according to one U.S. official, is caused by Israel's "intrusive involvement" in the program.

Prospects for the Future

A new chapter involving U.S. assistance to the territories opened in 1984, as a result of declarations by Secretary of State George P. Shultz and others concerning the need for "improvement in the quality of life," in the territories, and the coming to power, late in 1984, of the Peres government in Israel.

The U.S. thrust is now directed towards easing the burden of the Israeli occupation and stimulating economic activity, in this way strengthening moderate elements in the territories. The U.S. assistance program in the territories is regarded as one element that can help promote this concept, and the U.S. embassy in Tel Aviv has thus apparently stepped up its support for PVO projects with the Israeli authorities by pressing for more efficient handling of the approval process. Funding available for the economic development program was increased from $6.5 million in fiscal year 1983 to $8.5 million in fiscal year 1984, and $9 million in fiscal year 1985. The programming mode was also broadened, with grants for the first time going directly both to a Palestinian Arab organization—the Sun-Day Care Center in Gaza, headed by Gaza physician Dr. Hatam Abu Gazala—and an independent U.S. institution, the New York-based Institute for Middle East Peace and Development, headed by Prof. Stephen Cohen.

At first, Israeli officials responded to this increased U.S. interest by seeking to coopt it to their goals. In December 1983, for example, the government dispatched Binyamin "Fuad" Ben Eliezer, then the military administration's coordinator for the territories, to Washington, in an attempt to ensure Israeli control over any additional funds, and also reportedly to persuade Secretary Shultz to finance a $1.5 billion Israel-sponsored refugee resettlement scheme in the territories (*Al Fajr* March 14, 1984 and other sources). Nothing seems to have come of these approaches, but Israeli authorities did assure U.S. officials that the project approval process for the AID program would be improved and that answers would be provided in writing within two months—not, as often in the past, only orally.

As part of the Shultz thrust for improving "quality of life," the State Department sent a special mission to review the situation in the territories and to make recommendations on further steps the U.S. government could take. These recommendations have not surfaced publicly, but there are signs that they favor increasing the pace of economic development and stimulating Palestinian initiative, provided this does not jeopardize Israeli security.

While these explorations were going on, Israeli voters brought a Labor Party-led national government to power under the premiership of Shimon Peres. Indications are that the Peres government is more open to U.S. thinking on the subject than the preceding Begin/Shamir team. In his first official visit to the United States as prime minister in October 1984, Peres took the opportunity to meet with the Business Group for Middle East Peace and Development, a group of Jewish and Arab-American businessmen, to discuss possibilities of accelerating economic development in the territories (see *Jerusalem Post* November 9, 1984). At about the same time, Defense Minister Yitzhak Rabin told a Knesset Committee that his ministry had agreed in principle to the establishment of a Palestinian Arab bank in the territories, an issue that had long irritated relations between the Palestinian Arab community and Israel (*Jerusalem Post* November 1, 1984). Such signals have surely not been lost to American observers of the situation in the territories.

Both the U.S. and Israeli governments seem to have reached a watershed with respect to economic development in the territories generally, and the character and purposes of the AID program in particular. Both have in the past been prisoners of deeply embedded interests and attitudes. The U.S. government, following a policy of low profile and avoiding as far as possible official involvement, in effect permitted the PVOs to shape its assistance policy in the territories—a policy that at times ignored economic realities and went further in its identification with Palestinian Arab nationalism than seems to have been the mandate of the program. The Israelis, for their part, constrained by economic and political realities

and propelled by deep suspicions of the PVOs' motives, chose a policy
of inaction and obstruction that only added to existing tensions.

As partners in the larger effort to bring peace to the region, American
and Israeli policymakers have the opportunity to turn a page and enlarge
and improve the assistance program in the territories. This could indeed
be a meaningful instrument in the peace effort. But in order to succeed,
the U.S. government must grasp the policy reins into its own hands,
while Israelis must rid themselves of outworn suspicions and paternalism.

Notes

1. This study owes much to the cooperation of responsible officials in a
number of organizations and institutions involved, including: America-Mideast
Education & Training Services (AMIDEAST), American Near East Refugee Aid
(ANERA), Cooperative for American Relief Everywhere (CARE), Catholic Relief
Services (CRS), Holy Land Christian Mission (HLCM), Save the Children/
Community Development Foundation (CDF); U.S. Department of State; U.S.
Agency for International Development (AID); and the Office of the Coordinator
of Government Operations in Judea-Samaria and the Gaza District-Israel Ministry
of Defense. Officials of these organizations and institutions, despite the sensitivity
of the issues and the constraints placed upon them, provided me with information
and insights upon which a large part of this study is based. Among all the
sources used, those mentioned here were indispensable to the realization of the
study. In addition I wish to express my special appreciation to Clayton F.
Ruebensaal Jr. and Meir Yaskil of the U.S. Embassy Tel Aviv, Russell Misheloff
and Anne Gooch of the Near Eastern Bureau of AID/Washington, without
whose help, understanding and patience in supplying information and statistical
data this study could not have been completed.

2. The West Bank and Gaza areas under Israeli occupation are also referred
to as "administered territories," or simply "territories." The Israeli governmental
authority is sometimes referred to as the military administration, and more
recently, civilian activities have been placed under a "civil administration." In
the context of this study, the varying designations are not important and are
used interchangeably.

3. Examples cited include a long-pending ANERA proposal for an Arab
College of Medical Sciences polyclinic in Jerusalem and a Hebron Agricultural
Marketing Cooperative listed as "approved" by the Israeli authorities and "not
approved" by ANERA.

4. For example, Israeli authorities said they received implementation reports
from one PVO in February 1984 and returned them as inadequate in March
1984; by July 1984 they had heard nothing further and had taken no action.

5. The article stated inter alia: "The (Jerusalem US) Consulate employees
sniff out the territory and meet with Palestinian leaders who give them directives;
they then instruct the (PVO) bodies' directors as to whom to assist, and how.

We have here a joint political maneuver by the Consulate personnel and organization activists."

Bibliography

Books

Frisch, Hillel and Sandler, Shmuel. *Israel, the Palestinians and the West Bank.* Lexington, Mass.: Lexington Books, 1984.

Articles and Publications

Benvenisti, Meron. "U.S. Government Funded Projects in the West Bank and Gaza (1977–1983)." Jerusalem: West Bank Data Base Project, 1984.

Boynes, Wynta. "U.S. Non-Profit Organizations in Development Assistance Abroad." New York: Technical Assistance Information Clearing House, 1978.

Elazar, Daniel J., ed. "Judaea, Samaria and Gaza: Views of the Present and Future." Washington, D.C.: American Enterprise Institute, 1982.

"Palestinian Cooperatives on the West Bank and Gaza—Findings From a Study by U.S. Cooperative Representatives." September 1984.

Weinbaum, M.G. "Politics and Development in Foreign Aid: Economic Assistance to Egypt, 1975–1982." *Middle East Journal*, Autumn 1983.

"West Bank Mayors: U.S. Policy is Always Against Palestinian Interests." MERIP Reports, No. 83 (December 1979).

Voluntary Organization Periodicals and Reports

AMIDEAST. Annual Report, 1983.

America-Mideast Educational and Training Services, Inc. "An Assessment of Education in the West Bank and Gaza Strip." July 1979.

Catholic Relief Services. Jerusalem/West Bank. Annual Public Summary of Activities 1982—Statistical Information.

Community Development Foundation Background Sheet, October 20, 1983.

Holy Land Christian Mission International. Pamphlet, 1984.

Government Publications and Reports

Israel Economic Planning Authority.
"Economic Survey of the West Bank." December 1967.

Israel Ministry of Defense.
"Judea-Samaria and the Gaza District: A Sixteen-Year Survey (1969–1983)," November 1983.

U.S. Agency for International Development (AID).
Report on AMIDEAST: "Evaluation of West Bank/Gaza Program. Project No. 298-0147, March 23–April 3, 1981."

Report on ANERA: "An Evaluation of Five Annual Grants for Work in the West Bank and Gaza." NEB-0150-S-00-1055-00, September 1981.

Report on CARE: "Audit Report on CARE PL 480, Title II Food Distribution Program in Israeli-Occupied Territory (Gaza/El Arish/Sinai), July 1, 1967–February 20, 1968."

U.S. Embassy, Tel Aviv.

"Background Paper on U.S. Government-Funded Assistance Programs in the West Bank and Gaza," 1983–1984.

U.S. General Accounting Office (GAO).

"U.S. Economic Aid for the West Bank and Gaza—A Positive Contribution." Report of July 5, 1978.

U.S. House of Representatives.

House Report No. 93-1471. "Foreign Assistance Act of 1974, Report of the Committee on Foreign Affairs."

House Report No. 94-53. "Foreign Assistance and Related Programs, Appropriation Bill, 1975, Report of the Committee on Appropriations."

House Report No. 95-274. "International Security Assistance Act of 1977, Report of the Committee on International Relations."

"Foreign Assistance Legislation for Fiscal Year 1979 (part 5). Hearings before the Subcommittee on Europe and the Middle East of the Committee on International Relations," February/March 1978.

Newspapers and Periodicals

Al Fajr
Ha'aretz
Jerusalem Post
The New York Times
Yediot Acharonot Weekly

About the Contributors

Mordechai Gazit is a research associate at The Leonard Davis Institute for International Relations at the Hebrew University of Jerusalem, and formerly a senior Israeli diplomat with U.S. experience.

Eytan Gilboa is a senior lecturer in the Department of International Relations at the Hebrew University of Jerusalem. His most recent book, *American Public Opinion Toward Israel and the Arab-Israeli Conflict*, is to be published in 1986.

Menachem Hofnung is a Ph.D. candidate in international relations at the Hebrew University of Jerusalem.

Leopold Yehuda Laufer is a research associate at The Leonard Davis Institute for International Relations, and at The Harry S. Truman Institute for the Advancement of Peace, at the Hebrew University of Jerusalem.

Gabriel Sheffer is the associate director of The Leonard Davis Institute for International Relations and senior lecturer in political science at the Hebrew University of Jerusalem.

Index

ABC. *See* American Broadcasting Company

Administered territories. *See* Gaza; Golan Heights; West Bank

Afghanistan, 62

AFME. *See* American Friends of the Middle East

AID. *See* United States, Agency for International Development

Aid leverage. *See* Economic assistance, leverage

AIPAC. *See* American-Israel Public Affairs Committee

"AIPAC Congressional Handbook," 150

Airborne Warning and Control System Surveillance Aircraft (AWACS), 28, 116, 118–119, 137, 151

Algeria, 99

Allon, Yigal, 114

Ambivalence, 21–28

America-Mideast Education & Training Services (AMIDEAST), 179, 180(table), 183–185, 192, 193, 194

American Broadcasting Company (ABC), 65, 67–68

American Friends of the Middle East (AFME), 183

American Institute of Public Opinion, 39, 51, 52, 61, 63, 65, 67–68

American-Israel Public Affairs Committee (AIPAC), 146–150

American Near East Refugee Aid (ANERA), 179, 180(table), 187–189, 193, 194, 198(n3)

American Schools and Hospitals Abroad program, 169, 170(table), 173–174

AMIDEAST. *See* America-Mideast Education & Training Services

Amitay, Morris, 148

Anderson, Robert, 91

ANERA. *See* American Near East Refugee Aid

An Najah University, 183

Anti-Israeli groups, 28–31

Anti-Semites, 30, 33(table)

Arab College of Medical Sciences, 198(n3)

Arab-Israeli conflict
  American attitudes toward, 43, 44(table), 45–46, 47–52, 53, 56(table), 74(table)

Arabists, 29–30, 32, 33(table)

Arab lobby, 28–29, 32, 33(table), 183

Arab nationalism, 197

Arafat, Yassir, 25, 65

Arms control, 96–97, 102, 103, 104

Arms sales. *See* Military assistance

Assimilation, 9

Austin, Warren, 86

AWACS. *See* Airborne Warning and Control System Surveillance Aircraft

Badeau, John, 100

Baghdad Pact, 89

Bar-Zohar, Michael, 93

Begin, Menachem, 12, 30, 53, 54, 55–56, 58, 59(table), 61, 62–63, 65, 84, 197

Ben Eliezer, Benyamin "Fuad," 175–176, 197

Ben-Gurion, David, 89, 91, 93, 95, 96–97, 153

Benikke, Vagh, 153

Berglas, Eitan, 84

Bethlehem University, 173, 174, 180–181(table), 182, 183

Bir Zeit University, 183
Black Muslims, 22
B'not Yaacov Hydroelectric Project,
    152–153
Bowles, Chester, 96
Briera, 10
Brookings Institution, 52
Brothers of the Christian Schools,
    174
Brzezinski, Zbigniew, 53
Business Group for Middle East
    Peace and Development, 197

Campbell, John, 93
Camp David peace process, 24, 60,
    62, 143, 144
Canada, 60, 92
Cantril, Albert, 38
CARE. *See* Cooperative for American
    Relief Everywhere
Carlucci, Frank, 146
Carter, Jimmy, 13, 22, 54, 61, 74–
    75, 84, 114
    Arab lobby and, 28
    economic assistance under, 137
    Middle East policy, 115–116
    military assistance under, 85, 115–
    116, 117, 118, 121–122
    peace process and, 52–53, 60, 115,
    122
    PLO and, 62
    United Nations and, 27
Cash transfers, 133–134
Catholic Relief Services (CRS), 166,
    171, 172–173, 178, 179, 180–
    181(table), 182, 193
Catholics, 21–22, 27. *See also*
    Christians
CBS. *See* Columbia Broadcasting
    System
CDF. *See* Save the Children/
    Community Development Fund
Central Intelligence Agency (CIA),
    86
Chicago Council on Foreign
    Relations, 58
Christians, 12–13, 21–22, 27,
    32(table)
Church, Frank, 148
CIA. *See* Central Intelligence Agency

CIP. *See* Commodity Import
    Program
Cohen, Stephen, 196
Cohen-Orgad, Yigal, 160
"Collaboration," 185, 187
Columbia Broadcasting System
    (CBS), 55
Commodity Import Program (CIP),
    133
Community Development Fund. *See*
    Save the Children
Conference of the Presidents of the
    Major Jewish Organizations, 9,
    147
Consensus, 3, 4–5, 6
Cooperative for American Relief
    Everywhere (CARE), 166, 171,
    172–173, 178, 179, 182, 189,
    193
Cooperative programs
    military, 17–19
    strategic, 62–63
Council for Higher Education, 185
Council of Churches, 21
CRS. *See* Catholic Relief Services
Cyprus, 158
Czechoslovakia, 43, 83, 87, 91, 103,
    104

de Gaulle, Charles, 103
Democracy, 14–15, 37, 140, 141,
    143
Democratic Party, 13–14, 22,
    32(table), 94
Dependency, 158–161
Development assistance, 130, 131,
    144, 162(n7), 186, 187–188,
    196–197. *See also* Economic
    assistance
Dewey, Thomas, 41
Dine, Tom, 147, 148, 149
Dulles, John Foster, 45, 90, 91, 92,
    93, 153, 154

Eagleburger, Lawrence S., 168
Eban, Abba, 90, 92
Economic assistance, 24–26, 84–85,
    125–163
    application control, 175–178, 192,
    195, 197
    under Carter, 137

congress and, 136, 137–140
development, 130, 131, 144,
162(n7), 186, 187–188, 196–
197
under Eisenhower, 144
leverage, 151–157
policy, 140–151
politicization of, 169, 171–178
review process, 136–137
Eden, Anthony, 90
Education, 183–185
Egypt, 17, 112, 155
American attitudes toward, 49, 54,
55, 56–57, 60
arms procurements, 43, 83, 87,
91, 92, 95, 96, 97, 100
conflict with, 43–50, 51
economic assistance to, 145
military assistance to, 28, 115–116,
119, 121, 144
negotiations with, 5, 24, 51–52,
53, 54–63, 73, 113, 156, 167,
191
Soviet Union and, 49, 50, 89, 90–
91, 95, 101, 102, 104, 106, 110,
111
Sudan and, 3
Syrian experiment, 93
U.S. relations, 1, 90, 105, 106
Eisenhower, Dwight, 45, 74–75,
152–153
aid leverage, 153–154
economic assistance under, 144
military assistance under, 84, 89–
93, 94, 95, 100, 121
Eisenhower Doctrine, 92
Elath, Eliahu, 86
Energy crisis. *See* Oil embargo
Epstein, Eliahu. *See* Elath, Eliahu
Eshkol, Levi, 98, 99, 103
Ethiopia, 100
Euromoney, 158
"Evenhandedness Doctrine," 144–
145
Export-Import Bank, 130, 131, 146,
162(n7)

F-15 planes, 114, 116, 117, 121
F-16 planes, 114–115, 116, 117–118,
121
Falwell, Jerry, 13

Fawzi, Mahmud, 106
Feisal (king of Saudi Arabia), 50
Feldman, Meyer, 96
Food assistance, 171(table), 171–173,
178, 189–190, 194
Food Assistance (PL 480), 131
Food-for-Peace program, 130, 166,
169, 170(table), 171–173, 179,
189, 195. *See also* Cooperative
for American Relief Everywhere
Food-for-Work program, 166,
171(table), 172, 173, 189, 194.
See also Cooperative for
American Relief Everywhere
Ford, Gerald, 1–2, 52, 84, 85
Middle East policy, 113
military assistance under, 112–115,
118, 121, 142
Foreign aid. *See* Economic assistance
France, 44–45, 60, 87, 88, 89, 92,
95, 99, 103, 104, 105, 130, 153
Free trade zone, 2
Freij, Elias, 175
Frisch, Hillel, 184
Fundamentalist protestants. *See*
Christians

Gallup polls. *See* American Institute
of Public Opinion
Gaza, 5–6, 14, 60, 161
settlement policy, 26
U.S. aid to, 165–200
Gazala, Hatam Abu, 196
Gazit, Mordechai, 5
Gemayel, Bashir, 67
Geneva Conference, 111
Germany, 157–158. *See also* West
Germany
Gilboa, Eytan, 4–5, 6
Golan, Matti, 155, 156
Golan Heights, 14, 30, 47, 62, 63,
117, 143
Great Britain, 41, 43, 44–45, 60, 86,
87–88, 89, 90, 93, 99, 105, 153
Greece, 92
Gromyko, Andrei, 103
"Guidelines for Preparation of an
Emergency Economy," 160

Habib, Philip, 67
Hadassah, 9

Haig, Alexander, 117
Hamilton, Lee H., 145
Hannah, John, 139
Harman, Avraham, 95
Harriman, Averell, 100, 101
Harris, Lou, 47, 51, 55, 69
Hawk missiles, 95–96, 98, 100, 101,
    121
Hebron Agricultural Marketing
    Cooperative, 198(n3)
Henderson, Loy, 85
HIAS, 15
Histadrut, 24. *See also* Labor
HLCM. *See* Holy Land Christian
    Mission International
Hofnung, Menachem, 4
Holocaust. *See* World War II
Holy Land Christian Mission
    International (HLCM), 174,
    178, 181(table), 183, 193, 194
Hooks, Benjamin, 23
Hoover, Herbert J., Jr., 153
Hurvitz, Yigal, 160
Hussein (king of Jordan), 100, 105–
    106

Institute for Middle East Peace and
    Development, 196
Intelligence capabilities, 18
Interim agreement, 52
International Security Assistance Act,
    133, 139
Investment traps, 3–4, 25
Iran, 89, 100
    hostage crisis, 61
    Iraqi war, 3
    Jews in, 16
    revolution, 18, 61
Iraq, 97
    arms procurements, 87, 95, 101,
        102
    coup d'etat, 93
    Iran war, 3
    nuclear reactor raid, 2, 16, 62,
        117, 156
    U.S. military assistance to, 89, 90,
        92
Israel
    American perceptions of, 14–28,
        30–31, 32(table), 33(table), 37–
        82, 143

Black Hebrews in, 23
debt service, 159(table)
dictatorships and, 30–31, 33(table)
economy, 158–160, 196
establishment of, 40–43
Ministry of Labor and Social
    Welfare, 166, 173, 174, 178,
    179, 182, 184, 185
science and technology in, 16–17,
    20
stability of, 15, 18
strategic importance of, 17–19,
    110, 141–143
U.S. recognition of, 41, 141
Israel Bonds, 83, 125, 157, 158
Israel Defense Forces, 58, 89, 97,
    112, 121, 141
Israel Economic Planning Authority,
    166
"Israeli Economy and Debt
    Repayment Prospects, The," 136
Israeli-Egyptian Political Committee,
    55
"Israel's Requirements for U.S. Aid
    for Fiscal Year 1981," 158
Italy, 158

Jackson, Henry, 11
Jackson, Jesse, 23, 25
Jarring, Gunnar, 107
JDC. *See* Joint Distribution
    Committee
Jerusalem issue, 27, 33(table)
Johnson, Lyndon, 14, 84, 85
    military assistance under, 99–104,
        105, 110, 121
Joint Distribution Committee (JDC),
    9, 15
Jordan, 47, 55, 87, 88, 93, 97, 110,
    111, 155, 158
    assistance management in, 166,
        178
    development assistance to, 144
    development budget, 166
    military assistance to, 89, 92, 93,
        100, 101, 102, 104, 111, 119,
        145
    Palestinian crisis, 17
    peace process with, 6, 165, 191
    U.S. relations, 1
    West Bank influence, 192

Kahan, Itzhak, 68
Kahan Commission, 68
Katzenbach, Nicholas, 102
Kenen, I. L., 144, 147–148
Kennedy, Edward, 148
Kennedy, John, 22, 84, 85, 93, 99–
  100, 107
  Middle East policy, 94
  military assistance under, 93–98,
  121
Kfir plane, 110
Khomeini, Ruholla (Ayatollah), 61
Kirkpatrick, Jean, 151–152
Kissinger, Henry, 1–2, 51–52, 106,
  108, 109, 110, 111–112, 113,
  114, 142, 155–156, 157, 160,
  167
Kluznick, Philip N., 95
Komer, Robert, 100, 101
Kosygin, Alexei, 102

Labor, 24, 33(table)
Labor Party, 24, 53, 64
Laufer, Leopold Yehuda, 5–6
League of Nations, 41
Lebanon
  civil war, 46, 62
  evacuation of, 24, 25, 67
  invasion of, 2, 5, 14, 18, 24, 26,
  29, 38, 63–72, 116, 118, 156
  military assistance to, 89, 93, 102
  multinational force in, 67
  Palestinians in, 17
  retaliatory attacks against, 19
Leverage. *See* Economic assistance,
  leverage
Levering, Ralph, 73
Libya, 3, 102, 106
Likud government, 10, 13, 24, 53,
  64. *See also* Begin, Menachem
Lutheran World Federation (LWF),
  166, 171
LWF. *See* Lutheran World Federation

M-60 tanks, 121
McCloy, John, 97
Marshall Plan, 129
MCC. *See* Mennonite Central
  Committee
Media, 64–65, 75

Meir, Golda, 84, 98, 99, 106, 108–
  109, 110, 111, 112, 121
Mennonite Central Committee
  (MCC), 166, 171
MESRF. *See* Middle East Special
  Requirements Fund
Middle East Armament Committee,
  92
Middle East Special Requirements
  Fund (MESRF), 167, 168,
  170(table), 178, 191
Military assistance, 2, 5, 20, 28, 62,
  83–123, 132
  under Carter, 85, 115–116, 117,
  118, 121–122
  under Eisenhower, 84, 89–93, 94,
  95, 100, 121
  under Ford, 112–115, 118, 121,
  142
  under Johnson, 99–104, 105, 110,
  121
  under Kennedy, 93–98, 121
  leverage, 151–157
  under Nixon, 104–112, 115, 118,
  121, 142, 155
  under Reagan, 116, 117–119
  restrictions on, 83–84, 85–88, 89,
  90–92
  under Truman, 85–89, 130
Military Sales Credits, 134
Modernization, 101, 109
Mondale, Walter, 60
Moral Majority, 13
Morocco, 102
Moslems
  in Jerusalem, 27
Mount of David Crippled Children's
  Hospital, 173–174, 183
Muskie, Edmund, 148
Mutual Defense Assistance
  Agreement, 117

Nasser, Gamal Abdel, 43, 44, 46,
  47, 49, 90, 92, 96–97, 100,
  104, 130
National Broadcasting Company
  (NBC), 55, 56, 61
National interests, 2–3
National Opinion Research Center
  (NORC), 39, 45

NBC. *See* National Broadcasting
Company
Near East Council of Churches
(NECC), 166
Near East Report, The, 149
NECC. *See* Near East Council of
Churches
Neo-Nazis. *See* Anti-Semites
New Israel Fund, 10
Nicaragua, 31
Nixon, Richard, 84, 85, 104, 114
aid leverage under, 154–156
military assistance under, 104–112,
115, 118, 121, 142, 155
NORC. *See* National Opinion
Research Center
Northern Tier, 89

Occupied territories. *See* Gaza; Golan
Heights; West Bank
October War. *See* Yom Kippur War
Oil embargo, 50, 111, 155
Operation Litani. *See* Lebanon,
invasion of

Pahlavi, Mohammed Riza (shah of
Iran), 61
Pakistan, 89
Palestine Liberation Organization,
17, 21, 24, 25, 29, 53, 57–58,
62, 64, 65, 67, 72, 117, 192
Palestinians, 5, 6, 14
in administered territories, 165,
168–169, 174–175, 176–177,
186, 187, 188–189, 190–193,
194–196, 197
American attitudes toward, 21, 30,
142
American blacks and, 23
Jordan crisis, 17
moderate, 26
peace process and, 6, 53
self-determination, 10, 19, 26, 27,
161
in United States, 29
Patton tanks, 99, 100, 121
"Peace for Galilee" operation, 143,
148, 156
"Peace Now" movement, 10, 69
Peace process, 29, 33(table), 51, 63,
107, 165, 191

American attitudes on, 54, 55,
56(table), 57(table), 58(table),
59(table), 61
Camp David, 24, 60, 62, 143, 144
Carter and, 52–53, 60, 115, 122
economic assistance and, 141
Israeli stance, 26–27
military assistance and, 108, 120,
142–144, 155–156
Peres, Shimon, 99, 196, 197
Pershing missiles, 114
Phantom fighters, 103, 104, 105,
106, 108, 109–110, 116, 121
Philippines, 125
Philo-Semites, 11–12, 27, 32(table)
Pioneering ethic, 14–15
PLO. *See* Palestine Liberation
Organization
PLO-Jordan Fund, 192
Pollard espionage scandal, 2
Pompidou, Georges, 106
Private voluntary organizations
(PVOs), 166, 168, 169, 171–
173, 175–190, 191–192, 193–
195, 197–198, 198(nn 4, 5)
Protestants. *See* Christians
Public opinion. *See* Consensus
Public opinion polls, 37–38, 72–73
PVOs. *See* Private voluntary
organizations

Qawasmeh, Fahd, 175, 191
Quandt, William, 109

Rabin, Yitzhak, 84, 97, 102, 104,
106, 108, 109, 110, 112–113,
114, 115, 197
Reagan, Ronald
American Jewish community and,
13
assistance leverage under, 156–157
foreign aid policy, 146
Israeli relations under, 149
Lebanon war and, 65
Middle East strategy, 61–62, 63
military assistance under, 116,
117–119
philo-Semitism of, 11
United Nations and, 27
Reagan initiative, 26, 30, 147

"Report on the Israeli Economy and Debt Repayment Prospects," 158
Republican Party, 13, 22
"Requirements for U.S. Aid," 136
Rogers, William, 106, 107, 109
Rogers Plan, 107, 108
Roll, Charles, 38
Rubin, Gail, 57
Rusk, Dean, 94, 102, 103
Rustin, Bayard, 23

Sabra massacre, 66(table), 67, 68(table), 73
Sadat, Anwar, 38, 50, 53–54, 55–56, 58, 59(table), 61, 63, 73, 104
Sanctions, 152–157
Saudi Arabia, 55, 60, 100, 102
  American presence, 89
  AWACS sale, 28, 116, 118–119, 137, 151
  military assistance to, 28, 92, 115–116, 118–119, 121, 137, 145, 151
  U.S. relations, 1, 13, 118
Save the Children/Community Development Foundation (CDF), 179, 181(table), 185–187, 188, 193, 194
Schlessinger, James, 113
Security Assistance Act, 140
Security Supporting Assistance (SSA), 133
Shamir, 197
Sharett, Moshe, 85, 86, 91
Sharon, Ariel, 3, 64, 66(table)
Shatila massacre, 66(table), 67, 68(table), 73
Shawa, al, Rashad, 188
Shazar, Zalman, 108
Sheffer, Gabriel, 4
Shertok, Moshe. *See* Sharett, Moshe
Shultz, George P., 168, 196, 197
Sinai, 25, 47, 114, 115, 117
Sinai Campaign, 44–46, 47, 64, 92, 153–154
Six Day War, 14, 38, 46–49, 50, 63, 72, 73, 84, 102, 103, 107, 130, 141, 165, 171, 178, 179
Skyhawk planes, 100–101, 103, 105, 106, 108, 109–110, 121
Society of Friends, 21

Somoza regime. *See* Nicaragua
South Africa, 24
South Vietnam, 125
Soviet Union, 44, 46, 49, 50, 52, 53, 61, 89, 91, 94, 111, 120
  aggression by, 3
  arms sales by, 95, 100, 101, 102–103, 104, 106, 111
  Egypt and, 49, 50, 89, 90–91, 95, 101, 102, 104, 106, 110, 111
  Jews in, 3, 9, 15–16, 139
  threat of, 17
  U.S. assistance policy and, 61–62, 102, 103, 104, 105, 106, 110, 141
SRC/C. *See* Survey Research Center
SSA. *See* Security Supporting Assistance
Strategic Cooperative Agreement, 142, 143
Sudan, 3
Suez Crisis, 44
Sun-Day Care Center, 196
Supporting Assistance Program, 133
Survey Research Center (SRC/C), 39, 46
Syria
  conflict with, 47, 50, 91
  disengagement, 51, 112
  Egypt and, 50, 53, 93, 97
  Jews in, 16
  Lebanon war and, 62, 67
  Soviet Union and, 49, 89, 95, 100, 101, 102, 104, 110, 111
  U.S. relations, 106, 111, 155, 167

Technical assistance, 131
Technology transfers, 19–20, 32(table). *See also* Military assistance
Terrorism, 18
  Arab sponsored, 43
  Israeli actions against, 19, 32(table)
Trade, 19–20, 32(table), 34(nn 2, 3), 162(n2). *See also* Technology transfers
Trend analysis, 38
Tripartite Declaration, 88
Truman, Harry, 40–41, 92, 129, 141
  economic assistance under, 130

military assistance under, 85–89,
130
Tunisia, 102
Turkey, 89, 92, 100, 158

UAR. *See* United Arab Republic
Uganda, 19
UJA. *See* United Jewish Appeal
Union of Charitable Societies, 182
United Arab Republic (UAR), 96
United Jewish Appeal (UJA), 9, 83,
125
United Nations, 2, 29, 88, 153, 154
influence of, 27
Israel establishment and, 41–42,
43
position resolution, 40(table), 85
Relief and Works Agency
(UNRWA), 167, 183
Special Committee on Palestine
(UNSCOP), 42
United States
Agency for International
Development (AID), 136, 158,
172, 174, 179, 182, 183, 184,
186, 187, 189, 190–191, 192–
194, 197
Arab community, 28–29
arms supply role, 110–111
black community, 22–23, 25, 28,
33(table)
congress, 136, 137–140, 148–149
Foreign Assistance Act, 103
interest groups, 7–36
Jewish community, 4, 8–11, 13,
14, 15–16, 27, 29, 31, 32(table),
34(n1), 41, 86, 146–147, 150
liberals, 23–24, 33(table)
See also Economic assistance;
Military assistance

UNRWA. *See* United Nations, Relief
and Works Agency
UNSCOP. *See* United Nations,
Special Committee on Palestine
"U.S. Congress: A Guide to Citizen
Action, The," 150

Values
shared, 4–6, 14, 32(table)
Vance, Cyrus, 116
Veliotes, Nicholas, 143
Vietnam, 4, 49, 125

War of Attrition, 49–50, 73, 106,
107
Washington Post, 65, 67–68, 69
Weinberger, Caspar, 118, 120
Weizman, Ezer, 100, 137
Weizmann, Chaim, 86, 129, 141
West Bank, 5–6, 10, 47, 60, 161
occupation of, 14
settlement policy, 26, 27
U.S. aid to, 165–200
West Germany, 99. *See also* Germany
World War II, 11–12, 41, 141

Yankelovich, Skelly, and White, 51,
52, 61
Yariv, Aharon, 96
Years of Upheaval, 155
Yemen, 95, 97, 100
Yom Kippur War, 23, 24, 49, 50–51,
63, 106, 111, 112, 120, 121,
141, 144, 154, 155, 166
Young, Andrew, 23

Zionist Organization of American
(ZOA), 94
ZOA. *See* Zionist Organization of
America